A DIFFERENT JOURNEY
VIETNAM 1965-1973

A DIFFERENT JOURNEY
VIETNAM 1965-1973

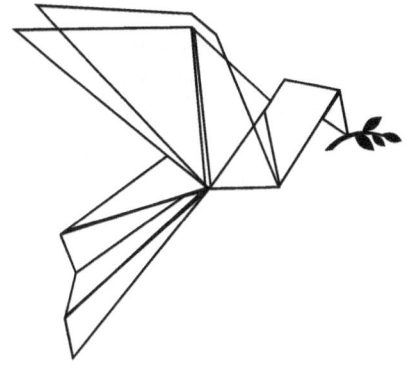

RICHARD A. BERLINER

Lystra Books and Literary Services,
Chapel Hill, North Carolina

ISBN: 979-8-9921363-0-2, hardback
       979-8-9877247-7-4, paperback
       979-8-9877247-9-8, ebook

Library of Congress Control Number 2024926037

Cover Art and Book Design by Joanna Lynn Holloway.
Book Layout by Andrea Reider.
Author's current photograph by Joanna Lynn Holloway.

Published by Lystra Books & Literary Services, LLC
391 Lystra Estates Drive, Chapel Hill, NC 27517
lystrabooks@gmail.com

To my parents, Milton and Nancy

CONTENTS

Part I

Encounter and Disillusionment

Gặp Gỡ và Vỡ mộng
—

Part II

The Children

Những Đứa Trẻ

—

Part III

Words Take Flight

Lời nói Cất Cánh

—

Part IV

Voices of the People of Vietnam

Tiếng Nói của Nhân dân Việt Nam

—

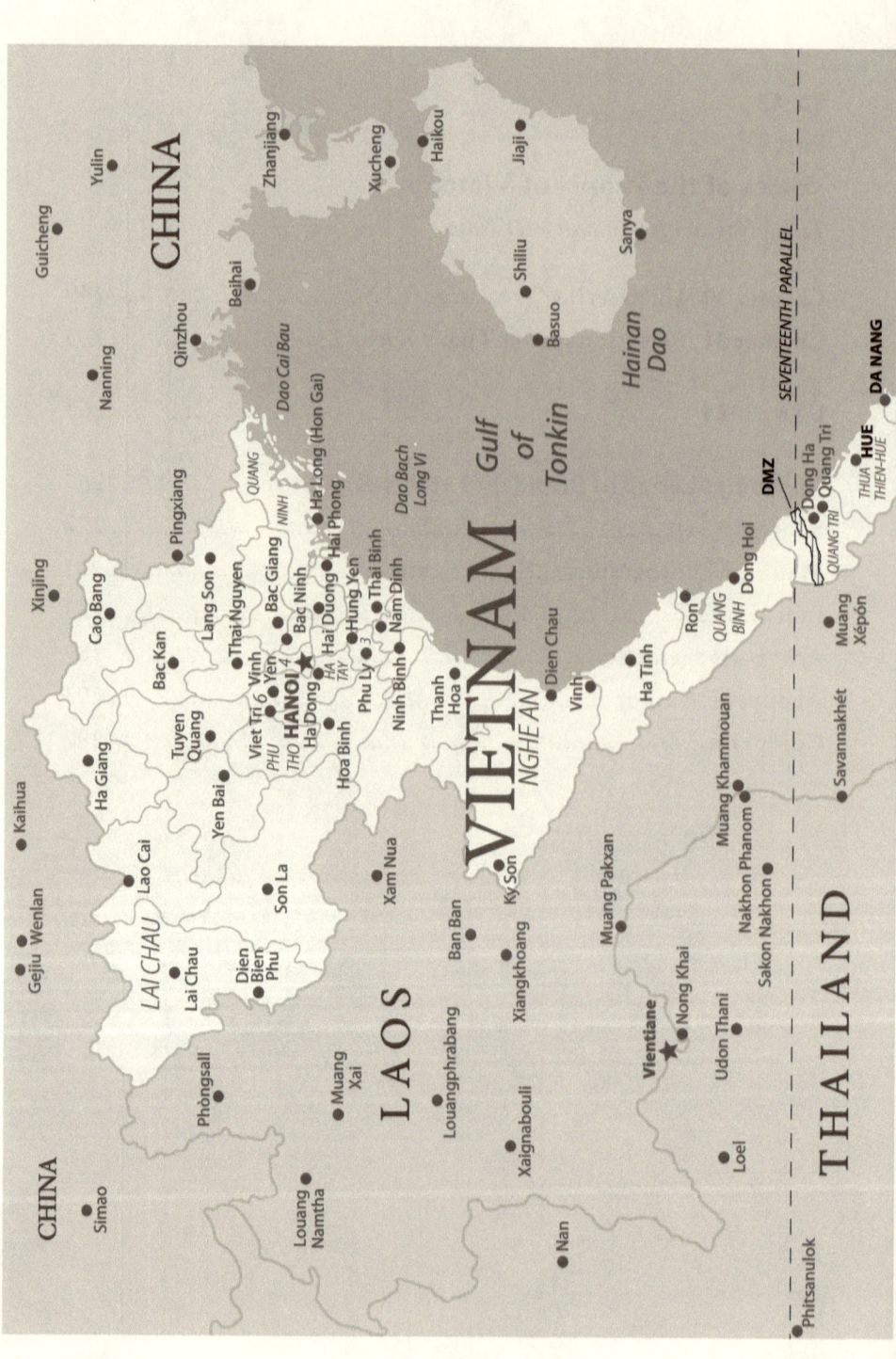

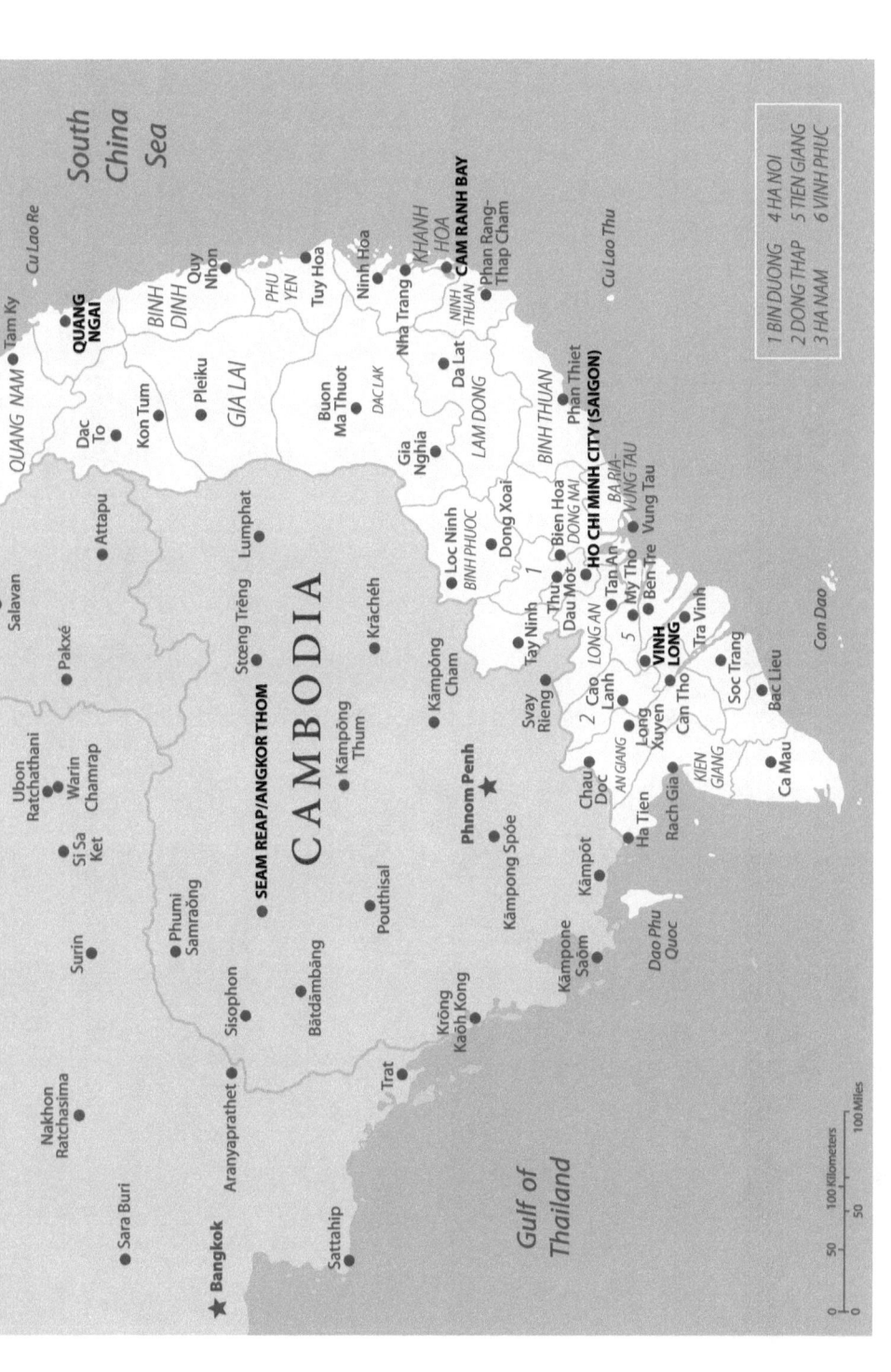

ABBREVIATIONS

ARVN   Army of the Republic of [South] Viet Nam

CIDG   Civilian Irregular Defense Group

COR   The Committee on Responsibility to Save War-Burned and War-Injured Vietnamese Children

DMZ   Demilitarized Zone

GVN   Government of [South] Viet Nam

IVS   International Voluntary Services

JUSPAO Joint U.S. Public Affairs Office

MAC-V   Military Assistance Command – Vietnam

NLF   National Liberation Front (Communist insurgency in South Vietnam)

NVS   National Voluntary Services (South Vietnamese program, similar to US VISTA program)

USAID   United States Agency for International Development

VC   Việt Cộng (Military arm of the National Liberation Front)

USA, 2023

"Are you a veteran?" the smiling young woman in the supermarket checkout line asked. "There's a 5 percent discount for veterans."

I thought, "Am I?" In a way, yes, but not in the way she means it.

"Are you a veteran?" the stony-faced man at the Lowe's checkout stand asked. He was about the right age. Perhaps he too had been in Vietnam, had witnessed the chaos at the embassy during the Tết Offensive.

"Am I a veteran?" I asked myself, considering the sign hanging over the last open parking space, "Reserved: Veterans only."

The question, each time, brought back a flood of memories of the three long years I spent in Saigon, roughly three times as long as most US military personnel were stationed in Vietnam.

I thought of the helicopter rides, each a potential target of Việt Cộng anti-aircraft fire.

I felt again—though at a distance of decades—the numbing anxiety upon learning that a good friend and colleague had been captured in Cambodia, a land that swallowed up news of captives' fates like a deep eddy in the Bermuda Triangle. I recalled the faces of the children I was trying to rescue, paralyzed by bullets or burned by napalm, as fire dropped from the skies with no artificial intelligence magic to ensure it landed only on "the enemy."

I remembered my visit to Mỹ Lai, joining colleagues trying to fill in the blanks for people back home, who were just beginning to hear about the massacre that would become a seminal event in turning the tide of opinion back home against the war.

How different my life would have been if I had not decided to go to Vietnam in 1966 to work as a volunteer aid worker. Since then, each time someone has asked, "Are you a veteran?" a part of me of me has wanted to say "Yes."

And yet, each time I have said "No," passing up the vacant parking space, the discount, the chance to meet another person who had served in Vietnam. And each time I thought how serving one's country sometimes means choosing not to fight—even in the middle of a war.

PART I

Encounter and Disillusionment

Gặp Gỡ và Vỡ mộng

"We don't know when the bombs will explode.
We feel that we are on the edge of time."

Thích Nhất Hạnh

CHAPTER 1

How It All Began

September 1966. Saigon's Tân Sôn Nhất Airport was like any other international airport, except for the sea of green uniforms sporting M-16 semiautomatic rifles, the heavy military equipment, and dozens of choppers flying in every direction. No doubt about it. We were in a war zone. There was no turning back.

Of course, it should have come as no surprise. There had been intense fighting in Vietnam since the fall of 1964, when President Lyndon Johnson cited the Gulf of Tonkin Incident to justify expanding the US role in Vietnam. Indeed, my journey to Vietnam began only because of that war. I set out to Vietnam not as a soldier but as a volunteer with the International Voluntary Services.

Most of the men and women journeying with me had similarly volunteered to come to Vietnam not in spite of the war but because of it. Some men who had gained Conscientious Objector status came to perform the required alternative service.[1] The rest of us came because of a desire to serve, to learn about another culture, or perhaps simply for the adventure of living in a developing nation halfway around the world.

---

[1] Men of draft age who opposed all wars on religious or moral grounds could avoid being drafted if their local draft boards, after investigating the sincerity of their asserted pacifism, designated them as Conscientious Objectors, or COs. While not conscripted for military duty, COs were required to serve two years in an approved alternative service position, such as a hospital orderly, social worker, or janitor in a nonprofit organization.

For me, the pivotal moment came in June of 1963 when a Buddhist monk, Thích Quảng Đức, set himself on fire at a busy traffic intersection in Saigon. It was an horrendous but not unique action, undertaken to protest the South Vietnamese government's persecution of Buddhist monks. I was finishing my freshman year at Earlham College, a private Quaker school in Indiana. When I saw that image on television, Vietnam became an inescapable part of my life.

The next semester I joined informal study groups at Earlham and began to read books by Bernard Fall, seeking to learn more about Vietnam.[2] The more I learned, the more I realized that the US had been involved in Vietnam since the end of World War II, when it supported France's efforts to recolonize the country, against the wishes of the Vietnamese government. I learned that the US had been involved in writing the Geneva Accords in 1954, which divided Vietnam into two countries, North and South. The Accords stated that an election would be held to reunify the country. It never happened.

In the wake of the Geneva Accords, the US supported an anti-communist propaganda effort that persuaded more than one million Vietnamese Catholics, including many of the educated elite of Vietnam, to migrate from the North to the South.

The rebellion against the French was led by Hồ Chí Minh, known affectionately to his followers as Uncle Ho, who by this time was firmly in the communist camp. Hồ Chí Minh had firsthand knowledge of the United States, having spent time in New York and in Boston in the 1920s. He even used the American Declaration of Independence as a model for a similar declaration for his country. But when the United States denied his request for help in removing the French colonial rulers from his country, he turned to Russia and China for assistance.

In the years that followed the signing of the Geneva Accords, Ho cemented his establishment of a communist government in North

---

[2] See, e.g., Bernard B. Fall, *The Two Viet-Nams: A Political and Military Analysis* (Frederick A. Prager, 1963); Marcus Raskin and Bernard B. Fall, *The Viet-Nam Reader: Articles and Documents on American Foreign Policy and the Viet-Nam Crisis* (Vintage Books, 1965).

Vietnam, while leaders of the Roman Catholic church, who had represented less than 20 percent of the population of the united pre-war Vietnam, assumed control in South Vietnam. The battle lines were drawn.

While the US had obviously been aligned with the South Vietnamese from the outset, it was not until the Gulf of Tonkin Incident in August of 1964 that US involvement came to the forefront of public consciousness in the States. Two North Vietnamese ships and a US destroyer exchanged gunfire in the waters of the Gulf of Tonkin. The parties disputed which side had initiated the confrontation. Although only the North Vietnamese suffered casualties, the incident became the trigger for a new and different level of American engagement. Citing the incident, President Lyndon Johnson sought and obtained congressional authorization to aid any country in Southeast Asia under threat of communist aggression. Of course, this meant Vietnam. The deployment of US troops, many of them draftees, signaled the commitment of large numbers of US troops on Vietnamese soil and the beginning of general public opposition to a war that ultimately touched the lives of every American.

As anti-war sentiment began to increase in the US, I found that what had begun as an effort to satisfy my curiosity about the war had become personal. While on a semester abroad in Denmark in 1964, I was often questioned about why the United States was fighting in Vietnam. I had no answer. As a reporter for *The Washington Daily News* in the summer of 1965, I covered one of the first demonstrations against the war, led by Yale professor Staughton Lynd, a Quaker pacifist and social activist. That same summer I found myself standing in the White House Rose Garden listening as President Johnson sought to explain why the United States was in Vietnam.

The *News* had received word that the president would deliver a speech at a local hotel to the International Platform Association, whose president, Drew Pearson, was a personal friend of Johnson's. Confident that President Johnson would not actually appear at the meeting, the assignments editor sent me—a rising college senior usually assigned to the crime beat or general local features—to the hotel in lieu of the paper's usual White House reporter. The editor was right: the president failed to appear. But the editor had not anticipated that the White House would send busses to the hotel to gather up everyone in attendance for a ride to 1600 Pennsylvania Avenue. And that included me.

It was rather a shock to me, a college student spending the summer as a local reporter, to get to cover a presidential speech. And in the Rose Garden, no less, not some crowded hotel ballroom. The president appeared jovial and calm. "When Drew Pearson invited me out to his farm to address this organization, I thought you might like to come here instead," he said. "I spent just about my whole life on a farm, and I don't want to go back until I have to."

The audience settled back for a spoonful of platitudes. What we got was the beginning of an ongoing debate that dogged Johnson for the next three years.

The president declared: "America wins the war she undertakes, and make no mistake about it." While asserting the country's determination to win, however, he also said that the US was "going to do everything we can ... to negotiate an agreement that will allow the people [of South Vietnam] to breathe free and independently, independent of any ideology of ours or anyone else." Commenting on critics' demand for withdrawal, he said: "I wonder why, oh why, oh why, people do not concern themselves about a country that is being invaded and about to be swallowed up ... [W]e are trying to do the reasonable thing and say that power, brute force, and aggression will not work."[3]

I am sure that, for some in the audience, President Johnson's powerful and cohesive message justified the US's increasingly substantial role in Vietnam's civil war. But, by then, I was having doubts.

Those doubts traveled with me as I returned to Earlham for my senior year of college, and I knew I would not volunteer to join the

---

[3] Richard Berliner, "President Had a Platform," *The Washington Daily News*, August 3, 1965.

miliary. With graduation looming, I faced a choice: take my chances of getting drafted, an increasing likelihood for all men of draft age, or find an alternative path that did not require me to become part of the US military. The latter entailed limited options. I had long thought I would join the Peace Corps, a two-year voluntary service program established by President John F. Kennedy in 1961. I considered going to graduate school in journalism and following in my father's footsteps, or going to the London School of Economics in hopes of meeting up again with a girl I had met in Denmark, or joining VISTA, the domestic Peace Corps. But my preferences were not the only factors at work. The Columbia School of Journalism put me on a waiting list, the London School of Economics turned down my application, and the VISTA program wanted to send me somewhere in the southwestern United States, which no doubt would have been hot and dry.

Before applying to the Peace Corps, I learned that the International Voluntary Services (IVS) was recruiting volunteers for two-year terms of service in Vietnam. IVS had begun sending volunteers overseas in the mid-1950s, and the organization had served as a model for the Peace Corps a decade later. The two organizations' goals were similar: to send out agents of change who lived humbly among the people they served and by their presence transferred knowledge and skills that would enhance the life of the villagers.

IVS, after receiving a recommendation from one of my Earlham professors, offered me a position. I accepted immediately. I later learned that several of my classmates had made a similar decision, signing on with either IVS or the American Friends Service Committee, a Quaker organization.

Unlike VISTA, IVS offered the adventure of the Peace Corps coupled with the opportunity to learn firsthand about US involvement in Vietnam. Besides, if I was going to a hot climate, tropical was better. At least, I thought, the annual monsoon season would provide some break from the heat. But I still had to win a deferment from my local draft board. Fortunately, the board approved my IVS assignment as grounds for deferment, viewing the work as critical to the interests

Earlham College graduates, Class of 1966, who went to Vietnam as humanitarian service volunteers after graduation. From left: Steve Swift (IVS), Jay Worrall (IVS), Mark Peacock (American Friends Service Committee), Rick Swigart (IVS), and the author (IVS). (Vietnam, 1967)

of the United States. That—coupled with the knowledge that IVS worked through a contract with the US Agency for International Development (USAID)—should have been a red flag. Was I becoming part of the US effort to save Vietnam from communism? More about that later.

I made plans to meet with other IVS recruits at Harpers Ferry, West Virginia, in August 1966. There we began preparing for our new lives. In that first week we heard presentations on the history and culture of Vietnam and the organization and mission of IVS itself. Between lectures we played basketball and drank Dr. Pepper in the hot August sun. I remember thinking one day that I was probably drinking the last Dr. Pepper I would get to enjoy for two long years.

From Harper's Ferry, our itinerary included two days in Hong Kong on our way to the Philippines and the International Rice Research

Institute in Los Baños, a small town outside of Manila. There our cultural orientation continued.

Those weeks were intended to help us ease into a new culture, but in truth, life in the Philippines felt in some ways more American than Asian. Everyone we encountered spoke English, and the music playing on local radios was pure Motown. One night I was bemused to find myself drinking—yes—Dr. Pepper, in the heart of the Philippines. I thought, these two years might prove to be less foreign than I had anticipated.

Finally, in mid-September, we left Manila for our final destination.

A short three hours later, we deplaned at the Tân Sơn Nhất Airport in South Vietnam. Suddenly, the feeling of excitement turned into intense apprehension. There was, indeed, no turning back.

CHAPTER 2

Meeting A New Country

"Here's where we turn around."

"Why?"

"It doesn't feel right."

A week had passed since my IVS colleagues and I first landed at Tân Sơn Nhất. We had stayed in Saigon one night and then flown to Vĩnh Long, in the Mekong Delta, for six weeks of intensive language training. It was now Sunday, and we had a break from classes. Jim Linn, an IVSer stationed in Vĩnh Long, agreed to take three of us new arrivals for a drive in the country. The day was sunny and the heat bearable.

But we didn't get far. "It doesn't feel right," Jim explained. None of the us knew what he was talking about. It seemed like a beautiful Sunday afternoon in the countryside. We felt relaxed after six days in the classroom and were looking forward to the day's outing.

Jim had been in Vietnam more than a year and had learned to rely on his instincts to keep safe. A seasoned IVS volunteer, Pete Hunting, had been killed twelve months earlier while driving from Vĩnh Long to Sóc Trăng, sixty miles south. Hunting had just passed a US military convoy and was crossing a bridge when he was fired at by Việt Cộng soldiers. They had set up to ambush the convoy; he just happened to be an easy target. Hunting knew the area well and knew that the road was considered unsafe from time to time.[4]

---

[4] Jill Hunting, *Finding Pete: Rediscovering the Brother I Lost in Vietnam* (Wesleyan University Press, 2009).

We had to remind ourselves that we were in a country at war, a war often fought from rice fields with grenades or behind the trees with sniper fire. We had to develop our own antennae to know when things "didn't feel right." Jim turned the Land Rover around, and we went back to Vĩnh Long without incident.

Our one-night stay in Saigon gave us our first encounter with Vietnamese food. We arose the next morning to a bowl of breakfast *phở*, a soup consisting of beef or chicken broth with thin slices of beef or chicken, bean sprouts, cabbage, mint leaves, rice noodles, and spices. If we dared, we could top it with a dash of *nước mắm*—Vietnamese sauce made from fermented fish—for good measure. This soup turned out to be a southern Vietnamese staple, served in the morning or late at night, and quite appetizing. Though strange to Americans in 1966, *phở* has since become not only a staple in Vietnamese restaurants in the United States, but a dish embraced by chefs of all persuasions. For a bunch of US volunteers in 1966, it marked the first of many unexpected encounters that would change our lives. So far so good.

After finishing our *phở*, we headed to the airport for the thirty-minute flight south to Vĩnh Long, in the Mekong Delta. Once out of Saigon, our eyes feasted on the flat expanses of rice paddies, the landscape crisscrossed with canals and dotted with sampans. The fields appeared to be covered almost completely with water. The city of Vĩnh Long looked very small from the air, and the airport was only a small building with one runway. Our next stop was a comfortable two-story villa where six of us would spend the next six weeks, becoming immersed in the Vietnamese language and completing our training. This was now home.

A high wall surrounded the house and garage. Inside were three bedrooms, two bathrooms, and a large living-dining room with high ceilings. Even with the six of us, augmented by three other volunteers and leaders during the daily training sessions, it seemed incredibly roomy and inexcusably comfortable given our reasons for coming to Vietnam. Especially the air conditioners in each bedroom. But we knew it was temporary.

I accepted the comfort as being conducive to learning Vietnamese. Language study meant repeating words and forming sentences for six hours a day. Except for the fact that the language is written with the Roman alphabet, Vietnamese is nothing like American English, and we learned only about the structure and sounds of the language. We finished the training with a modest vocabulary to get us started. Learning Vietnamese took me the rest of the time I was in Vietnam, and even then, I only scratched the surface.

Vietnamese is a monosyllabic tonal language that relies on five tones (six in the northern part of the country) to distinguish meaning. Fortunately for us, the modern written language had been converted to Latin letters in the seventeenth century by Portuguese missionaries and modified by the French in the 1800s. The tones are indicated by diacritical marks attached to vowels, which means that, at least in theory, anyone who can read English can pronounce Vietnamese words if he or she understands the tones. The main challenge is in pronouncing the sounds correctly. Each word may have as many as five or six meanings, depending on the intonation. Mispronunciation can be dangerous. On one occasion I asked a young lady why she was laughing (*cười*) at me. What she heard was, "Why do you want to marry (*cưới*) me?"

We ate all of our meals at the house unless we chose to venture out and eat at one of several restaurants in town. My favorite eatery overlooked the Saigon River, where we drank coffee in the morning and Algerian wine at night and enjoyed a cool breeze. I sat for an hour one Saturday watching Vietnamese families pull up to the dock in their sampans, unload their goods, and take them to the nearby market. Some families sat in their sampans to eat a meal and then motored off into the swirling water.

A Vietnamese woman prepared our meals, which included a variety of vegetables, some meats and—always—white rice.[5] Miniature bananas were the standard dessert. I ate rice twice a day and quickly

---

[5] Prior to the war, Vietnam was a major exporter of rice.

gained proficiency with chopsticks. I also overcame my revulsion to the rather repugnant odor of *nước mắm* and added it to my bowl regularly, if sparingly. My biggest complaint was not being able to get enough exercise to match my consumption. This changed once I received my permanent assignment, when bicycling and walking became my primary modes of transport for the first few months. I went from 165 pounds to 150 pounds during my first two-year stay in Vietnam.

My mother commented that the children in the pictures I sent home looked very healthy. A US medical doctor stationed in Vĩnh Long told me it was because of the *nước mắm*, full of vitamins and minerals. I don't know if that was true, but I kept eating the exotic condiment, and the only health problems I had while living in Vietnam were common colds and an occasional bout with athlete's foot. A US Army doctor treated my feet. I treated my colds by breathing in the scent of eucalyptus leaves in a public steam bath—and by eating more *nước mắm.*

Our limitations with the language did not keep us from exploring the town of Vĩnh Long at night and on weekends. This modest-sized city of 25,000 people grew on a riverbank and was the provincial capital of Vĩnh Long Province. The US had early on established a helicopter base on the outskirts of the city, which meant that by 1966 several bars had opened to cater to US soldiers. The bars were a good place for us to run through Vietnamese phrases learned that day, as long as we were willing to keep buying "Saigon tea" for the women hired by the bar owners. Bar girls, as they were called, sat with GIs and encouraged them to buy drinks in exchange for table companionship. The women avoided getting drunk by drinking only Saigon tea, a dark drink, purportedly alcoholic, but actually just water doctored to look and smell like a real drink. The women earned money based on the amount of alcohol consumed by the GIs.

The soldiers were often drunk. Occasionally, they started fights with the South Vietnamese soldiers, members of the Army of the Republic of Vietnam (ARVN). At first, I was critical of this behavior but soon realized that I had no idea what the US soldiers' lives were like during the day, how many went on patrols, made reconnaissance flights, or worked behind desks. No doubt they felt the strain of being in a war zone in a country where the children loved you, but most of the population did not, and where the battle lines were not clear. Getting drunk and fighting, though disturbing to the local community, might have been a natural outlet for the inevitable stress.

The war played like background noise for us IVSers. It was out there, but we had no real knowledge of what was happening. When the US committed 180,000 troops to Vietnam in 1965, some IVSers extended their tours. "I just want to see if it [a massive infusion of US soldiers] will make a difference," one IVSer said. But a year later the future for Vietnam was no more certain.

(Letter home: October 21, 1966)[6]

In the short time I have been here, my conception of the war continually grows cloudier until the only thing I can be sure of is how senseless it all is. VC [Việt Cộng] terrorism is heavily emphasized in this area as justification for the war. And the fact that I, an American, should look at each Vietnamese I meet as a potential threat, and consequently, my enemy, has a strange impact. With some knowledge of recent history, it is easy to see how the Việt Cộng developed the grievances that they are fighting for, their appeal to a large proportion of the population, and the necessity of fighting underground, even though their suffering is so prolonged—from loss of life or loss of means of economic survival.

---

[6] While I was in Vietnam, my journalist father insisted I write detailed letters home at least weekly. These were usually handwritten. I learned later that my mother had typed and saved all of those letters, a resource that proved invaluable in writing this memoir. Throughout the text are excerpts from that collection, providing a contemporaneous record that I could never had provided without her maternal diligence.

The Việt Cộng were primarily southern Vietnamese who chose to oppose the existing government in Saigon through guerilla warfare and peasant education. They were supported by the communist North Vietnam government, which supplied weapons and eventually overall leadership.

I decided to look at each Vietnamese as a potential friend and sought every chance to learn something about the people while studying their language. An early opportunity came when a fellow IVS volunteer and I visited the home of Miss Nga, a young woman whom we had met in the market. Nga sold fourteen-day-old eggs, which are a treat I think only Vietnamese enjoy. Another seven days, and they would have hatched. Chris Lumbo, from the Philippines, and I made repeated efforts to garner an invitation to Nga's home. Visiting after dark for our first visit would have been highly frowned upon, but we finally succeeded in getting an invitation to visit at 9 a.m. on a Sunday.

We went to the market at the appointed time and met Nga's two younger sisters, who had come to guide us to her house. We had planned to walk, but a sudden rain led Chris and me to crowd into a one-person cyclo, a cart pulled by a motorbike with a rain hood over the passenger seat. The two girls continued to walk, laughing at the sight of two big foreigners sharing a single cyclo.

We arrived a few minutes later at their thatch-roofed house, only to discover that Nga had gone to the market in a neighboring town. She had asked her mother to suggest that we come back in the afternoon. The presence of two foreigners in this house was unusual, however, and the family wouldn't let us leave. We had met Nga's mother in the market previously and apparently had her approval. Soon we met the rest of the family. There were eight children in all. Nga's father was living permanently in Saigon. One son was on leave from the navy, two sons were in school, and a fourth son was in diapers. Nga worked with her mother in the market. The sisters who had greeted us earlier attended school (one was doing math problems while we were there), but they were often called upon to trundle off to the market to sell eggs and "*nem*," pork wrapped in banana leaves. Nga, who spoke some English, took typing lessons when she was not busy helping her mother.

(Letter home: October 24, 1966)

Sunday morning passed quickly, mostly learning Vietnamese songs with the young girls directing our efforts. When the time approached noon, the family invited us to stay for a hefty meal of rice, cabbage, and some sort of meat that was mostly bone. By the end of lunch, we were quite full, as our hosts continued to fill our bowls with hardly recognizable foods. I am quite sure that three weeks earlier, I would not have wanted to eat anything in my bowl, but our cook at the IVS house changed that. I was first under the impression that she was a remarkable cook. Now I believe that cooking is not taken lightly in any home.

We left after lunch, which is siesta time, but at six, we crowded back into the small living space in the house, illuminated by one fluorescent light hanging from the ceiling. We talked with Nga for quite a while and drank beer with her brother. Before leaving, we had to promise to come back the next day and take pictures. I am not sure if it is vanity or delight in the sound of the camera clicking but having one's picture taken has much appeal here.

As I grew more comfortable with town life in Vĩnh Long, I looked for opportunities to venture further afield. An opportunity came up to join a US Military Provincial Health Assistance team for a one-day visit to several small villages outside of the city. First stop: Long Thành, population 2,000. Next was a slightly larger village called Phú Quới.

We reached the first village via a one-lane dirt road, winding through bamboo trees. At last, a taste of village life. I was apprehensive about being in a remote area, but I was caught up in the beauty and serenity.

Few people walked the road, but as soon as our team set up a large tent, women and children came out of nowhere and formed a line. Word must have gotten out early. The medical team was here to provide quick medical checkups. I walked up and down the line, drawing giggles from the children.

"Our biggest item is soap," medical specialist Paul W. Ritter of Morocco, Indiana, told me. "Almost everything we find here comes from poor sanitation." Soap came to Vietnam in all sizes and shapes, much of it donated by large hotel chains. Each child was told to *chà mạnh*—rub hard—with the soap. The team also gave plenty of injections of penicillin for serious cuts or rashes. The jabs proved to be very popular. Some people were caught coming back for seconds. While the team's medical members gave examinations, Airman First Class Jerry Kirk, of Bakersville, California, examined teeth. Kirk had a month of medical training, including two days of dentistry, before coming to Vietnam. "I wouldn't pull children's teeth, though. They jump around too much for me." He did manage to pull ten badly decayed canines without breaking a root the whole day.

At Phú Quới, the perfume of tropical flowers and the odor from Chinese soup drifted into the spacious recreation center where the team worked. Village elders rewarded the team with oranges, mangos, and coconut milk as they worked.[7] The war seemed far removed.

I learned about the US war effort from conversations with US military persons and the seasoned IVS volunteers. Defense Secretary Robert McNamara had announced in 1966 that he had no intention of moving more troops into the Mekong Delta, where we were living, as most of the fighting was further north, closer to the Demilitarized

---

[7] Richard Berliner, "Our Biggest Item Was Soap," *The Washington Daily News*, December 14, 1966.

Zone (DMZ).[8] But it was clear that this was not the case. The US was expanding military outposts in this area and building a totally new base nearby.

I found it difficult to understand the strategy of concentrating more and more troops in the Mekong Delta. The purported political goal of the US was to win the hearts and minds of the population in support of the South Vietnamese government. This could only be done effectively by supporting the efforts of South Vietnamese troops in eradicating the presence of the Việt Cộng. It seemed that the more directly US troops became involved, the more estranged the Vietnamese became.

The Việt Cộng also pursued the goal of winning hearts and minds, but they did not amass large armies in the South as they had done in the North. Using guerilla tactics, they attacked Government of [South] Vietnam (GVN) outposts, often at night and often killing GVN village "heads." If they failed to encounter GVN troops, the Việt Cộng ran mandatory village meetings and listened to the concerns of the villagers.

(Letter home: November 3, 1966)

In the delta, much of the work is psychological, the ultimate victor being the side that is most appealing. An American colonel told us that a victory in the South would be much more achievable if the Vietnamese troops and not the Americans were responsible. One possible reason for sending more troops to this region is that American advisors and soldiers tend to be rather impatient with the Vietnamese. There is little camaraderie between the two forces. Americans are called gun-happy, and Vietnamese are said to be afraid to shoot. Probably both are true.

---

[8] The DMZ, located at the Seventeenth Parallel, separated North Vietnam from South Vietnam. See map on pp. xiv and xv.

The fighting was always in the back of my mind, but I could not know how close or how threatening it was. Some nights the windows shook from a far-off blast, some nights they shook more because the blasts were closer. More high-flying jets seemed to be passing through the area. But Vĩnh Long remained secure and life went on.

As we wound up our language study in Vĩnh Long, we began to speculate about the next phase of our lives. We jokingly bet on who would be sent to the most remote village or the least secure area of the country. This was one way of dealing with our anxiety. As I wrote then, "The reality of our situation has probably yet to sink in." But surely, I thought, we would not be targets. We were there to help, and we did not carry guns. We heard that an IVSer had received a note from a Việt Cộng soldier saying that they were aware of our presence and that if we stayed away from the US military, we should not feel threatened. But would anyone know who we were and that we were not armed when they saw us driving down a lonely two-lane country road or even walking through the densely populated slums of Saigon?

Two volunteers were killed while I served in IVS, but it was never clear if they were targeted by the Việt Cộng or by ARVN soldiers. One was Dave Gitelson, known among the Vietnamese as the "Người Mỹ nghèo" or "poor American" because he lived in a remote village, enjoyed very few amenities, and often went around barefoot. Dave met with Senator Edward Kennedy during a visit to Vietnam in 1967 and told the senator he had strong misgivings about the war. He also reported on abuses by US troops involving Vietnamese civilians. The press reported the conversation, and there was some speculation at the time of Dave's death that ARVN forces had killed him in retaliation for that action.

Despite these anxieties and the constant presence of warfare, I was anxious to get started. As I explained in a letter home dated November 22, 1966: "I don't see the war as a complete obstacle to my doing any work here because life does go on, and some semblance of order is maintained—at least in the cities. It's not hard to imagine what could be accomplished with only poverty and ignorance to fight."

Reflecting on those words now, I realize I went to Vietnam with a Westerner's stereotypical view of what it meant to work in a developing country. I was accepted into IVS while still completing my last trimester of college and preparing for comprehensive exams. I had committed to teaching in the US-based Upward Bound program the summer after I graduated. I did nothing to prepare for Vietnam.

In my mind, I had a *National Geographic* image of bamboo shacks with no running water, dotted along dusty dirt roads. I assumed that the "natives" were largely ignorant of basic sanitation practices and would welcome any suggestions that Western civilization had to offer. I don't think I even visualized what urban life might be like because I was so sure I would be a half day's walk from a telephone in the closest town. The early reports from returning Peace Corps volunteers did nothing to dispel this image. Nor did my college courses on Japanese history suggest that Vietnam, with its 4,000 years of history, might be intellectually equal to Japan.

So, with few skills but a big heart, I thought all I had to do was show up.

Surprise. Many Vietnamese were highly educated, and those without formal education possessed street smarts. Farmers might not have known about new, improved strains of rice or advanced ways to filter water, but their knowledge of ancient farming techniques and medicine was extensive. Too often, well-meaning Americans, both military and civilian, encouraged the adoption of Western practices without realizing that those practices ran counter to the local culture and were doomed to failure.

A striking example concerned the use of chopsticks, the standard eating utensil in Vietnam. Food was often served family-style, from large bowls in the middle of the table. Diners typically reached for food with their chopsticks, selected an item, and brought it back to their individual small bowls of rice. Then they mixed the food items with the rice and consumed it by holding the bowl to their mouths and shoving the food in with the same chopsticks.

Concerned that this method spread germs, the American military tried to teach the Vietnamese to use spoons, forks, and knives, instead of chopsticks. This was a hard sell, particularly since Western-style silverware was made from material that was not readily available.

The North Vietnamese also recognized the health risks in eating from a common bowl, but their alternative was more practical and less intrusive. Instead of promoting the use of silverware, the North Vietnamese encouraged people to reach for food from the serving dish with the large end of the chopsticks and put food in their mouths with the other end.

I don't know how successful they were, but one thing, at least, was evident. Americans were trying to impose a Western practice while the North Vietnamese were building on local traditions to improve lives.

I also know that Vietnamese food does not taste as good when eaten with a fork.

While I was studying in Vĩnh Long, IVS was still trying to sort out where to place me. There were three work areas: agriculture, community development, and education. I opted for community development. The term is amorphous and there was no manual. IVS simply placed volunteers in areas where the leadership team thought he or she could do something worthwhile and let the volunteer figure it out. At a minimum, it did try to connect the volunteer with a Vietnamese counterpart who might provide direction. But the volunteer was generally left alone for the first few months.

As assignments were given out in Vĩnh Long, there was talk about sending me either to Saigon or to one of the northern provinces. I still found the idea of living in a remote village attractive but realized that a placement in Saigon would give me a front-row vantage point from which to observe the political dynamics that shaped the war effort. It also meant that I would meet Vietnamese people close to me in age and education. I could learn firsthand how the war shaped their lives. So when a slot opened up working with a youth organization in Saigon, I jumped at the chance. I had just come from teaching high school students in the summer Upward Bound program in Indiana and had enjoyed working with that age group. This seemed a good match for my admittedly limited experience, and I was excited about the chance to once again be working with teenagers and young twenty-somethings. The placement in Saigon was confirmed and language training ended.

I was finally off to my new home—Saigon.

CHAPTER 3

Total Immersion

Before arriving in Saigon, I was filled with the youthful idealism common to new volunteers. I had given little thought to the practical challenges of the situation—including the need to find suitable housing. IVS volunteers received about $80 per month for food and housing, which was more than adequate when living in smaller cities or towns, untouched by abnormal housing demands. But US civilian contractors with monthly salaries many times the size of the IVS stipend had driven housing rents up throughout Saigon, and it seemed everything was out of reach for the volunteers. The IVS leadership thought they had solved my housing problem when they received a request to have someone act as resident manager of a walled-in, gated villa that served as transitional housing for US government personnel. The villa came complete with a cook and cleaning staff—and air-conditioning—and became my first lodging. Not what I had envisioned.

I had misgivings about the arrangement from the start. The clincher came when an American government worker began complaining about the quality of the breakfasts being served. I did not come to Vietnam to make life more comfortable for Americans. After two weeks, I had had enough and complained to the IVS leadership. "I came to Vietnam to be among the people, not shut off from them," I told them. The proverb, be careful what you ask for, would prove to be right on target.

IVS chief Don Luce worked out a deal with the National Voluntary Services head, Nguyễn Hy Vân, for me to rent a three-room house on a small alley, next to a stagnant creek in the heart of one of Saigon's poorer neighborhoods.[9] I would live there, sharing the house with two Vietnamese youth leaders and with frequent visitors.

This time there was no wall or gate and no air conditioning, but we did have electricity and running cold water. A sparsely furnished front room served as a common living area. The next room had two sets of bunk beds separated by a curtain, the beds for men on one side and those for women on the other. At the back of the house were a small kitchen and a bathroom. After one sweltering sleepless night on a bunk bed draped with mosquito netting, I commandeered the long chest in the front room and put a roll-up mattress on top. The breeze from a ceiling fan kept the mosquitoes away, so no need for mosquito netting. I was quite comfortable living there for the next year. The only amenity added to the house after a few months was a discarded refrigerator. It stayed empty most of the time.

After settling into my new home, I reported to work at the National Youth Council, a coordinating committee for twenty-six Vietnamese youth service groups active throughout the South. I was there to support youth volunteerism in the countryside, but I had no idea what I should do on day one. I am not sure the director of the National Youth Council, Trần Ngọc Bảo, knew either. But together we determined that initially I could use my writing skills to help the council communicate to the world outside Vietnam the importance of supporting Vietnamese youth in their quest for peace. Because two outside mega-powers, the US and the USSR, were pulling the strings on the war, it made sense to mount a worldwide response in support of peace.

---

[9] The National Voluntary Services (Thanh Niên Thiêm Chí), or NVS, was a South Vietnamese program much like the VISTA program in the US. Organized in 1965, NVS sponsored student volunteers who worked in rural areas of the country, primarily assisting villagers with sanitation, vegetable production, and education.

We launched an English-language newsletter: *YOUTH BULLETIN— Voices of Vietnamese Youth.* I assisted the leadership in communicating with similar organizations throughout Asia. I wrote letters and newsletters that tried to reflect what the council's leader, Trần Ngọc Bảo, wanted to say without inserting too many of my own views. The content was often critical of the South Vietnamese government and the American war effort, but our efforts were never stymied by the South Vietnamese government.

In addition to working with the newsletter, I met with Vietnamese youth leaders and visited their work sites, sometimes lending a hand physically and other times just listening and affirming their ideas. I also taught a class in English at the College of Agriculture two nights a week. I could not claim that any of my work had substantial impact on the lives of the Vietnamese. But I enjoyed myself and felt important.

I thought I had a good rapport with the students in the classroom until one said he thought my feet were dirty. I looked down and, sure enough, the sandals I wore did nothing to keep out the dust from the streets. I wore sandals because they were cooler than shoes, and I thought they would help students identify with me better. Wrong. The profession of teacher was greatly respected, and teachers were expected to stand out in dress and manner. The next day I switched to my brown leather brogans. But I did not adopt the normal attire of teachers — a long-sleeved white shirt and dark trousers — opting instead for the much cooler short-sleeved shirts and khakis I had brought with me from the US.

Many Vietnamese youth had an insatiable urge to learn English, often because the US military and the South Vietnamese government offered extremely attractive job opportunities for English-speaking Vietnamese. By 1966, there were more than 300,000 Americans in South Vietnam. The US presence had become so dominant in places like Saigon that the whole economy was dependent on it. English was the ticket to a better life. But this was not the motive of every Vietnamese. One Vietnamese man, fluent in French and Japanese as well as English, told me, "We always should learn the language of our enemy."

(Letter Home: December 2, 1966)

*In Saigon alone we have created thousands of jobs at
the administrative level, such as secretaries, interpreters,
and warehouse supervisors. The US presence also
supports a legion of cyclo drivers, shoeshine boys, and
bar girls. It has stimulated the creation of thousands
of businesses that started because of the availability
of capital. Many of these involved the sale of black-
market goods that seemed to originate on US bases.
One Vietnamese friend remarked that the prosperity
Saigon is now enjoying is a superficial prosperity,
based entirely on the American presence. When the
Americans leave, he said, the prosperity will fade away.
But no one is talking about the US pulling out.*

My two housemates, Thọ and Quỳnh, wanted to practice English
whenever possible, which posed a problem. I wanted to practice
Vietnamese. We used both in conversations. I became acquainted with a
private English teacher who invited his students to picnic at the zoo near
the Saigon River on Sundays. He was a robust man with a constant smile
and was delighted when I accepted his invitations for a picnic lunch on
occasion so that his students could practice their English. In return, they
gave me lunch. Picnicking at the zoo near the Saigon River on a Sunday
was almost like home. Another scene in contrast to the raging war in
the countryside.

My work with the Youth Council was challenging but left plenty of
time for me to get to know the city of Saigon, once known as "the Paris
of the Orient." The city comfortably held 500,000 people in the 1950s,
with parks and wide boulevards and French architecture, reflecting
a hundred years of French colonial rule. By 1966, its population had

grown to three million people, and the air was full of dust and smog from large military vehicles and motorcycles.[10]

Despite the growing population and the constraints of war, the city functioned reasonably well. Electricity was only occasionally disrupted. The public sewer system worked for the most part, and traffic police kept the streets clear. Wedding parties showed up at restaurants, and funeral processions were constant. Life went on. The best time of day was early morning before the sun drove temperatures into the nineties. The French had left a legacy of coffee and French bread, so there were ample cafés and soup shops where one could dine outdoors before heading to work. I ate many of my meals in one of the Vietnamese or Chinese restaurants. But once in a while I went with American colleagues to one of the two or three French restaurants in the city, establishments way above my price range.

Even on a volunteer's stipend, however, I could always find adventure at the large market at the corner of Le Văn Duyệt and Trần Quý Cáp in Saigon. It was typical of markets in every city in Vietnam, only larger than most. Within the market lay a rabbit-warren of small shops selling dry goods, small appliances, fresh eels, live chicks, brooms, and baskets—almost anything one might want for normal everyday living. But for a Westerner visiting the market for the first time, the real action was outside the market.

(Letter home: March 1, 1968)

Small food shops line the outer walls on two sides of the market, completely open on the street side to an array of metal tables and wooden stools. Each shop is selling a single food item from various kinds of soups, dried squid, pig skins, to name but a few. Strong odors come from bubbling pots, blending in with the odors of stale produce in the market and from garbage lining the edge of the streets.

---

[10] By 2023, the Saigon population had increased to more than nine million.

There is an invisible line between the tables that mark the boundary between each soup shop, usually discovered when one tries to attract the attention of a girl taking orders from a table on the left or right. The only rewards are cold stares and empty plates.

From four a.m. until midnight this area is alive with the transients who come to eat and the intransient sellers who spend almost every waking minute of their lives within the confines of the market. The transient set is varied: students taking a break from daytime classes, soldiers in the evening on leave, and the night club set for one more beer or a glass of Martel whiskey with soda, along with a bowl of súp cơm —rice soup. They say it settles the stomach.

There is another permanent set at the market, a variety of people and children that help create a circus-like atmosphere. The stream of activity can blow one's mind, better than any light show. Neo-bar girls, with little of the makeup but all the flirtatious qualities, do most of the serving. This is not a job, but their life. So, the pace is never too hurried. They strut among the tables, better than Hazel ever did.[11] But don't misinterpret. Any attempted advances only lead to a bitter next cup of coffee.

Everywhere you look you see someone trying to sell something. There is the permanent news stand with a variety of thin magazines emphasizing romance stories (soldiers off to war is a common theme) and the current celebrities that can be seen on television or on record jackets. On the flanks are women selling bread, C rations (illegal), and American cigarettes by the carton (illegal). There is a sandwich wagon selling bánh mì— half a loaf of French bread stuffed with chopped pork, tomatoes, cucumbers, onions, red peppers—sprinkled with black pepper,

---

[11] A reference to a song popular at the time, "Hazel's Hips," written and sung by Oscar Brown Jr. and later recorded by Chaka Khan.

garlic sauce, and other spices. A fruit stand sits next to the sandwich wagon. The specialty this time of year is watermelon. In what little concrete space is available among the tables a woman spreads out a sheet and steams clams on her charcoal stove. Next to her a woman is heating fourteen-day-old eggs (the feathers are just beginning to form). All you need is a spoon and a strong stomach.

Young children, some as young as five, run in and out of the rows of tables selling peanuts, shrimp bread, and lottery tickets. An elderly crewcut woman, whose legs are apparently crippled (you never know for sure), moves about on a wooden dolly, between the children and the tables, asking for money. She is one of the many beggars in the area who have taught the very young children how to beg for food as well as money. Her teeth are blackened from chewing betel nuts.

And then there are the shoeshine boys—Vietnam's never to be forgotten wartime symbol.

Anyone can be a shoeshine boy if he has enough money to buy or rent a box with accessories and works himself into a territory. The latter is the most difficult. This food market complex is one of Saigon's many territories and is divided into several small territories by yet again invisible lines. Each shoeshine boy knows where his territory begins and ends and dares not encroach on another's. I talked with one boy who could not break into a territory in Saigon, despite its vastness, and made the 150 Km trip to Vũng Tàu to try his luck. He said he knew somebody there. But two weeks later he showed up back at the market. "No work," he said.

This soup shop complex is a "poor" area. There are no bars or American military installations in the area and few foreigners venture here. Only local inhabitants have their shoes shined but not at a rate that foreigners pay. [I was initially a prime target but quickly learned always to wear sandals when coming to the market.] *Because it is a poor area few homeless boys hang around the market. What is left are children of families who live nearby, a majority of whom live in the market itself. If there are no shoes to shine a boy won't starve here. Every piaster they make is turned over to their mothers or aunts to add to their slim earnings. Those without relatives are cared for by the merchants in the complex. This is true in almost every territory, an extension of the extended family structure.*

The children look for the slightest of distractions. Fights are inevitable in this crowded complex, but they end as abruptly as they start. Drawing is a popular activity—often Batman themes—as is playing with cards. When a traffic accident occurs in the intersection children immediately gather around and listen to the ensuing arguments. (When accidents occur in Vietnam the vehicles involved are left exactly where they landed, sometimes for over an hour, until cause is determined, and settlement is made.) Then back to the turn, a turn around the tables to look for new shoes to shine and then something else to fill the long hours.

I continued to follow the progress of the war and attempted to understand US strategy. During my time in Vĩnh Long, I had learned that there were active US combat troops in that area, in the Mekong Delta southwest of Saigon. US Navy boats stopped the Vietnamese sampans traveling up and down the canals. Vietnamese military checked for the movement of supplies by the Việt Công, the communist guerillas fighting in South Vietnam. The Việt Công, known generally as "the VC," actively engaged in firefights along the banks of the rivers. Our military recognized that most enemy activity in the area was being waged not by North Vietnamese coming from the north but by southern indigenous Vietnamese forces identified as VC. So it left the bulk of the combat there to the ARVN. The US military preferred to think of themselves as advisors rather than combatants, supporting the existence of a functioning government capable of taking care of its people.

The advisory effort in the Mekong Delta was managed by the Military Assistance Command-Vietnam (MAC-V), which divided the US forces into subsector advisory units. A large unit stayed in each provincial capital, and smaller teams of five to ten US soldiers were in district towns in the provinces in areas that were secure. In some instances, the soldiers lived with Vietnamese troops.

A key weapon in the US war effort was propaganda, carried out primarily by JUSPAO, the Joint US Public Affairs Office. JUSPAO's mission was to persuade VC members to join the *Chiêu Hồi* (the Returning Patriot) program and to encourage uncommitted Vietnamese to support the government in the South. JUSPAO printed an enormous number of books and pamphlets, as well as American novels, such as *The Yearling* by Marjorie K. Rawlings, translated into Vietnamese. I was never sure how a novel about a deer published in the US in 1938 supported the war effort.

The work of JUSPAO overlapped with the work of USAID, whose goal was to assist in building an economically stable government. IVS, in fact, received much of its funding from USAID. As the war was heating up in 1964 and 1965, the Johnson administration sought to send Peace Corps volunteers into the country. Not surprisingly, this plan encountered considerable resistance from members of congress, who feared it would hurt the image of the Peace Corps in other countries.

For that reason, the administration turned to IVS, which had been working in Vietnam since the mid-50s. Through USAID, the US channeled considerable funds to IVS for its work in Vietnam. IVS quickly expanded its cadre of volunteers, increasing from forty to more than a hundred volunteers by the time I arrived in the country, and planned to add 100 more over the next twelve months.

Thus, USAID and IVS worked in parallel, one overtly governmental and the other a private nonprofit aid group funded increasingly by the US government. The goal of USAID was to enhance the economy through infrastructure improvement, public works, and economic development at the local level. Unlike IVS, however, USAID's work was hampered by the cultural distance between its staff and the people they sought to aid. Because of their lack of language ability and their generally luxurious lifestyle, the American provincial representatives were cut off from all but the more highly educated class of Vietnamese.

Time magazine painted a very different picture for its readers in the States, glossing over the vast economic and cultural distance between US representatives and the local populace. *Time* was distributed to US troops through JUSPAO, and its frequent inaccuracies became very apparent to those of us on the ground. Some USAID officials were able to break through the social and economic barriers and become fully acquainted with the needs of the Vietnamese people, but not many.

The lack of direct contact with Vietnamese by USAID officials may be one of the reasons funds were directed to IVS. IVS volunteers were known for their language skills, willingness to live in remote areas, and ability to develop personal relationships with Vietnamese. Few IVSers possessed guns. Instead, they relied on their personal contacts to advise them of the occasional need for caution. The US government did not attempt to direct our efforts. I wrote at the time that "USAID imposes few restrictions on IVS volunteers. I am surprised at how much independence IVS has been able to maintain."

It did not occur to me at the time that USAID possibly benefited from IVS in other ways. IVS supported every volunteer's effort to stay in touch with families and friends and offered to mail out a monthly newsletter to up to a hundred people. Those newsletters no doubt contained a wealth of information about what was happening in Vietnam. Were they shared with USAID, or with the CIA?

Robert Minnich, an IVS volunteer stationed in Bính Hòa near Saigon, went to the USAID office one day to pick up his mail and saw a report he had written on the desk of a USAID officer. He was shocked. "I was working with some Vietnamese youth who the government thought might be draft dodgers," he told me. "Whatever I wrote might in some way come back to hurt my colleagues. I don't think I wrote another newsletter after that."

IVS leadership worked hard to disassociate IVS from the war effort. There was no doubt the US government believed that IVS could assist in the battle for "hearts and minds" by showing a positive side of US involvement, but I was learning more and more about how the US war was doing the opposite. Increasingly my Vietnamese friends were telling me the US had to go. "We don't like the communists. But you are destroying our country. We just need the war to end."

My friends were not telling me that I had to go home, though some might have felt that way. After a year, I wasn't sure I was ready to leave and thought there was some benefit to my staying. Other IVSers shared that ambivalence, and a year into my tour, senior IVS staff began resigning in protest of the war.

While working with student groups in Saigon, I had opportunities to travel into other parts of the country and into neighboring Cambodia, where I discovered extraordinary beauty and a rich heritage. During those months I increasingly realized the extent to which the US involvement in what was to have been a military endeavor was, in fact, penetrating and bringing change to the deepest and most remote areas of life in Southeast Asia.

CHAPTER 4

Exploring the Country ...
And Christmas

My language group had been in Vietnam for just a few months when IVS arranged for us to spend three days in Vũng Tàu, a beach resort town on the South China Sea. This was our first trip away from our stations; the IVS leadership described it as a "mental break."

This was most important for IVSers working in remote areas, where they had little opportunity to escape being the center of attention in their village in those first few months of their tours. I was experiencing a different kind of culture shock, now living in an overcrowded city with a barely tolerable decibel level and unable to communicate with most people I met. I needed a break just as much. But the trip was much more than a break. It was an eye-opener to how the US military kept soldiers in the game. And how the US presence was disrupting the norms and culture of the Vietnamese people.

Vũng Taù sat on the South China Sea and sported miles of sandy white beaches and blocks of bars and tattoo parlors. Once a resort town frequented by French expatriates and Vietnamese alike, it had become the only in-country rest-and-recreation (R&R) site set up by the US military. Rest and recreation. More like free-flowing beer and women and beach time, twenty-four hours a day.

The US army thought this was necessary to keep up the morale of the troops. Fight four or five months, then take a three-day break from the war. Anything to help draftees get through the thirteen-month in-country commitment. Additional breaks were offered for those who extended their stay. Apparently with little regard for what it did to this once peaceful town.

The army provided housing for the US soldiers in Vũng Tàu. The women, bars, and related establishments followed on their own. Children roamed the area, offering to shine shoes and sell postcards. American music spilled out on to the streets. The atmosphere was festive and raunchy.

Our free time was limited by the hours we spent watching CIA propaganda films about the government-sponsored Revolutionary Development Program and by other group activities planned for the weekend. A fellow IVSer asked one of our American presenters if the US had any concern about the way it was disrupting the traditional life of the town. His answer was that change is inevitable and people will get used to it. Called it modernization. This was subtle indoctrination about why the government supported IVS in Vietnam.

But none of that kept us from squeezing in time for the beautiful beach. The breeze from the ocean offset the heat of the sun.

I left Vũng Tàu with a sense of relief and questions. Would all of Vietnam be "modernized" like Vũng Tàu?

My first exposure to Vietnamese youth in action came in December and took me to another world. The US and North Vietnamese armies agreed to a Christmas truce, and a group of Vietnamese Buddhist students took full advantage. They planned a work camp in a village not far from the mountainous city of Đà Lạt, near the edge of the Central Highlands.

I was surprised by the agreement of a truce at Christmas, particularly since one army was predominately non-Christian. I was also concerned that we were being naïve in expecting that the truce would be honored. Despite my doubts, I boarded an Air Vietnam flight on the morning of December 24 and flew to Đà Lạt.

The flight took less than two hours, going from a city close to sea level to a town 5,000 feet above sea level. I knew as soon as I got off the airplane why Đà Lạt was such a popular vacation destination.

(Letter home: December 28, 1966)

Đà Lạt, an old resort city, is beautifully situated on rolling hills quite different than anything I had seen since our stopover in Alaska on our initial flight to Asia.... Fields of vegetables crowded the scarce patches of flat terrain, and the smell of flowers was everywhere. Girls walked around in the traditional white áo dài *but wore heavy sweaters over them—almost as colorful as in Scandinavia.[12] Besides the freshness of the air the most striking thing was the lack of noise, mechanical noise, that drones continually in Saigon.*

The city was home to Đà Lạt University, one of Vietnam's major universities, as well as the summer residence of Vietnam's last emperor, Bảo Đại. Đà Lạt appeared to be surprisingly untouched by the war. There were a few Vietnamese soldiers in the town, but I saw no US soldiers during our stay. I assumed that the US kept its presence there to a minimum because of the historical significance of the city or simply because there seemed little strategic advantage to placing military camps on the side of a mountain covered with vegetable gardens and strawberry patches.

While temperatures in Saigon hovered in the upper eighties during the dry season, Đà Lạt's temperature ranged from fifty-five to

---

[12] The *áo dài* has been a traditional mode of dress in Vietnam for hundreds of years. In its basic form it is a long-sleeved, ankle-length tunic, often made of silk, with side slits up to the waist, that is worn over slim trousers. While girls of high school age usually wear white, women often wear the *áo dài* in prints and bright colors for festive and formal occasions.

seventy degrees Fahrenheit throughout the year. It felt like eternal spring. But I did not linger long in the city. I connected with the Saigon students, who had arrived the day before, and boarded a bus that carried us further up the mountain to Suối Thông village. The air was considerably cooler than in Đà Lạt. We arrived in early afternoon and the students immediately built a large fire outside of an open-air schoolhouse that served as our camp for two days. I put on the one sweater and jacket that I had brought to Vietnam and ended up wearing them both for most of the visit.

Suối Thông village was off-limits to Americans not on official business, but no one seemed to question my presence. Montagnard refugees lived in the village, one of many set up by the government to help the mountain-dwellers avoid US air strikes.[13] The US military frequently dropped bombs and napalm[14] in the mountains to interrupt the flow of weaponry and soldiers moving from North Vietnam down the Hồ Chí Minh Trail into the South.[15]

The Montagnards were largely nomadic and found village life to be an alien experience. But they seemed to adapt. Many of the men were conscripted into the army and assigned to work with units of US military, who reported that they found the Montagnards easier to work with than the Vietnamese soldiers.

---

[13] Montagnard was the French name that referred to all the minority tribes living in the mountains. The word literally means "mountain people." There were actually twenty-nine separate tribes, all ethnically different from the Vietnamese and each with its own language. There were approximately 600,000 Montagnards in South Vietnam in the 1960s.

[14] Napalm is a flammable substance contained in canisters that immediately ignites upon impact. The US military used it to burn vegetation in order to expose opposing troops, as well as to kill the enemy directly, but its use was not limited to isolated areas. The residue that remained continued to contaminate the soil for many years to come and caused birth defects in newborn children.

[15] The Hồ Chí Minh Trail was a network of jungle trails that led from North Vietnam into the South, some going west into Laos, on Vietnam's northwestern border. The trails were the major supply line for troops and equipment from the North to the South.

The work camp was organized to help the villagers build a community building. I soon discovered that our visit to the village was less about manual labor and more about bringing good cheer and joy to the village children. After settling into the camp, we wrapped small gifts—cookies, candy, toys—to pass out to the children. This was my first Christmas away from home. Not surprisingly, my thoughts turned toward my family, 12,000 miles away, and Christmases in our small but comfortable three-bedroom, one-bath home in the suburbs of Washington, D.C. I was in a state of melancholy when I heard musical sounds coming from one of the nearby huts. Not just any music, but clearly the tune of "Silent Night."

"This must be my imagination," I thought. But then my Vietnamese colleagues began talking about the music. A few of us decided to explore its source and walked down the hill to the tin-covered building from where it was coming. I was not expecting what we discovered. A group of villagers was sitting on benches while a few others stood at one end of the one large room and led them all in the singing of the Christmas carol. When the villagers saw us, they immediately escorted to the front bench, as the choir began to sing, again, "Silent Night," in their native language of Co Ho. The service then ended, leaving me feeling flushed and full of—yes—joy, and nostalgia.[16]

As I wandered around the village after the service, I heard rhythmic sounds akin to jazz and, seeking their source, came upon five elderly men playing copper gongs of different sizes. They pounded the gongs with their fists and then turned the gongs to create variations in the tones. Soon several of my work-camp colleagues joined me, and the men put on a full-fledged concert—the same rhythmic beat for about twenty minutes.

---

[16] Later one of the villagers told me that, in fact, the small hut where we had joined in singing the Christmas carols was one of four churches in the village and that the whole community had been converted to Christianity by Protestant missionaries. I did not learn if the missionaries were French, American, Vietnamese, or from some other country or when the conversions occurred.

(Letter home: December 28, 1966)

Although the beat was the same it never became
monotonous. And with my Western orientation I
could almost hear an alto sax taking off with melodic
variations, but never overpowering the rhythm section.

After an early Christmas Eve dinner of minced-meat sandwiches, I was hustled off with two others in our group to another church for another Christmas service. This church, like the first, was built of wood, with a hard mud floor and tin roof. The village elders, all men, wore brightly colored ties and sat in the front on one side of the room on hard wooden benches. They quietly nodded their approval as congregants came to the front and recited their lines, which I assumed to be their part of the Christmas story.

(Letter home: December 28, 1966, continued)

Each recitation, delivered very fast and in a determined
fashion so as not to miss a line, was interspersed by singing
from a large choir of boys and girls from 10 to 25 years
old. The sound of familiar hymns such as "O Come, All Ye
Faithful" and "The First Noel," translated into Co Ho, filled
the church with a certain gaiety as a soft wind whistled
through the pine forest. Only one girl failed to remember her
lines. She hurriedly left the stage in deep embarrassment.

After this second service I took a stroll around the village of well-built huts, surrounded by pine trees and small patches of corn and upland rice. But I soon had second thoughts about wandering by myself as darkness approached, fearful that I might be mistaken for an intruder by one of the indigenous Montagnard Popular Force Guards who protected the village. So I headed back to the camp, where I found a large bonfire ablaze, surrounded by children dancing and laughing in delight.

After watching the children a few minutes, I decided to teach them the game of Stoop Tag, a standard game of tag in which one becomes safe not by touching a tree or returning to home base, but by stooping quickly before being tagged by the one who is "it." I thought my Vietnamese was good enough to explain the game to the children, but they were Montagnards, so my Vietnamese was as useless as English. I then tried to use pantomime and imitation. The children soon caught on to the idea that they were safe if they stooped, and they quickly began to jump up when my back was turned. But they never quite understood that when they were caught it was their turn to be the chaser. I got a lot of good exercise that night!

To the delight of the children, we distributed gifts and candy and sang songs led by the Vietnamese students. As the night wore on, the village families began drifting away and, when the last of them left, we sat down to a late-night supper of curry and sweet soup.

I soon fell into a heavy slumber but was roused about 5 a.m. by a hearty rendition of "Zum Gali Gali," sung with gusto by the village children in their native Co Ho. I could not understand the words, but I recognized the tune as that of an Israeli folksong that was popular at summer campfires back home in Maryland. I don't know when or how they learned that song. Apparently, they realized that we enjoyed hearing it, and they returned to our quarters every half-hour to sing another round. Or perhaps they decided that it was a good way to rouse us out of bed. Whatever their motivation, there was no more sleep for us that night.

After a breakfast of a rice and salt dish and another church service, we left the village with great fanfare. By the following day I was back in the sweltering heat and dust of Saigon, still feeling soothed from two days of peace in the mountains. I knew I would never again celebrate Christmas without recalling that village in the mountains of Vietnam and the sound of "Silent Night" wafting out in a strange tongue to draw a homesick American into the Christmas spirit.

CHAPTER 5

More Travels, More Travails

With my return from Đà Lạt to Saigon came an abrupt reminder that the war had not gone away during my sojourn in the mountains. On the first full day back, I was one of several IVSers asked to assist in refugee resettlement in the provincial capital city of Bình Dương, thirty miles north of Saigon. Bình Dương had become a refugee holding area when a joint US-Vietnamese military operation forced 6,000 people out of their villages in the region. Villagers received short notice that their homes were to be destroyed and their villages demolished. Large military trucks brought families, mostly women and children, from their villages to Bình Dương. There were few men and boys over the age of twelve on the trucks; they likely had already been recruited or conscripted by ARVN or the Việt Cộng.

Clearing the villages appeared to be part of a strategy aimed at starving the enemy by separating anti-government forces from the villagers, thereby cutting off the enemies' food supply. The plan probably backfired, as the abrupt disruption of the villagers likely did more to generate antagonism toward the South Vietnamese government than to reduce supplies for the National Liberation Front.

For one long day, we helped the families as they tried to make new homes in tents that were a hundred feet long and ten feet wide. The tents were lined up in rows on an empty field and surrounded by barbed wire. It was hard to distinguish the "resettlement" from a prison.

I was appalled. Appalled at the action by our military and appalled that IVSers had assisted in its operation. What made it worse was knowing that this kind of operation was happening all over the country. Families poured off the trucks at the camp, looking exhausted and bewildered. Every member carried a bundle in their arms, whatever they had managed to gather when the evacuation order came. Their lives had been shattered.

I had volunteered to assist because I wanted to observe this part of the war effort. But the irony of my involvement was not lost on me. We had come to Vietnam to help make lasting improvements in the lives of the Vietnamese. But in this type of action, we only aided the war effort by temporarily mitigating the pain caused by our government.

I knew I had to see more of Vietnam if I was going to get any better understanding of what was really going on. For some months I had been working in Saigon with members of South Vietnam's National Voluntary Services (NVS). Hoping to learn firsthand the effects of that work in the countryside, I set out to visit NVS work sites in An Khê and Phan Rang, provincial capitals north of Saigon.

My journey began at Tân Sôn Nhút air base in Saigon, where I boarded a US C-130 military transport plane to fly to Quy Nhơn for a one-night stay before catching a smaller military plane to An Khê, in Bình Định Province. After the beauty of Đà Lạt, Quy Nhơn was a huge disappointment. The city was located near the coast, halfway between Saigon and Đà Nẵng, and I had visions of walking on a sandy beach and drinking *café sua* while watching the sun rise.[17] But the city was slightly inland; the rainy season was still in full force; mud covered the sidewalks while the roads were a mess due to heavy military vehicles. The city seemed to be completely overrun with American and Korean soldiers. Dozens of bars and restaurants lined the streets, where droves of prostitutes solicited customers. After four months in Vietnam, I no longer found the scenes surprising, but they were still deeply disturbing.

---

[17] The French introduced coffee and hot milk to Vietnam when they colonized the country in the mid-nineteenth century.

Prostitution was one of the few ways available for women uprooted by the war to support themselves and their families. The scenes called to mind one of the most famous Vietnamese literary works, an epic poem written in 1820 by Nguyễn Du, called *"Truyện Kiều."* In the poem Truyện Kiều sells herself into marriage to save her family, only to discover that her husband is a pimp who forces her into a life of prostitution. Kiều became a folk legend and hero because of her sacrifice. There were an estimated 300,000 prostitutes in Vietnam at the height of the war. The US military no doubt realized early on that it could not prevent soldiers from taking advantage of their services. In some towns, following French practice, the US military even set up facilities to confine the practice, and medics regularly checked the women for venereal diseases. In An Khê the facility was referred to by soldiers as "the plaza."

After one night in Quy Nhơn, I boarded another military plane for the twenty-minute flight to the landing strip near An Khê, located further inland in a slightly mountainous region. I waited there almost two hours in drizzling rain before catching a ride to the town. While waiting, I talked with various US military personnel and learned more about the area. An Khê was largely populated by people who had been forced off their land so the US military could create free-fire zones—areas where the military could bomb at will without concern for civilians on the ground. The people were categorized as refugees and given small plots of land on which to grow vegetables, but the plots were too small to support the families, and most of the refugees appeared to work for the US military. I saw long lines of people walking to and from the base each day, picks and shovels in hand. One IVS volunteer, Bob Spencer, was trying to provide an alternative. He promoted chicken-raising and helped some families build chicken coops. He was one person trying to take the long view when most people around him just wanted to survive day-to-day.

I spent most of my time in An Khê at the NVS compound, a thirty-minute walk from town. About twenty young Vietnamese men and women lived together in a sprawling farm building, pursuing various projects. My language ability was still quite limited, and the youth in this group were not as fluent in English as my counterparts in Saigon. I spent a lot of time observing.

Some of the NVS workers ran an abbreviated school for children who were engaged in the shoeshine business. Shining boots of soldiers was a big source of income for families, particularly during the muddy rainy season. Many children were sent from their homes in nearby villages to the town, where they became street urchins, to be closer to their customers. The NVS program was providing some normalcy in the children's lives, as well as food once a day.

Other volunteers provided medical treatment for minor cuts and bites, operated a dispensary to distribute medicine, and managed a demonstration farm where they grew vegetables. But they had yet to work out an effective way to involve a significant number of An Khê's residents, so their impact was still limited.

I left An Khê with some feeling of optimism that there were Vietnamese youth who were willing to volunteer their time and who believed they could make a difference if given sufficient resources and respite from the war. They were the reason I sweltered in Saigon helping to support what they did.

That sense of optimism followed me to my next stop, an NVS project in Phan Rang in Ninh Tuấn Province, located in the central part of the country. The area was one of the loveliest I had visited.

(Letter home: May 13, 1967)

Phan Rang is probably the most peaceful city in Vietnam and one of the least affected by the American presence (at least, in my experience). It is located near the sea, with the clearest blue water I have seen, and nestled among rolling foothills. Even the sounds of F-105 bomber jets flying into nearby Cam Ranh Bay are muffled by the hills. The climate is mostly hot and dry with only a soft sea breeze providing relief. There is almost no rainy season. Remnants of the Cham civilization, which reigned over the area six hundred

years ago, sit on top of a small rocky mountain nearby.
Approximately 10,000 Cham people, who are more ethnically
akin to Cambodians than Vietnamese, still live in the area,
but none appeared at the myriad of burial temples of their
ancient kings during my visit. After travelling by shrines
and temples while on a two-week vacation in Japan, it was
very strange to visit an almost equally impressive ancient
site with no people or concession stands around. No doubt
that day will come (when peace comes to Vietnam).[18]

An enchanting place, yet even here I encountered the incongruities
of a war with no geographical battle lines.

"Why did that boat just latch on to ours?" I asked Quáng, the NVS
volunteer accompanying me.

"It's an American navy boat," he said looking out a window. "You
tell me."

We had just embarked on a closed ferry, heading from Phan Rang
for a small island off Cam Ranh Bay where refugees were being
dumped. We wanted to see if NVS could do anything to help out. It
was still early in the morning, and our boat was crammed full of day
laborers and merchants. Suddenly two US soldiers came down the
narrow staircase and began slowly walking down the aisle—looking
closely at each passenger.

"I think they are checking for weapons or bombs," Quàng said.

No one on the boat said a word as the soldiers moved cautiously
toward the back. Then they saw me—and stopped. First, they looked
surprised. Then relieved. They glanced around the boat one more time
and then turned around and left. Apparently, they thought the boat
must be safe if there was an American on board.

On the island we found refugees, as rumored, but saw little that
NVS could do to help. And so we returned to the NVS compound,
about ten kilometers outside the city, where NVS volunteers were

---

[18] Tourism in Vietnam today is big business.

Woman boarding local ferry going to refugee island. (Cam Ranh Bay, 1967)

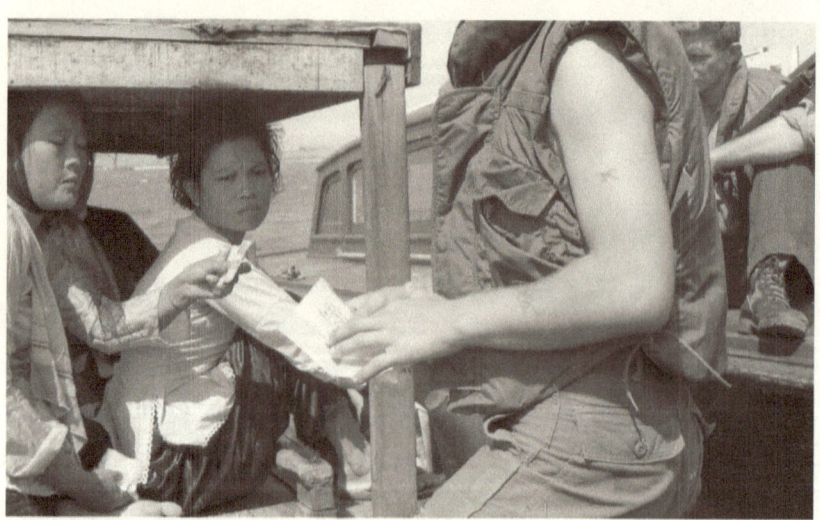

US military personnel checking papers of persons going to refugee island on local ferry. (Cam Ranh Bay, 1967)

Refugee camp on island. (Cam Ranh Bay, 1967)

working with three Japanese agriculture technicians, seeking to carve out an experimental farm. The task was daunting. The land was very parched and dotted with native cactus, the only plants that seemed to thrive in the dry conditions. Despite a discouraging apathy among local farmers, the NVS workers succeeded in demonstrating that, with enough irrigation, the land could support vegetables and rice. But the experiment ended abruptly when the US military bombed the area, completely destroying the farm and injuring one of my former Saigon housemates, Miss Lan, and another of the project's residents. When I learned what had happened, I felt sad and empty, empty because it was no surprise that months of planning and implementation had come to such an abrupt end.

The author on ferry returning from refugee camp. (Cam Ranh Bay, 1967)

CHAPTER 6

The Imperial City

My travels through South Vietnam had greatly increased my appreciation for the country's beauty and my understanding of the impact the war had on the people. But nothing prepared me for the rich journey into history that came in the summer of 1967, when I encountered Huế, the Imperial City.

(Letter home: August 11, 1967)

Huế, the Imperial City, exudes a sense of history and timelessness from the throne room of the Imperial Palace to the nearby rice fields irrigated with pedal pumps made of bamboo. The beauty of the Sông Hương (Perfume River), fragrantly clear and refreshing, continually haunts strangers and inhabitants alike as one realizes that the river itself is Huế and sets the atmosphere. Sampans move leisurely under the stone and steel bridges along banks of lotus flowers, the flower of Vietnam. Áo dài clad women crowd the ferry boats, bound for market. Tall and sturdy stands the wall built by Vietnam's first emperor, Gia Lông, to hold back the Chinese [in 1804]. It surrounds the entire inner city of peasant homes.

The city of so much turbulence last spring that forced the evacuation of all American personnel here moves peacefully through the day to the rhythm of bicycles that crowd the roads and the presence on almost every corner of Nuốc Mía

*stands (sugar cane water), which promise to quench an ever-
present thirst.[19] A short swim in one of the many canals off
the river, a ride through the straw villages, a moment of rest
at the Từ Dàm Pagoda, under the Bodhi tree—the same kind
of tree under which Buddha found enlightenment centuries
ago—and time slips away.... Only at night in fact are there
reminders of the present. They come from two oversized
Vietnamese tanks that rumble through the city at high speed
to remind the people that the South Vietnam government
is protecting them. And from the noise of bombs seemingly
creeping closer to the city's gates. The bombs are perhaps
a reminder that no one is ever safe in a war zone. Today
I ate ice cream with a new friend, Xoa. His family's home
was destroyed two months ago by the bombs of the army.*

The monsoon season was over, and Saigon was again hot and dusty. But I found some respite in Huế. I knew that Huế had a long history of political activism and was the site of the first demonstrations by Buddhist monks in the early 1960s. Thus I was not surprised to find store fronts covered with election posters lauding candidates for the presidency and national assembly.

Having entertained a somewhat romantic vision of a pristine historic capital, however, I was disappointed to find that the streets were similarly filled with the trappings of commercialism. Several shops displayed televisions as well as cameras for sale. Few homes in Vietnam had their own television, and those that did often positioned the screen so that it could be seen from the alleys and streets in front of the houses. Vietnamese soap operas seemed to be very popular. There were few signs of the war that raged outside the city's edge.

I came to Huế to participate in a student work and seminar camp with over a hundred Vietnamese youth from various parts

---

[19] In the spring of 1966, Huế was the site of widespread protests against the South Vietnamese government for its treatment of Buddhists. Protestors at one point burned a building the US had been using in Huế.

of the country, including Saigon and Đà Lạt. The air was fresh. We flew to Đà Lạt to pick up about twenty youth affiliated with the National Voluntary Services as well as IVS volunteer Chris Jenkins and were greeted with the ever-present coolness of Đà Lạt. But the relief from the heat didn't last long. As soon as we landed at Huế's Phú Bài airport and boarded busses for the twenty minute ride to Huế, the Đà Lạt students shed their turtleneck sweaters. Another IVSer, Len Ackland, joined us in Huế.

We had planned to spend the night in Huế and then take a Vietnamese navy boat to the island of Cù Lao Re, but we learned that the nearby Vietnamese Navy base had been overrun by the Việt Cộng. There was no boat to take us on the long trip to the island. It was unclear when a boat might appear, so we were left on our own to explore the city. This was the first time many of the students from Đà Lạt and Saigon had been to Huế, and we quickly became tourists together.

We walked through the Imperial Palace, built over several years starting in 1804, and a nearby pagoda. The palace had some interesting ornamentation but was not particularly impressive, except that it had been preserved for so long. It had also suffered from years of neglect because of the war.[20] The moat surrounding the palace was covered with lotus plants. Young women moved among the visitors selling a Huế delicacy, *sữa trứng nóng với đường*, a type of hot custard served with sugar. The presence of these women was the only visible sign that tourists still frequented the palace.

We also toured the main city of Huế across the river and passed by significant landmarks. We saw the burned-out United States Information Service library, a target of the anti-American riots the year before. Out of spite, I assumed, the US refused to restore the building or even clean up the site. We stopped at the Từ Dàm Pagoda,

---

[20] Six months after my visit, the walled city was one of the sites of a three-week battle during the 1968 Tết Offensive. The fighting destroyed much of the wall and reduced some of the buildings to rubble. I returned to Vietnam in 1999 and was pleased to see that restoration was well underway.

a base of operations in 1963 for Buddhists challenging the Ngô Đình Diệm government. And we walked past the oldest high school in Vietnam, Trướng Quốc Hoc, where Hồ Chí Minh and Ngô Đình Diệm, Vietnam's most significant leaders in the twentieth century, had attended school.[21]

We had come to Huế not as tourists, however, but to organize a work camp, so we soon shifted our focus to the walled village inside the grounds of the Imperial Palace. There we took on a series of improvement projects at an elementary school. We dug holes, carried dirt, cut bamboo, and performed other tasks as needed to repair a bridge, build a children's playground, and build a six-stall latrine.

The young student leaders, all in their early twenties, assigned us to teams with responsibility for meal preparation and cleanup. Each of us had a stab at cooking, and it was then that I noticed some chickens in cages. For the first and only time in my life, I participated in the entire process of cooking a chicken, from its encounter with the chopping block to adding spices to the broth. It was almost enough to turn me into a vegetarian. I was very impressed with how smoothly the students ran the camp, which I attributed to a clear division of responsibilities.

Our days ended with a cooling-off on the wall next to the canal. My new young friends Tuấn, Quàng, and Mạnh poured buckets of water

---

[21] Hồ Chí Minh formed the Communist Party of Vietnam while in exile in China in 1930 and led the Việt Minh's fight for independence against the French, a war that culminated in the Battle of Điện Biên Phủ. He emerged as the official leader and prime minister of the northern half of a divided Vietnam in 1955. By the time he was seventy-seven years old in 1967, "Uncle Ho" served more as the spiritual leader of North Vietnam's efforts to conquer the South, rather than as the chief military strategist. Responsibility for handling day-to-day governance and waging the war had passed to Lê Duẩn and Võ Nguyên Giáp.

Ngô Đình Diệm fled to France when the French came back to assert control over Vietnam after World War II, but he returned to Vietnam in 1954 to assume the position of prime minister under Emperor Bảo Đại. The next year, Diệm defeated the emperor in a referendum. The United States reportedly played a significant role in elevating Diệm to power. Originally seen as a populist, his continued misuse of power triggered a coup d'état by his own generals in 1963 that led to his death.

over me, which was a welcome relief for some aching muscles that I had not used in a long time. Often this was followed by a glass of *nước chanh đá*—iced lemonade. I fervently adhered to not drinking local tap water because of potential contaminants, but I was less cautious when it came to iced fruit drinks.

During our long breaks after lunch and sometimes after dinner, I strolled with fellow work campers along the deteriorating wall and through the rice fields and vegetable gardens that separated the houses. The children in the village, who had become accustomed to our presence and followed us around, called out *"Cù Tèo,"* the Vietnamese name given to me at a campfire the night before. This was a familiar name often given to the youngest son. Chris, Len, and I were about the same age, so I don't know how I warranted it, but hearing the children call me that was so much better than being called "you, you, you," which is how children frequently addressed me in Saigon, a foreigner in their midst.

Language was a barrier for me as well as for my new Vietnamese friends. Each of us tried what we knew, which meant I was asked seemingly one hundred times a day if I had slept well, if I was tired yet, if I was hungry yet, if the food was good, and so on. Fortunately, this rather wearisome exchange faded by the end of two weeks as we grew more comfortable with each other and our cultural differences. The only rather awkward moment came on the first night as I was setting up my tent. There were a few boys hanging about in furtive discussion, and I finally figured out what they wanted to know. Who was going to get to spend the night with me in my tent? I was aware that physical contact among males was not a sexual act but rather a way of showing friendship. This was often expressed by holding hands with a companion while walking down the street, and there were a few times when I willed myself to participate in that ritual. I did, however, have my limits and told the boys, *"Tôi ước được ngủ một mình."* ("I wish to sleep alone.") I was never asked again.

There were a few special moments that occurred at the camp. One happened the second evening, after midnight, while some of us were sitting on steps next to a very swampy part of the river.

(Letter home: September 3, 1967)

A few of us were chatting and listening to the mortar
fire in the distance when Đào pulled out a violin from his
sack and proceeded to entertain us for the next hour or so. A
cloud-speckled sky, lit up by a near full moon, added to the
sur-reality of listening to Mozart and Haydn in the northern
reaches of South Vietnam. The sound of crickets and mortars
blended extremely well, and even the pesky mosquitoes were
forgotten for a while. Đào, from Huế, has been studying for
four years at the conservatory there, as well as for many
years before, becoming quite proficient on the instrument.

We completed our work in Huế and then moved to a place on the
coast twenty miles to the east, where we camped on the beach and spent
two days in seminars discussing the role of youth in the future of the
country. Much of the discussion centered on the distinction between
politics and public service. But the substance of the talks escaped me.

Returning to Saigon, I reflected on the work-camp experience,
particularly the joy of working with others in trying to make a
difference in the community. What I did not understand, and missed
completely, was that the work-camp experience for some of the
Vietnamese participants was an absurdity—trying to make a difference
with so much destruction and need all around. This was expressed in a
long poem by Trần Đại that begins as follows:

I have to build a latrine.
While the people starve
Begging impatiently
For a handful of corn
Enough to feed them[22]

---

[22] This poem was included in a collection of poems and letters given to me, as
I prepared to leave Vietnam for the last time, by a Vietnamese soldier sympa-
thetic to the National Liberation Front. He hoped that I would get the collection
published in order to help Americans understand the agony of this war. The full
text of the poem as well as others is printed in Chapter 31.

CHAPTER 7

Tết, February 1967

Tết 1968 was to be climactic. The memory is lodged in the minds of Americans and Vietnamese who lived through it, and for their loved ones back home.

But my first Tết in Vietnam, in 1967, was just another three-day festival marking the lunar New Year. I was still pondering the contrasts between the beauty of the Imperial City and the realities of contemporary Vietnam when I returned to Saigon in time to join in preparations. Like Christmas in the US, the festivities start long before the actual three-day event. My first encounter with the celebration was as a somewhat honored guest at a party thrown by my students at the College of Agriculture. It was held in our classroom, now draped creatively in crepe paper and boasting refreshments appropriate for the occasion. (No alcohol!) The party gave us an excuse to overindulge in, among other things, *mứt Tết*, a seasonal favorite consisting of candied fruits and vegetables, from sliced coconuts to sweet potatoes, frosted with cane sugar.

To my great relief, I did not have to sing a song, as had been previously threatened, but the students did invite me to give a speech. In a combination of Vietnamese and English I told them how happy I was to celebrate the New Year with them and how glad I was to be a part of their lives. Some of the students, knowing that they would not be able to go home for the holiday because of the war, expressed their sadness. But for the most part it was a festive occasion.

My next party was a more formal affair, hosted by a former IVS volunteer who was then working with USAID. Among the guests was Henry Cabot Lodge, the US ambassador to Vietnam, as well as several other US officials and Vietnamese youth leaders. Ambassador Lodge left early, accompanied by his military police entourage and Vietnamese officials, and suddenly it was party time. A Vietnamese band played American rock-and-roll songs, and firecrackers began exploding throughout the streets of Saigon. The South Vietnamese government had banned fireworks for fear they would be confused with the sound of small-arms fire, but it was the season of Tết, and no mere governmental edict could restrain the enthusiasm and celebratory spirit that had reigned for centuries at this, Vietnam's most important holiday. The decorations might have been traditional Vietnamese, with Tết-related paraphernalia, but the atmosphere was like the raucous New Year's Eve celebrations I was accustomed to on the other side of the world.

For the Vietnamese, Tết is not only a time to celebrate the New Year; it is also a time to reconnect with one's ancestors. For the three days, ancestral spirits descend upon households and take up residence. No one is allowed to sweep the floor for three days, for fear of brushing out these spirits. Candles are lit in homes and in the pagodas, marking a time of reverence. Visitors are welcomed and special candies and cakes are served in celebration. Adults wrap new paper money in special sleeves to hand out to the children. All is right with the world. And in 1967, the world of Saigon, as I had come to know it, stopped for those three days.

In the days leading up to Tết, school children performed plays highlighting important historical events. Shop owners and landlords festooned their buildings with long strings of firecrackers that they, or perhaps the neighborhood teens, periodically ignited. Dragon dancers moved up and down the streets to the sound of drums. Street markets, with long rows of tables displaying candies, fruits, clothes, and crafts, popped up overnight. I bumped into one market that was crowded with hordes of people and illuminated by strings of colored lights powered by generators. It felt like carnivals back home, but it had a limited life. When I returned the day before Tết officially began, it was practically empty, peopled with only a few last-minute shoppers and vendors packing up their wares. The Tết festivities were moving from the streets into homes.

The restaurants closed early the day before Tết officially began and remained closed throughout the three-day holiday. Fortunately, one of my students invited another IVSer and me to join her family for dinner. This was the traditional dinner on the eve of Tết, when the people invite their ancestors to return to their homes to be with their families. Before eating, the family set out portions of each dish of the meal at the base of an altar for the ancestors. It was an elaborate ritual, and by the time we sat down for dinner, the food was cold. But it was still delicious.

It was important to understand the customs of Tết because ignorance could lead to a misstep with dire consequence. I learned that the first visitor after midnight on the first day of Tết determines the fortunes of the household for the coming year, particularly whether they will encounter good luck or bad. When I realized that the evening was getting late, my friend and I departed, just a half hour before midnight. We didn't want the responsibility of determining that family's fate for the next twelve months!

The city was still alive, so we headed to Chợ Lớn, the Chinese part of town, which had its own traditions. Arriving at midnight, we encountered masses of people celebrating; dragon dancers and drummers blocked the streets and firecrackers pierced the night air. Most of the action in the Chinese community on this day was outside of the pagodas. Many celebrants were anxious to learn their fortune for the year, which they did by shaking numbered joss sticks in a wooden container.[23] Eventually one joss stick would emerge from the

---

[23] Joss sticks, also known as incense sticks, are narrow sticks of wood, about eight inches long, wrapped in a combustible material infused with an aroma. Vietnamese Buddhists light them and place them at altars created in their homes to honor deceased relatives.

container and fall to the ground. The celebrant would exchange the fallen joss stick for a piece of paper with the corresponding number on it. And that small piece of paper would announce the shaker's fortunes for the entire coming year. I decided I was better off not knowing.

On the first day of Tết, all was quiet throughout the city. This was a day for families to gather in their homes and for outsiders like me to stay indoors. I have no memory of how I used that time, probably writing and reading letters from home. But I couldn't wait for the public celebrations to begin again.

The Vietnamese devoted the second day of Tết to visiting friends and honoring ancestors at the local pagodas, burning pungent incense purchased from street merchants. Devout Vietnamese also burned incense in homage to Buddha and, in one pagoda, in honor of Le Văn Duyệt. A war hero from Vietnam's war with the Chinese many centuries earlier, Duyệt was entombed outside Saigon.

There was a recent tradition in Saigon after the first day of Tết, reminiscent of New Year's celebrations in the States. Family obligations fulfilled, ancestors honored, fortunes pronounced, some people of Saigon seemed with one accord to pack the movie houses. Joining in the fun, I saw *Bonnie and Clyde* at a single-screen theater, the dialogue in French with Vietnamese, Chinese, and English subtitles. Not surprisingly, the subtitles covered half the screen.

Tết in Saigon, 1967, a time of parties in the days leading up to the New Year, three days of ritual and celebration, and then, almost as an anticlimax, life returned to normal—or at least, as normal as a city in the middle of a war can be.

CHAPTER 8

Life in Saigon, 1967

In the year following that Tết celebration, it seemed that politics was always on the minds of people in Saigon. The city had four or five daily Vietnamese language papers and one daily paper in English, *The Saigon Daily News*. Much of the news dealt with upcoming elections. I stubbornly bought one Vietnamese language paper every day, thinking I just might be able to glean some insight, but that rarely happened.

Much of the news dealt with demonstrations and marches. I came across one march involving a thousand or so school children. One student told me that his school administrator had ordered him to participate, but he did not know why. The official reason for the demonstration was to protest the formation of a Vietnamese government-in-exile in Paris. These ex-patriots were hoping to gain the attention and the support of key government leaders in the US. Doubtless the South Vietnamese government sought, through such demonstrations, to show the people's widespread support for the existing government and the relative lack of support for those seeking to install a new government, one less supportive of the war.

Reminders of the war were never far away, and the reminders did not always come in the way expected. One day I received word from a friend, Minh-Tuãn, that his brother, a soldier in the South Vietnamese military, had been killed in battle. I visited Minh-Tuãn's home soon after and encountered a family in shock. A large picture of the brother hung on the wall. Candles burned on a table under the picture, along with some of the soldier's possessions. I knew of no way to express my sorrow.

Two weeks later, on April 9, 1967, Minh-Tuấn's father, having lost his soldier-son to the war, showed up at my house and handed me a letter written that day. His English was imperfect, his print very neat. The letter brought me news of what had happened to my friend in those intervening two weeks.

Dear Mr. Dick Berliner

My son, Minh-Tuấn was arrested by the National Police 237 Cong Hoa Saigon Street from 31-3-1967. Sine [since], my son is not released.

I please you intervene for my son, thus he can free and come back to home.

As you know, I am recently losse my youger son (death in battlefield).

I am very suffering.

Before my bitterness situation,

I hope you to pay attention for my family interfere for my son.

Please accept here my grateful,

Your sincerely

Cát Cảng Tiến

A father grieved for two sons, one killed in combat in support of the government, the other arrested by the same government for alleged anti-government activity. The way of a civil war.

Young men like Minh-Tuấn were often arrested for no apparent reason in Saigon. Other IVSers and I assumed that the South Vietnamese government believed them to be opponents of the government and in some way involved in trying to bring it down. I did not know my friend well enough to know why he was picked up, but after reading his father's letter I did make some inquiries at the national police headquarters. I could not even get an acknowledgement that he was there. To our great relief, he was released a few weeks later. He never talked to me about what had happened.

On another occasion I was awakened by a sharp knock on our front door, well after midnight. Two policemen stood at the door, asking for one of my housemates, Thọ. When he appeared from the next room, the police told him to get dressed because they were taking him to the police station. With a sense of bravado, I started pulling on my pants and announced that I would accompany him. The police seemed confused, not quite sure how to handle my intrusion.

Fairly quickly they decided not to persist in taking Thọ into custody, instead telling him to come by the station the next day. He agreed. Thọ was not arrested, but he never explained to me what the incident was all about. I felt the sentiment expressed so clearly in the movie version of Graham Greene's *The Quiet American*: "When you come to Vietnam you learn a lot quickly. The rest you have to live."[24]

Some weeks after the Tết celebrations had begun to fade into memory, while I was still trying to understand what had happened to Minh-Tuấn and my housemate, life changed again—monsoons!

In Vietnam, the monsoon rain starts off in short spurts, lasting fifteen to twenty minutes. In such weather it was normally easy to find shelter in a café or shop and wait it out. But, as the monsoon season progressed, the spurts become marathons, and for all the creatures that roamed the streets of Saigon —including me— there was no escaping a complete drenching. The dust on the sidewalks turned to mud, but even during this time the sun eventually emerged to steam up the streets. And the temperature shot up. As the rains became heavier, I worried that the small river at the end of my alley might overflow its banks. It never happened. But the nights did become cooler, which meant I could sleep without the fan spinning over my head—except for those pesky mosquitoes.

---

[24] From *The Quiet American*, a 2002 film distributed by Miramax Films, based on the 1955 novel of the same name by Graham Greene.

On Sundays, I sometimes sought relief from the heat between rainstorms at the only public swimming pool in the city. Many Americans in Saigon had memberships at the prestigious Cercle Sportif or other private clubs that offered swimming, tennis, and dining, but I had neither the money required to join nor any interest in spending my time with other Americans.

The public pool, while quite large, was always overcrowded, and the water never quite cold enough to be refreshing. By the time I left the pool and biked to my house, the slight relief found in the pool's water had dissipated. It was as if the refreshing swim had never happened.

As the monsoon season dragged on, I realized that things were changing politically in Saigon. The police made more mysterious arrests as spontaneous protest marches became more frequent. College students organized a sit-in hunger strike in the School of Architecture to protest the arrests. The strike continued for several weeks until the police finally stepped in and put an end to it. Buddhist monks joined in the fray, marching to protest the adoption of new laws that appeared to curtail their rights.

In the midst of the unrest, the National Youth Council program director, Trần Ngọc Bảo, decided to run for a place in the national senate. As a result, work at the council, my principal arena of responsibility, ground to a halt. My focus then shifted to visiting NVS sites and IVS volunteers on behalf of the IVS leadership.

When I was not travelling for IVS, I spent a lot of time talking with youth about the future of Vietnam. A new housemate, Hùng, helped fill in a lot of gaps in my understanding of what was going on around me. Hùng was a student of architecture who had moved to Saigon to finish up his project for his degree. But once in Saigon he, too, found that he could not escape the reality of the war. He participated in the hunger strike at the School of Architecture, and we shared long, late-night talks about the corruption that permeated the Vietnamese-US relationship. All of this diverted him from his work, and I was not surprised when he announced one day that he would not make the deadline for submitting his final project report. I remember feeling somewhat guilty at the time for taking Hùng's attention away from his project during those weeks, but in retrospect I realized that his path reflected an essential reality of life in Saigon in the late 1960s. There was little incentive for the people, especially young men, to make plans, to set goals, to work toward meeting deadlines, because the nature of the war made life so uncertain.

Despite the growing chaos around me, I was generally upbeat about my situation, but at times my mood would shift from my natural optimism to moments of despair.

(Letter home: July 25, 1967)
Life in our house has become progressively more enjoyable as my Vietnamese ability increases and as I become pretty much accepted as just another member of our happy family, by the people with whom I live and by the frequent visitors.

But then, two short weeks later, I wrote my parents in a very different vein.

(Letter home: August 6, 1967)
I am deeply sorry that I caused such consternation by not writing for it certainly wasn't intentional. I am not quite sure why I have been writing less, except that I find that I have less patience with writing.... Much of this is due to a general depression I have been in for some time, not from a dissatisfaction with the day-to-day affairs of my life, although they seem greatly detached from what is consequential in this world, but from even being able to define what is

consequential. After reading The Little Prince *recently (what matters in life is a little flower all alone on a faraway planet who needs me) I have doubt I have been even thinking in the right direction. Violence seems to be the order of the day from China to Hong Kong to Burma to Indonesia to the Middle East to Nigeria, to the Congo, Vietnam, and in American cities.... Adding to the distemper of the situation is the budding crisis of materialism that appears in the form of crippling strikes in the affluent nations of North America and Europe. I'd like to think that my view from Vietnam is distorted, shaped by sensational media that thrives on disorder, but more and more it seems that this is not the case, that we are walking towards the middle of nowhere because there is nothing else to do. The way I am impacted is frightening. I become intolerant with intolerance, react violently to violence, and become cynical to a world plagued by cynicism. I find myself choosing sides (usually the wrong side) and thus become part of the factionalism that precipitates crisis.... President Johnson in response to the Detroit riots remarked: "We have endured a week such as no nation should live through, a time of violence and tragedy." Vietnam had endured centuries, the most violent and tragic being the present. "Unbelievable" someone remarked, "Americans shooting Americans." But for some reason shooting non-Americans in Vietnam became acceptable....*

Vietnam now is the best place for me to be. For in Vietnam exists a nation of people who have learned to endure hardship, but more importantly have learned to incorporate seemingly contradictory elements of the universe into a unified whole, which sees clear relationships among everything that exists (living or not living). These relationships have little to do with the cause-effect association that we (Westerners) use to explain things. The result is a sense of harmony that exists in the Universe that can only be overshadowed but

not replaced by the disharmony that man has created.
Consequently, I see in my friends an incredible reserve of
power that allows them to endure hardship and see light
where the dark prevails. I think what I see in them will
better prepare me for dealing with life's complexities.

I do know one thing for sure. What matters in life are
two parents that appreciate knowing whether their son is safe
and healthy in a world where we can no longer take these
things for granted. I am sorry if I sometimes forget this.

Looking back, I realize I may have been overdramatic. But the letter
did elicit the most heartfelt letter I had ever received from my always
stoic father.

(Letter from my father: August 16, 1967)
I was greatly moved by your letter. I must confess I had
the same choking feeling I had on the day you left almost
a year ago. In a sense I was again saying goodbye to a boy
facing adventure, uncertainty but with quiet courage and
idealism. Now I am meeting a man who too soon perhaps has
come face to face with the human race's great dilemma—the
pull toward the material that leads to self-destruction and
the pull towards the spiritual transformation that comes
from the heritage left by men like Bach, Mozart, Einstein,
Shakespeare, and so many many more. In Vietnam it is not
easy to keep the focus on the latter, but as you wrote, the
Vietnamese have learned to endure hardship and at the same
time achieve an inner peace. Even far away from Vietnam
(but still close to the contradiction of luxury and misery
enduring side by side and, appallingly, being accepted by
most Americans as a way of life) it is possible to find peace
only by cultivating your own garden, in the words of, I
think, Santayana, while not remaining isolated from the
challenges of the sick society that is America's today. I, too,

*find myself more intolerant than ever of the bad manners,
the neurotic behavior, the disgraceful way people dress
when visiting the Capital or the White House or Kennedy's
grave, the obscenity of commercial television creating
a nation of morons! It is symptomatic of a breakdown
that seems to me to be linked to growing lack of respect
for law which is, of course, the bulwark of a democratic
society. But no matter how discouraging things are,
there is one great driving force that keeps us going—the
necessity for making a better world for our children, or for
making our children more capable of finding a measure
of happiness even in the world as it exists today. Despite
your discouragement, we know that you have too much
to offer to give way to discouragement. You have the rare
gift of compassion and the ability to convey it in words.*

My father's words provided some comfort. But more importantly
they expressed shared anxieties and perhaps a pathway for maintaining
sanity, one that he followed through literature and through the music
that were so essential to his life. We rarely talked about these things
after I returned.

Both my hope and my despair found expression in the music of a
Vietnamese musician, Trịnh Công Sơn, whose anti-war songs evoked
images of Bob Dylan. IVS volunteer John Schafer, who became a
renowned authority on Sơn, wrote that it was not just his songs that
made Trịnh Công Sơn so popular but also his public appearances. As
Schafer reported:

A watershed event was a performance at the Faculty of
Letters of the University of Saigon in 1965. Organized by
some of Sơn's friends, and attended by artists, intellectuals,
and high school and college students, it took place on an
open space behind the University. This was Sơn's first
performance before a large audience, and he has said that he

looked upon it as an "experiment to see if he could exist in the hearts of the people."... He got his answer in the form of an enthusiastic response.[25]

I met Sơn one afternoon in a Saigon café, with some Vietnamese friends. At twenty-seven, he looked far older than his years, no doubt due to his dark-rimmed glasses, slight mustache, and look of sadness. We talked with him awhile and then he pulled out his guitar and began to play and sing. His songs mourned the sadness of an endless war and the loss of a Vietnam that had become only a memory. His words still haunt me.

Love Song of a Mad Person

I loved someone killed in the Battle of Pleime
I loved someone killed in Battlezone D
Killed in Xoi, killed in Hanoi
Killed suddenly near the border

I want to love you, to love Vietnam
In the storm my lips whisper your name
And the name Vietnam
Bound together by our golden-skin tongue

And,

A Mother's Legacy

A thousand years slaves of the Chinese
A hundred years dominated by the French
Twenty years of daily civil war
A mother's legacy, to leave for her children

[25] John C. Schafer, "The Trịnh Công Sơn Phenomenon," *The Journal of Asian Studies* 66, no. 3 (August 2007): 597–643.

A mother's legacy, the sad country of Vietnam
A mother's legacy, a forest of dry bones
A mother's legacy, a mountain of graves

Teach the children truthful speech
Mother hopes for her children won't forget the color of their skin
Children don't forget the skin color of the old Vietnam
Mother waits for her children to come home
Mother hopes that her children far away
Oh, children of the same father, will forget hatred[26]

The first song was sung to a mournful tune, almost a dirge. The second song had an upbeat, dance-like tune that could be sung with gusto, totally masking the content. It was written in 1965 during the early stages of the US's massive military involvement, and by 1967 youth in work camps throughout the South were singing the song.

In another song with upbeat lyrics, entitled "When My Country Has Peace," Sơn recites all the places inside Vietnam that he will be able to visit when Vietnam has peace, all the places where fighting and killing occurred. His early lyrics never strayed far from the war at that time, but it was not the kind of music smiled upon by either the North or the South Vietnamese governments. Both sides used music to rally the population, but their music was militaristic, upbeat, and always in praise of the motherland. Not songs that evoked the pain of war.

Sơn become a very popular writer and singer of love songs after the war and into the twenty-first century. His recordings often featured a female vocalist, Chánh Lý, whose voice was described as heavenly. But it was not until 2017 that the Vietnamese government finally lifted the censorship that had, through all those years, allowed his songs to slip, only one or two at a time, onto the public airwaves of a united

---

[26] John C. Schafer, *Trịnh Công Sơn & Bob Dylan: Essays on War, Love, Songwriting, and Religion* (Press at Cal Poly Humboldt, 2024), 611, 614. Songs translated from Vietnamese to English by John C. Schafer and Cao Thị Như Quỳnh.

Vietnam. When he died in 2001, thousands of Vietnamese joined in a spontaneous songfest to celebrate his life and contributions to the music of Vietnam.

Other voices of discontent began to emerge in 1967 and 1968. One was Professor Lý Chánh Trung, a professor of philosophy at Saigon University. He was known for his staunch advocacy for peace and often appeared at student rallies. Because he was a Catholic, he was given more latitude by the government than were most Vietnamese critics of the war.

Thích Nữ Nhất Chi Mai protested the war in a different manner. She set herself on fire. A thirty-three-year-old elementary school teacher and student at the Faculty of Letters, University of Saigon, Mai was among fifty-nine students and teachers who signed an appeal for peace in March 1967. Mai chose to take her appeal one step further. On the eve of her self-immolation she wrote:

I voluntary sacrifice myself in order to ask that: My sacrifice be understood, that it is for the peace of the nation; that it is for the humanitarian cause and justice.

Following the sacrifices of Morrison [American professor] and Venerable Quảng Đức,[27] I pray that:

—The flame which will burn my body will reduce the ambitions and hatred, which are throwing so many people into despair and cause so many mournful scenes to the people.

—Humanity will bathe in the freshness of the mercy of Buddha and the love of Christ and the humanism of Man kind.[28]

---

[27] Norman Morrison, a Baltimore Quaker, set himself on fire at the Pentagon in protest of the war on November 2, 1965. Quảng Đức was a Vietnamese Buddhist monk who immolated himself in 1963.

[28] Thích Nữ Nhất Chi Mai, "Hear My Distressful Cry," *Youth Bulletin: Voices of Vietnam Youth*, no. 3 (June 1, 1967). She is also known as Phạm Thị Mai. At the time of her death she was a Buddhist nun.

CHAPTER 9

Doubts and Discontent

When I decided to join IVS, I was unfamiliar with the organization's history and the complexities of its role in a country divided by a multiplicity of differing political philosophies, dialects, climates, lifestyles, ethnic identities, religions, and war. But as I became increasingly enmeshed in the lives of the Vietnamese, I also became more aware of the ambiguous role and mission of IVS in Vietnam.

IVS had its roots in the US religious peace community in the 1950s, as Quakers, Mennonites, and leaders of the Church of the Brethren envisioned an organization that would provide technical assistance to people in less developed countries. These founders believed from the outset that IVS's success could only be measured by the degree to which its members succeeded in transferring skills and knowledge that would empower indigenous people to build their own future. Vietnam was an agrarian country, so when IVS came to Vietnam in 1955 it sought to recruit volunteers from US farm communities who not only knew about animals and plants but also had sufficient experience or training to educate others in appropriate technologies. Many of the first volunteers had backgrounds in animal husbandry and crop production. Some had served as agricultural extension agents in the US. Some came with additional skills in mechanical engineering. Most, if not all, were equipped to provide hands-on assistance upon arrival.

In the early '60s, IVS added education as a specialty and began to recruit volunteers who could partner with Vietnamese on curriculum development, school construction, and support for classroom teachers. The goal was to provide technical assistance to Vietnamese educators, but this focus shifted somewhat as the increased US military presence led to a greatly increased desire on the part of the Vietnamese to learn English. IVS responded by recruiting volunteers qualified for specific classroom roles, including sending at least one volunteer to a specialized training program in teaching English as a Foreign Language before she landed in Vietnam.

Even with this expansion, IVS remained a relatively small program in Vietnam until the war began heating up in earnest in 1964. In the mid-'60s, IVS expanded again to include another official track, community development. This was an amorphous designation, and most volunteers were already participating in some form of community development, along with their regular assignments. But by creating this category IVS could broaden its appeal while recruiting volunteers with less specific skills. I applied for a position in community development without much understanding of what that might entail.

Ironically, the funding that enabled IVS to expand its network of volunteers in Vietnam might have come because of the relative success of the US Peace Corps, which by the mid-1960s had become a symbol of US willingness to assist the countries in the world in most need. President Johnson wanted to send Peace Corps workers to Vietnam, apparently with the hope that their presence would convey a more benign and compassionate image of the US, offsetting the increasing role of the US military in the country. He may have been convinced that the Peace Corps could help directly in winning the hearts and minds of the Vietnamese.

But Congress brought Johnson's plan to a halt due to concern that it would politicize the Peace Corps and create problems in placing Peace Corps volunteers in other countries. The Administration thus did the next best thing. It poured considerable resources into IVS, channeling funding through USAID. When I arrived in South Vietnam in 1966, the number of volunteers had more than doubled over the previous year to 100. Over the next twelve months it reached its peak of 186 volunteers in the country.

No doubt the White House and the US military expected that IVSers would become a direct extension of the war effort. This was evidenced in a letter General Westmoreland sent to Warren Rogers, Washington editor for *Look* magazine and a friend of my family, in response to a query from Rogers about me.

Westmoreland wrote:

> It was good to get the information about Richard Berliner. The young man arrived in Saigon on 27 September and is to spend his first six weeks in Vinh Long studying the Vietnamese language.... Such men serving here with the various volunteer agencies are making a significant contribution to our overall effort. I shall endeavor to meet Richard on one of my visits in his vicinity.... Tell Dick my ambitions do not extend further down the road than the success of our efforts in Vietnam.

It must have been natural for US officials to assume that any American working in Vietnam was there to support the war effort. After all, protesters in the US were refusing the draft and going to jail or relocating to Canada—not volunteering to go to Vietnam. But the newest IVS recruits came with more on their minds than helping a developing country to prosper.

When IVS expanded into education in 1962, "the character of IVS volunteers began to change," noted Hugh Manke, the last director of IVS's program in Vietnam. "They brought with them a higher level of political awareness than the agriculturalists had. This personnel shift later became an important part of the radicalization of the organization."[29]

New volunteers came straight from college campuses where anti-war activity had been building since the Gulf of Tonkin Incident in 1964. We came to help, but we also came with a lot of questions about the war. We wanted to find out how the Vietnamese felt about being caught in the middle of what was another battlefront in the US's continuous effort to combat the spread of communism. And we came determined to maintain our independence from the entity that was paying most of our bills—the US government.

For most IVSers this was not difficult. Although I was working with Vietnamese youth whose allegiances were important to the US effort, I was never asked to convey information or do anything that seemed overtly related to promoting US government interests. IVS mailed my newsletters to the hundred or so names I provided and never questioned the content. My occasional letters were somewhat direct in criticizing the US role, particularly the involvement of US authorities in Vietnamese domestic politics.

In 1967, several IVSers, myself included, decided to show our opposition to the US presence by burning our military PX cards in front of the US embassy.[30] This was done more as street theater than as a meaningful gesture, since we rarely used the PXs. The government-issued PX card was, for us, a symbol of the US presence in Vietnam, bestowing privileges on Americans and further insulating them from the realities of how the war was affecting the Vietnamese people.

We did not tell the press of our actions, and the only notice of the event was taken by an elderly man from Hungary who showed

---

[29] Hugh Manke, "The Expulsion of IVS—Another Casualty of War," *War/Peace* (December 1971).

[30] "PX" is short for the "Post Exchange," a kind of general store on military bases. The PX card granted access to the base store and was generally made available to all military and US governmental personnel. IVS volunteers also had access to the US military postal service, which significantly facilitated my correspondence with family back home.

up to lecture us on the horrors of communism. But it made us feel good.[31]

By the end of the summer in 1967, many IVSers believed that, even though they were not directly part of the war effort, they needed to express their feelings about the war. To do otherwise was to be complicit and, by association, supportive of the war. We held an all-team meeting in Saigon to discuss how IVS viewed its role in Vietnam; ways that volunteers might act to ensure their independence from the military; and changes IVS-Washington might make to show its independence from USAID, its chief source of funding.

The meeting offered an opportunity for volunteers to share feelings, and several concrete proposals did emerge from the gathering. One proposal was for IVS-Washington to accelerate its recruitment of non-US volunteers. (IVS already had volunteers from Japan, the Philippines, India, and a few other countries, but it was a small percentage of the team.) Another proposal was to wean IVS off funding from the US government. We agreed to meet again at the end of the year to talk about more concrete steps that IVS could take.

The frustration felt by IVSers came to a head after the Vietnamese presidential election failed to bring about any meaningful change in the country's leadership. Beginning in September, the top IVS leaders in Vietnam, in quick succession, submitted their resignations. The first was Willie Meyers, team leader of region IV, who wrote in his resignation letter:

The United States' policy and actions and their consequences

---

[31] Throughout IVS's time in Vietnam only one IVSer was removed from his post because of political protest. Hugh Manke used vacation time to fly to Washington to testify against the war before a congressional committee. (Subcommittee to Investigate Problems Connected with Refugee and Escapees, Judiciary Committee, United States Senate, April 23, 1971, 1–6.) A few months later he gave an interview to *The New York Times*, criticizing the Thiệu government. Shortly thereafter he was fired by IVS.

in Vietnam, with which we are ever more closely identified, have become so distasteful to me that I wish to be completely disassociated from them. Three major examples of this are: (a) The massive introduction of American troops and extensive bombing in the North and the South have greatly intensified the war and the suffering of the Vietnamese people.... (b) During the three years I have been here, since June 1963, the United States has steadily increased its authoritative role in the affairs of Vietnam until today very little sovereignty remains for the Government of the Republic of Vietnam.... (c) By far the most serious and intolerable action of the United States is that we have not sincerely and persistently sought to bring peace to Vietnam, but rather have brought more troops and bombs and war, and thus moved further away from the possibility of a peaceful settlement. This is *completely counter* to the interests and desires of the majority of the Vietnamese people [emphasis in original].[32]

Reflecting some years later on his decision, Meyers explained that he had concluded that he could no longer justify being part of "a sugarcoating on the undesirable effects of the American effort in Vietnam," but that he hoped to return when Vietnam "has a government that is free from foreign domination and a people that is free from the ravages of war."[33] After leaving IVS, Meyers became an international agricultural consultant and professor and did return to Vietnam on various missions after the war ended.

Meyers's resignation was soon followed by those of Don Luce, IVS's senior representative in Vietnam from 1961 to 1967 and the one who had arranged for me to live with local Vietnamese youth when I first arrived in Saigon; Gene Stultzfus, Luce's second-in-command; and

---

[32] Willie Meyers, Appendix IV, "Willie Meyers' Resignation Letter," in Thierry J. Sagnier, *The Fortunate Few: IVS Volunteers from Asia to the Andes* (NCMN Press, 2015), 349–351.

[33] Meyers, in Sagnier, *The Fortunate Few*, 351.

Don Ronk, one of four divisional team leaders in the country. Ronk stayed in Vietnam to report on the war. Luce, Stoltzfus, and Meyers returned to the US and began speaking out about what the war was doing to the Vietnamese people. They joined forces with The United Methodist Board of Christian Social Concerns in Washington, D.C., to form the Vietnam Education Project (VEP). Through the VEP, Luce and the others met with civic and religious groups around the country, testified before various US Congressional committees and before the Republican and Democratic Platform Committees, and established personal contact with over 150 members of Congress. The VEP facilitated the visits to Vietnam of more than a hundred members of Congress and arranged for them to meet with IVSers still in Vietnam.

Three days after I returned to the US for an extended leave a year later, VEP was still going strong. VEP asked me to be a featured speaker at a luncheon hosted by US Senator Vance Hartke from Indiana. Senator Hartke made the following remarks on the Senate floor later that day:

> Mr. President, today a number of senators, some members of the press, staff members of the Foreign Relations Committee, and some senators who could not attend, joined me in discussions on Vietnam at a luncheon arranged by my staff with the cooperation of the Vietnam Education Project of The United Methodist Church. Our guest speakers were Richard Berliner who returned only Sunday from two years with international voluntary services in Vietnam and Dr. David Marr of the University of California, and Tràn Văn Dĩnh, former ambassador from Vietnam....[34]

After my short assessment of why I thought the US should withdraw from Vietnam immediately, the bulk of the luncheon focused on Dr. Marr's analysis of lessons he hoped the US learned from Vietnam.

---

[34] 114th Cong. Rec. S 27519 (September 18, 1968).

A substantial part of VEP's efforts was to get the word out to towns and cities not reached by the major urban newspapers. I was interviewed by the *Montgomery* (Maryland) *Sentinel* on October 2, 1968. The paper ran an article with the headline: "'Anti-Americanism' Rampant in Vietnam, Returnee Says." On a visit to Boise, Idaho, my interview with *The Idaho Daily Statesman* led to an article with an eight-column banner headline: "Vietnam Visitor Brings Home Critical Analysis of Policies Aimed at Winning Over Native Populace."[35] VEP left no stone unturned and in October sent me to address the Audubon Society in Washington, D.C., at the Lincoln Auditorium. Other former IVSers in the US also spoke frequently for the VEP, while colleagues who had remained in Vietnam continued working as stringers, feeding information about the current state of the war to various US papers.

In a report on the VEP, William R. MacKaye of *The Washington Post* wrote:

> It is impossible to assess how far the Methodist project was responsible for the growth in number of influential Americans willing to accept an indecisive end to the Vietnam war. But it is apparent that the impact of the project ... was far greater than its [$100,000] budget might suggest.
>
> Perhaps of greatest significance, the project successfully blitzed its findings and opinions into newspapers, television, radio, and the consciousness of a wide array of community leaders.[36]

Whether by design or by accident, IVS became a channel for considerable information about the failure of the US war effort to reach political leaders back home. By strategically targeting both

---

[35] Ken Robison, "Vietnam Visitor Brings Home Critical Analysis of Policies Aimed at Winning Over Native Populace," *The Idaho Daily Statesman*, October 16, 1968.

[36] William R. MacKaye, "Methodists Push Viet Peace," *The Washington Post*, December 29, 1968.

opinion-leaders and smaller media markets, VEP enabled IVSers to convey considerable information about the failure of the US war effort to political leaders back home.

I was in total agreement with the reasons for the IVS resignations.

(Letter home: September 1967)

For some it has been a realization that as an organization or even as individuals we really have no purpose for being in Vietnam. The suspicions that have developed and the misunderstandings that have ensued make it difficult for any American to work in a country that is increasingly becoming more anti-American. Being mistaken for an emissary of American policy, one that has become increasingly detestable, is one reason for not wanting to work with government-subsidized IVS; living in Vietnam consuming more rice and adding more pressure on the Vietnamese from foreigners—with little hope of accomplishment— is one reason for not being in Vietnam at all. And the strongest, most compelling drive is to speak, now, about what is happening in Vietnam to the Vietnamese people.

Despite my own growing disillusionment with the role IVS was playing in Vietnam, I was not ready to leave. I did not think that I had been in Vietnam long enough to have any credibility back home. Luce, Stultzfus, and Meyers had lived collectively in Vietnam for sixteen years. I had been there less than one. I had developed friendships with Vietnamese who were actually comforted to know an American who did not support US policy. I wanted to continue learning what I could and hopefully figure out a way for the US to come out of the quagmire it was in.[37]

But I could not stay in Vietnam and stay quiet. Many others in

---

[37] Arthur M. Schlesinger, *The Bitter Heritage: Vietnam and American Democracy, 1941-1966* (Houghton Mifflin Company, 1967). "Quagmire" was a term used by Schlesinger to describe the US involvement in Vietnam as happening one step at a time until it was so deeply involved there was no way out.

IVS felt the same way. So, without regard to personal consequences, a small group of us decided to draft a letter to send President Johnson, expressing the need to bring the war to an end. I was charged with writing an initial draft of the letter, which then passed through many hands and many changes before being finalized. We decided to include as signatories all IVSers who wanted to sign the letter. We hatched a plan to take the letter by hand to every IVSers in the country, all within just a few days. So once again I headed back to Đà Lạt, where several volunteers were stationed. When I landed at the airport, the gravity of our actions sank in. Once again, I was struck by the beauty and peacefulness of Đà Lạt. But this time, I knew I was going to disrupt that peace for the volunteers living there. Only Chris Jenkins added his name on the letter.

On September 19, 1967, we sent the letter, signed by forty-seven IVS volunteers, to President Johnson, calling for him to *"End This War."* We also gave a copy of the letter to *The New York Times* and presented it to the US Ambassador to Vietnam, Ellsworth Bunker. It read in part:

> We are finding it increasingly difficult to pursue quietly our main objective: helping the people of Vietnam. In assisting one family or one individual to make a better living or to get a better education it has become evident that our small successes only blind us to how little or negative the effect is, in the face of present realities in Vietnam. Thus, to stay in Vietnam and remain silent is to fail to respond to the first need of the Vietnamese people—peace...

> We do not accuse anyone of deliberate cruelty. Perhaps if you accept the war, all can be justified—the free strike zones, the refugees, the spraying of herbicides on crops, the napalm. But the Vietnam war is in itself an overwhelming atrocity. Its every victim—the dead, the bereaved, the deprived—is a

victim of this atrocity.... Việt Cộng terrorism is real; so are the innocent victims of US bombing, strafing, and shelling...

We have flown at a safe height over the deserted villages, the sterile valleys, the forests with huge swaths cut out, and the checkerboard of long-abandoned rice paddies. We have had intimate contact with the refugees. Some of them get jobs at American military establishments and do fairly well. Others are forcibly resettled, landless, in isolated, desolate places which are turned into colonies of mendicants. Others go to the Saigon slums, secure but ridden with disease and the compulsion toward crime. These are refugees generated not by Việt Cộng terrorism, but by a policy of the war, an American policy...

In a refugee village, one of us heard an old woman say these words (translation): "These days of sorrow are filled with napalm, hate, and death. The rice fields turn brown. The new year brings a cold, clutching fear."

A young Buddhist teacher, on the eve of her self-immolation, made her last statement to express the anguish of the Vietnamese people: "You Americans come to help the Vietnamese people, but have brought only death and destruction. Most of us Vietnamese hate, from the bottom of our hearts, the Americans who have brought the suffering of this war.... The tons of bombs and money you have poured on our people have shattered our bodies and sense of nation."

The letter continues for a total of five single-spaced pages, with specific examples of the war's atrocities and more evidence that the longer that the US stayed, the more opposition it encountered. It expressed the sentiment of Vietnamese colleagues that, despite the opposition and fear of a communist government, the price of victory, if that were possible, was not worth the cost. The letter noted that progress in the war was measured by statistics—Việt Cộng killed, former VC who came over to the other side, villages secured. But there was no measure of the cost to the Vietnamese people.[38]

The letter concluded with five recommendations: (1) Stop escalating the conflict; start deescalating; (2) Stop the spraying of herbicides; the primary victims are children and older people; (3) Stop the bombing; it only stands in the way of negotiations; (4) Recognize the National Liberation Front; there will be no peace until all parties in the conflict are recognized; (5) Turn over the future of Vietnam to an international peace commission and be prepared to accept its recommendations. In short, stop allowing the US's proclaimed self-interest to undermine the Vietnamese people's right to self-determination.

Stories on the letter appeared in *The New York Times, The Washington Post,* and *Newsweek,*[39] and its text was read on the floor of the US House of Representatives and printed in the *Congressional Record.* Not surprisingly, *Time* magazine, whose publisher was a strong supporter of the war, dismissed it out of hand, reporting on it in a single-paragraph story. The story suggested that anyone with a typewriter and the ear of a local reporter could get a story in *The New York Times.* For five more years the war raged on, until finally, on January 23, 1973, the warring parties signed a peace agreement. The final agreement incorporated all of the steps urged in the IVS volunteers' letter, except the recommendation to allow an international peace commission to determine Vietnam's future.

After the letter's release, we braced ourselves for possible repercussions. Of chief concern, would we be told our services were no longer needed, either by the Vietnamese government, by the US government, or by IVS-Washington?

Somewhat to our surprise, nothing happened. Despite the

---

[38] The full text of the letter to President Johnson appears in the Appendix.

[39] "The Toughest Question," *Newsweek,* October 2, 1967, 32. *Newsweek* described IVS as "perhaps the most respected of the private relief agencies operating in South Vietnam."

prominence the letter received in major media, IVS-Washington was publicly silent. Its chief executive officer, Arthur Z. Gardiner, a former US State Department official, did make a trip to Vietnam and visited many of the IVS stations around the country. His main message: "Don't engage in politics." Politics, military action, human torment. These were not our responsibilities. Gardiner's decision not to take action against the signers of the letters may have been because his own view of the war was changing. Three months after the letter and resignation of the top management in Vietnam, Gardiner wrote a letter to *The Washington Post* that was very critical of the US war effort.[40]

Our letter did not change the course of the war. But it came at a time of insatiable demand on the part of the US Congress for firsthand knowledge of Vietnam, particularly from potential candidates for the US presidency.[41] The 1968 election was just around the corner. A few months after the letter was circulated, I was asked to arrange for Vietnamese youth leaders to meet with Senator Birch Bayh from Indiana, a Democrat, and Governor George Romney from Michigan, a Republican, both presidential candidates. Senator Bayh listened attentively during his meeting, as did Governor Romney in a separate meeting.

But things did not go well for the governor when he returned home. He used an unfortunate choice of words when he told the press back in the US that he had been "brain-washed" while in Vietnam. Gov. Romney was trying to convey the message that what the US military and embassy personnel conveyed to him about the war was bogus. Those official sources had highlighted the achievement of military victories in battle and stressed their belief that the war was going well, but Gov. Romney learned from Vietnamese students, from IVS volunteers, and non-military Americans in Vietnam that the US was losing the battle to gain support for the South Vietnamese government

---

[40] Arthur Z. Gardiner, letter to the editor, *The Washington Post*, February 20, 1968.

[41] The letter was also of interest to potential draftees and was posted on at least one college campus—Earlham College, my alma mater.

and increase popular opposition to the National Liberation Front and North Vietnam.

The press in the United States naturally focused on Gov. Romney's reference to being brain-washed, words that were quickly used against him in his bid for president. He ultimately failed to win the nomination.

CHAPTER 10

Protest

In the spring of 1967, Saigon cafes were abuzz. Students and youth leaders talked endlessly into the night about the coming elections. The military council that had been ruling the country since the 1963 ouster of Ngô Đình Diệm had announced that September 3 was the magic date—the first truly free election for a head of state in the history of South Vietnam.

When the military council took control of the country in 1963, it ended the Diệm government's forced relocation of rural families into strategic hamlets, something that had only alienated the population. Families returned to their homes and fighting subsided. But the country continued to be plagued by four years of instability and successive coup attempts.[42]

In 1965, the military council negotiated an agreement whereby Nguyễn Cao Kỳ and Nguyễn Vân Thiệu would become prime minister and chief of state, respectively. Thiệu and Kỳ, like their predecessor, Ngô Đình Diệm, promised free elections, but it was still two long years before elections were announced for the fall of 1967. At last, the people of South Vietnam were going to be able to choose their own leaders in a fair process—or so it was thought.

My Vietnamese colleagues were optimistic. On the political front, they believed that a free election would lead to civilian leadership

---

[42] See, Stanley Karnow, *Vietnam: A History* (Viking Press, 1983), 334-348, 378-386.

and political stability. On the military front, a massive build-up of US troops—focusing on preventing North Vietnam troops and supplies from entering the South and on helping the South Vietnamese military wipe out the Việt Cộng—offered hope for a quick end to hostilities. After one hundred years of French rule, four years of Japanese occupation during World War II, nine more years of fighting to liberate Vietnam from the French, the 1955 partitioning of the country into North and South, and a series of military dictatorships—after all that, it seemed that things were truly about to change.

In 1967, fighting was largely contained to the countryside. The main disruption in urban areas came from the large presence of American military personnel and soldiers now populating the bars and restaurants. US dollars were flowing, and American products illegally flooded the markets. Life was tolerable for urban dwellers, despite the increased number of peasants showing up in the cities.

I was still working as an IVS volunteer with the National Youth Council in Saigon. The council was not a political organization, but its leaders decided to play the role of watchdog to help ensure fair elections. Military leaders were not known to give up their positions of power readily, and there was widespread concern that the election might be stolen rather than lost. Council members thought they might be able to prevent this.

I was not pulled into this campaign, but continued to support youth service activity, particularly related to the National Voluntary Service program, whose work camps I had visited some months earlier. But I could not ignore the political fervor around me.

My Vietnamese colleagues spent hours in cafés speculating on who would run for office. There were hints that Thiệu and Kỳ would compete separately for the top slot. Rumors abounded that the very popular General Dương Vân Minh (by then a civilian) would return from exile in Bangkok to run. The former minister of economics, Âu Trung Thân, indicated he would run on a peace ticket. Trần Văn Hương, a sixty-two-year-old southern Confucian and former head of state in 1964, also announced. He was attractive to intellectuals but had little following outside the cities. Ultimately, Thiệu and Kỳ decided to run on the same ticket to oppose eleven other announced slates.

In order to qualify for the election, candidates had to be certified by the newly formed Constitutional Assembly. Initially the Assembly showed signs of independence, certifying General Minh with 90 percent of the members voting in favor. But a second vote removed the certification, apparently finding Minh ineligible because his running mate had at one time been a French citizen. Then Âu Trung Thân was labeled a communist and declared ineligible because neutralist and communist sympathizers were prohibited from being president. Vietnam's security chief, Nguyễn Ngọc Loan, bottle of beer in hand and accompanied by an armed guard, sat in the balcony of the Assembly Hall to watch the proceedings.[43] His presence did much to undermine the government's pledge of noninterference.

Enthusiasm for the election rapidly diminished over the summer because there was now little doubt about who would win. Kỳ and Thiệu decided not to campaign, but the rest of the candidates organized a barn-storming tour that called for all candidates to travel together to twenty-two cities in twenty-two days. The tour was quickly cancelled, however, when transportation promised by the government did not materialize. In response to accusations of trying to undermine the campaign, the government promised to behave, and the candidates again agreed to tour, this time to twelve cities in twelve days. The format was five minutes of speeches for each slate, ten minutes of questions, fifty-six minutes of radio and TV time in a country where electricity was still a luxury. The format might have seemed fair, but its design ensured that it would be invisible to 80 percent of the population.

My Vietnamese friends also speculated on the role the United States was taking in the election and on what its posture would be if a civilian

---

[43] Loan later received world attention when photographed shooting a Việt Cộng prisoner point-blank.

actually won the election. Most agreed that a civilian victory would not be acceptable to the military junta then in power. If a civilian was somehow elected, Thiệu and Kỳ would come up with some pretense for negating the election results. The US would then be in the position of having to support the continuation of a military dictatorship when one of its prime goals had been to support the development of a democracy in Vietnam. Some even thought that such a dilemma would force the US to pull out of Vietnam, but this was a minority opinion.

Perhaps fortunately for the US government, the Thiệu-Kỳ ticket won easily. Saigon students began mobilizing immediately to protest the election results.

(Letter home: October 2, 1967)
For the third time in eight days student demonstrations broke out in protest against the September 3ʳᵈ presidential and senatorial elections...The National Police applied unusual force in the use of clubs and tear gas to squash the activity. Several CBS cameramen were among the casualties, as was one badly beaten girl who bled profusely around her head as she was carried away by the police. Officially there were twenty-five people arrested, including the leader of the protest. But it appeared to be twice that number.

Premier Kỳ had banned all rallies and protests the previous day, but his edict did not stop several hundred students from gathering at the Student Union headquarters on September 24, carrying signs calling for the Constitutional Assembly to invalidate the elections. They set out to march to the Assembly Hall to confront the assembly. Their planned route took them down Duy Tân Street, around the large Catholic cathedral, and then to Tự Do (Freedom) Street. But early on they encountered a roadblock and a burley officer who exhorted the students to give up their protests. The students instead sat down in the intersection, but quickly scattered when other police arrived with clubs. A crowd gathered to watch the protests; some

The author with Thích Trí Quảng, organizer of 1963 Buddhist protest against the government of Ngô Đình Diệm. (Saigon, 1967)

became entangled in the chaos and were shoved to the ground. One CBS cameramen attempting to film the scene was attacked by four or five policemen with clubs and rifle butts. Surprisingly, he got up and walked away, but his camera lay shattered on the ground.[44]

Also on September 24, 1967, while students were protesting the election results, Buddhist monks led by Thích Trí Quảng staged a sit-in in front of the Independence Palace. Quảng had been a major force in the protest movement in Huế that had led to the overthrow of Ngô Đình Diệm in 1963 and protests in early 1966 and had been under house arrest intermittently since that time. I was able to observe

---

[44] Among those joining the students in the protest was David Marr, a former member of the US military, who carried a sign reading "US Students Also Demand Peace Now." Marr later became a distinguished professor of Vietnamese studies at the Australian National University; see the Sources section of this memoir for additional information on his works.

Quảng in action on several occasions and was impressed with his quiet command of the situation. On September 30, the Buddhists marched without incident to the Ấn Quang Pagoda to protest a new charter announced by the government regarding the rights of the Buddhist community. A large group of elementary students followed the monks in sympathy with their protest.

The changes in the charter, which favored the Thích Tâm Châu faction of the Buddhist church, did not seem so dire as to warrant the protest action. In fact, there was rampant speculation that Nguyễn Cao Kỳ, the newly elected premier, had instigated the protest in order to provide a pretense for him to declare martial law, consolidating his control over the country.

While the students and others in South Vietnam were angry with the new government, many youth at this time held on to the belief that a middle ground, called a "Third Force," would emerge and take power away from both sides. But there were no identifiable leaders with large popular support ready to step in to exert control or stage yet another coup. By mid-October, the protests had withered away. Hope for a middle ground surfaced again in April 1968, after the Tết Offensive, with the formation of the Alliance for National Democratic and Peace Forces, which had been in the making for some time. State Department memos suggested the US was aware of and perhaps even encouraged this development. The NLF recognized the political value of the alliance, but the Thiệu regime never did. Instead it chose to imprison its most prominent supporters.[45]

(Letter home: October 11, 1967)
> *Things are getting back to normal, but it has been an*
> *active two weeks for students and Buddhists in Saigon. Today*
> *I had an opportunity to talk with Thích Trí Quảng on the*
> *last day of his two-week sit-in in front of the Independence*

---

[45] Richard A. Berliner, "The Vietnamese 'Middle Ground,'" *Ripon Forum* V, no. 5 (May 1969): 24.

*Palace. The monks were able to get some of what they wanted
concerning the Buddhist Charter, mainly by threatening
to send over a thousand monks into the streets and staging
more immolations.[46] Students have not been so lucky. Six
more were arrested when they tried to hold a press conference
calling for the release of students already in jail... The
flare-up on Monday was my first real taste of violence in
this violent place, enough to evoke bitterness toward the
existing power structure... The students are too divided to
be an effective force, which means they will continue on
the same course without any real plan. It sometimes seems
like a game with everyone aware of the consequences but
not willing to take an alternative path to avoid them.*

Buddhist monks leading protest march against the South Vietnamese government.
(Saigon, Fall 1967)

---

[46] The self-immolations of Buddhist monks in 1963 focused the world's attention on the emerging crisis in South Vietnam. Vietnamese Buddhists continued
this practice over the years, although it was less noticed by the Western press as
time went on.

Buddhist nuns in protest march against South Vietnamese government. (Saigon, Fall 1967)

One last march occurred in mid-October, and while it passed without incident or apparent effect, it may have been the most significant event of the sometimes-chaotic election season. The march was held in honor of the legendary Vietnamese hero Emperor Quảng Trung (also known as Nguyễn Huế), who in 1788 had led a surprise attack against the Chinese invaders. That surprise attack began on the first day of the Chinese New Year—the same day that the Vietnamese celebrate their New Year, Tết.

The stream of marchers in 1967 extended for several blocks, waving large colorful banners with the Vietnamese colors of red and yellow, colors used by both the South Vietnamese government and the National Liberation Front. Had I studied more Vietnamese history, I might have seen this march as a perfect foreshadowing of what was about to come, and the march itself as perhaps a way of preparing the population for the most dramatic event of the war—the 1968 Tết Offensive.[47]

---

[47] Two centuries earlier, China had launched an invasion of Vietnam but paused fighting during the Chinese New Year celebration. Vietnam's New Year fell on the same dates, which led the Chinese commander to assume that Vietnam forces would be enjoying the annual celebration. He was wrong. Nguyễn Huế launched a surprise attack and defeated the Chinese army.

CHAPTER 11

Respite and Reflection

That Tết however, was still in a seemingly distant future. In October 1967, Saigon was in turmoil. Work at the National Youth Council had ground to a halt. It was a good time to take a vacation, and Cambodia was the perfect destination. A peaceful oasis on the otherwise troubled peninsula that was Southeast Asia.

Cambodia lies on the southwestern border of Vietnam, but while the topography at the border is seamless, the contrast between the two countries at that time could not have been starker. Cambodia, led by Prince Norodom Sihanouk, was a country at peace. Sihanouk had maintained peace since the signing of the 1954 Geneva Accords by ultimately recognizing that an alliance with the United States was a path to disaster. When the US began increasing its presence in neighboring states to repress insurgencies, Sihanouk remained wary of allowing the US to expand its influence into Cambodia. He remained so despite increasing pressure from the Khmer Rouge, an anti-government insurgency in his own country. As the US-communist struggles mounted to the east, Sihanouk formally declared Cambodia's neutrality and ended all US-based aid programs, including IVS, in 1963.

The Cambodian capital, Phnom Penh, was less than a sixty-minute flight from Saigon, but when I emerged from the plane it seemed worlds away. No soldiers stood guard around the airport. No manned sentry stations lined the city's avenues. The streets were free of the camouflaged jeeps and trucks and trails of fumes and intolerable decibels level that I had left behind in Saigon.

(Letter home: November 3, 1967)

Phnom Penh—it is called Nam Vâng (Golden South) in Vietnamese—presents an air of prosperity to this nation. Wide flowered and tree-shaded boulevards cut across and through a town of an almost equal number of Cambodians, Vietnamese, and Chinese inhabitants.... The central market stands a bit off center, with large streets such as Avenue de Gaulle radiating out in three directions. Smaller streets complete the symmetry, each lined with dry goods and cloth shops owned primarily by the Chinese and Vietnamese community. In true French tradition, restaurants spill onto the sidewalks, each covered with striped awnings and edged with potted bushes. One whole front of the market area is a small park with benches and narrow paths, completely negating suggestions that markets need to be odiferous and unattractive to be authentic.

Phnom Penh's main boulevard, Preh Norodum, stretched from the market at one end to the city's largest Hindu temple, Phnom Stupa, standing among numerous smaller stupas at the foot of a small hill topped with the Monument of Independence.[48] The mall beneath the monument extended as far as one could see, matching in size the mall in Washington, D.C.

Pedi-cabs, bicycles, and a few Czechoslovakian Jawa motorcycles dominated the roads. Sampans and small merchant ships filled the Mekong River, which begins in Tibet and traverses China, Laos, Thailand, Cambodia, and Vietnam before emptying into the South China Sea. A US helicopter shot down over Cambodian territory and a small US tank sat on the banks of the Mekong, reminders to Cambodians and foreigners alike of the increasing threat from the East. The danger of an expanding war.

---

[48] The monument celebrates Cambodia's independence from France, achieved in 1955.

Before leaving Saigon, I arranged to share my Cambodian sojourn with Roger Montgomery, a second-term IVSer then serving in a leadership position in Saigon. Roger was very comfortable with travel and exploration, and instead of joining me on the flight to Phnom Penh, he rode the 150 miles from Saigon on his Honda motorcycle. We met in Phnom Penh, where his motorcycle proved an invaluable resource for moving around the city and countryside. Although we could not afford to stay at the best hotel in Phnom Penh, nothing prevented us from going there during the day. We hung out by the pool, drank German beer, and talked with the English-speaking travelers staying at the hotel.

But the time was not spent solely in R&R. Our most notable experience in Cambodia came about totally by chance. We met a German physician working in Hué. He was a friend of an IVS volunteer in Hué and was curious to learn more about IVS and particularly the letter to President Johnson. He also knew that Wilfred Burchett, then living in Phnom Penh, would be interested in the letter.

Burchett was a seasoned Australian journalist.[49] I knew of his work from my studies at Earlham College. Burchett had written extensively about the war, working with material gathered during his frequent visits to North Vietnam. Western journalists frequently sought him out for his knowledge of the war from the perspective of the "enemy."

We jumped at the opportunity to meet him, but the process was an adventure in itself.

The German physician gave us a letter of introduction to Charles Meyers, a French citizen who was a longtime resident in Cambodia and a counselor to Prince Sihanouk, and said that Meyers could get us a meeting with Burchett. We were unsuccessful in seeing Meyers the next morning at his office but were told to go to his house that night at 6:30 p.m. Arriving right on time, we encountered not just Meyers but a small gathering, including the ambassador from Israel and a Russian

---

[49] Journalist and author of such works as *The Furtive War: The United States in Vietnam and Laos* (1963), *My Visit to the Liberated Zones of South Vietnam* (1964), and *Vietnam: Inside Story of the Guerrilla War* (1965).

who was teaching Chinese in Israel. Meyers welcomed us. We told him about our letter to President Johnson and our wish to take a copy personally to Burchett. He excused himself to call Burchett. While waiting for Meyers, we stood around and drank his gin and chatted with the gentleman from Israel and Meyers's Chinese wife.

After several failed attempts to reach Burchett by telephone, Meyers offered to drive us to Burchett's house. It was located nearby in the diplomatic section of town, tucked behind a high fence. Burchett, like Meyers, greeted us with great hospitality, offering Scotch from a US PX in Vietnam. He wanted to hear more about our letter to Johnson, and the conversation naturally shifted to North Vietnam. Burchett had just returned from there, and we were eager to hear what he had learned. While we were familiar with the shifting dynamics of the war in the South, we had very little information about what was happening in the North.

We listened intently as he described how the Vietnamese were surviving the onslaught of an overwhelming military power—the US Air Force.

(Letter home: November 3, 1967)

Burchette reports North Vietnam is surviving very well despite the bombings. About a third of Hải Phòng's (North Vietnam's second largest city) residential section is destroyed, but the population has been largely evacuated. There is now a system of personal cylindrical fox holes that are very strong and able to withstand the shock of almost anything but a direct hit. Although he was told that he would have several minutes warning before the bombing started, there were three separate attacks the night he was there—each with almost no warning. He said that radar picks up US planes leaving the Seventh Fleet, but because they are so numerous and may be going to a different part of North Vietnam, officials did not want to disturb the population every time a plane takes off. Hence the late warning.

He was surprised at the extensive amount of anti-aircraft fire thrown at the airplanes, from rocket launchers and individual rifles possessed by almost everyone able to carry one. After the night of bombing, a US broadcast said that they had destroyed a large military barracks. But the only thing that may have resembled a barracks, Burchett said, was a home for convalescents—long ago evacuated. We asked Burchett why there was such a difference in the official figures given by the US and North Vietnam regarding the number of aircraft shot down. He said that the US numbers may be low because it did not count planes shot down where there is no hope of saving the pilot, or planes running by remote control doing reconnaissance. On the other hand, the North Vietnamese numbers may be high because they count a plane twice if there is a dispute about which province it landed in, since it is quite an honor to have a plane shot down over one's province....

North Vietnam has an extensive dike system to manage the water coming down from the mountains. We asked about reports of US bombing the dikes, which potentially had catastrophic consequences. He said that if the US had bombed dikes in 1965, when the US first asked the French for a map of the dike system, which the French refused, it would have been a complete disaster for Hanoi and most of the Red River Delta. But North Vietnam had since built secondary and tertiary systems to protect the land and in the process achieved almost total irrigation in these areas. Rice production has increased every year for the past few years, now averaging five tons per hectare with three crops per year. In contrast rice areas in the delta (in South Vietnam) averaged less that 1.7 tons per hectare with one crop per year. Montgomery, who had an agricultural background, challenged his production figures for the North, saying they sounded awfully high, but Burchett stuck firmly to his numbers.

*We of course had many more questions and could
have gone on much longer, but Burchett's wife was getting
impatient to eat dinner, as it was now about 8:45 p.m. As we
were saying our farewells, he promised to call the press officer
for the National Liberation Front, which had an office in
Phnom Penh, and arrange an interview for us upon our return
from a visit to Kep, on the southeastern coast of Cambodia.*

Given Burchett's sympathies with the North, we assumed that not everything he had told us was completely accurate. But still he painted enough of a picture of how North Vietnam was coping with the war to let us know that it could probably endure anything the US deployed against it, except perhaps a nuclear bomb.

We learned later through the media that President Richard Nixon had proposed the use of nuclear weapons in 1972 but was talked out of it by Secretary of State Henry Kissinger.

Roger and I went to Kep, Cambodia, once a French resort town. The trip was uneventful and not unusual except for its proximity to Vietnam, just ten kilometers to the east. Residents told us that on clear nights they could see the lights of tracers in the sky, bullets that often precede bombing runs, on the Vietnamese-Cambodian border. If the wind was blowing from the east, they could hear the sound of the bombs. I learned later that the US was regularly dropping bombs in Cambodia, a fact hidden from the press.

We neither saw the tracers nor heard the bombs but spent our time on the beach as if Vietnam was a million miles away. Other than a bus full of very pale-skinned Russians on holiday from teaching at a technical school in Phnom Penh, we did not encounter any tourists and had the wait staff at a large French-style restaurant to ourselves. For two days we reverted to Western-style meals, including steak, lobster, and creamed vegetables. Quite a change from our rice-based diet back in Saigon. And upsetting to our stomachs.

Upon our return to Phnom Penh from Kep, we visited the press office of the Vietnamese National Liberation Front. While waiting in the reception area I noticed a display in a glass-enclosed case next to the wall, memorabilia of the war, remnants of the enemy. A US Army helmet, a bomb fragment, some dog tags. A picture of Hồ Chí Minh was on the wall. A picture of Mao Zedong was on another wall. It suddenly struck me that I was on enemy territory. I began to feel rather queasy. Was I being disloyal by even entering this building? Perhaps I could even be accused of cavorting with the enemy. But I was no doubt doing that every day in Saigon, where it was impossible to know who was an enemy and who was a friend of the US. We gave the press liaison a copy of the letter to President Johnson, exchanged a few words, and left. I never learned what the press office did with the letter, and I never told my supervisors at IVS of our subversive stopover at the press offices of America's sworn enemy.

Roger then returned to Saigon, but I could not leave Cambodia without visiting the place that many around the world know as the country's defining wonder—the ruins of Angkor Wat and Angkor Thom. Bidding adieu to Roger, I boarded a plane for the northern city of Seam Reap and two full days of exploring the ancient city.

About noon on my first full day in Seam Reap I set out, peddling a rented bicycle along a smooth road to the north of town. Rounding a turn, I suddenly saw, tucked among the trees, the first of the ancient temples. There were few people around (most having known the imprudence of setting out in the heat of the day), and I walked alone freely through the temple and climbed one of the ancient walls. Reaching the top, I looked around and caught my first glimpse of the vastness of the complex. I thought of the history I knew of the place and tried to imagine the area teeming with royalty and monks and the air filled with the noise of crowds and the clatter of horses and marching troops.

The walled city of Angkor Thom, encompassing some four square miles and at one time home to more than two million inhabitants, served as the capital of the Khmer empire from the ninth to the fifteenth centuries, C.E. During the empire's height inhabitants built elaborate Buddhist and Hindu temples within its walls. The Bayon temple alone has some two hundred giant stone faces carved into its towers. The Angkor civilization reached its peak in the 11th century and then began to erode due to foreign invasions. Thai forces captured Angkor Thom in 1431 and then abandoned it, leaving the city to be completely covered by vegetation. A French archeologist in search of rare butterflies discovered the city in 1861, triggering a restoration effort that lasted more than eighty years. The most dramatic of the temples, Angkor Wat, occupies the largest footprint of any religious monument in the world. In 1992 the United Nations declared the city a World Heritage Site.

My last stop was at this towering temple, Angkor Wat. Joining a small crowd in the courtyard, I discovered that Cambodia's head of state, Prince Norodom Sihanouk, was standing in the center of the crowd. The prince was not holding a press conference or escorting a foreign dignitary around the treasured ruins. He was, instead, holding a movie camera. One of the prince's hobbies was making movies, and as I approached, I heard him describing the movie to the crowd, in English. "I am making a tragedy," he said. "When my people are sad, they want only comedies. But when they are happy, like now, they want tragedies." He said that the movie was about a young princess being held captive inside the temple, waiting for someone—perhaps a handsome young prince—to rescue her. Even in Angkor Thom, it appeared, princesses were still doomed to await their princely rescuers.

After ten days of enjoying the history and serenity of Cambodia, it was time to return to Vietnam. This is how I would have remembered Cambodia if I had not revisited the country two years later, just after Prince Sihanouk was deposed and leadership fell into the hands of Lon Nol, a pro-US general who was expected to support US efforts in

Vietnam. On that visit I found military structures marring the wide, once open boulevards. Army jeeps sped by. No US soldiers but plenty of Vietnamese troops appeared in Phnom Penh. Although not widely known, the US was regularly bombing the Hồ Chí Minh Trail in Laos and was prepared to extend the raids to the south, into Cambodia.

Lon Nol would presumably support such efforts, but that did not keep him from being overthrown in 1975 by Pol Pot and the Khmer Rouge. Pol Pot, inspired by the Cultural Revolution in China and with China's support, attempted to turn Cambodia into a "socialist agrarian republic." He emptied the cities of their inhabitants, declared a war on intellectuals—including anyone who wore eyeglasses—and eventually slaughtered 1.5 to 2 million people, some 25 percent of the population. This included 200,000 to 300,000 ethnic Chinese, 90,000 Muslims, and 20,000 Vietnamese. Pol Pot's reign of terror continued both inside and outside the country, as Cambodian troops crossed the Vietnamese border numerous times and killed an estimated 30,000 Vietnamese. Finally, to stop the invasions and the killings in Vietnam, Vietnam invaded Cambodia in 1979 and drove out the Khmer Rouge.

I returned to Cambodia for the last time in 2000. The country was only beginning to recover from the trauma of the war years and was still deeply impoverished. There was no fighting or killing or foreign intervention. The government was stable, and tourists came in greater numbers. Some came to visit the museum school in Phnom Penh that the Khmer government had used as a torture chamber. But most came to visit the magnificent Angkor Wat and the other temples of Angkor Thom in Siem Reap.

The author. (Saigon, 1967)

CHAPTER 12

The Calm Before the Storm

With hopes of a new dawn and a democratically elected government seemingly dashed, life in Saigon had returned to some semblance of normalcy when I returned from Cambodia in late fall 1967. Nguyễn Vân Thiệu and Nguyễn Cao Kỳ, now president and vice-president respectively, were in firm control, having won the election handily, not by resorting to illegal vote-counting or voter-suppression, but by the simple expediency of making sure the electoral council did not certify the candidacies of their more popular opponents. In a move to consolidate power, the new government swiftly imposed strict censorship measures on the Vietnamese press, measures that led to newspapers routinely being printed with large expanses of blank space. While we could not know what content had been censured, the extent of the mandated deletions was clear for everyone to see.

IVS workers in the countryside began reporting increases in anti-American sentiment among their Vietnamese friends and acquaintances, but members of the Western community in Saigon continued about their business, frequenting the downtown restaurants and enjoying cultural events. The National Ballet of Germany held a two-night performance, sponsored by the Goethe-Institut.

(Letter home: November 30, 1967)
*They performed a few classical dances (Le Cygne Noir),
but most dances were neo-classic, modern, and sexy. One
Vietnamese Catholic priest stayed for the whole performance*

but left hurriedly, speechless, after the final act. I realized
at intermission that the performances were not intended
for a Vietnamese audience, and, in fact, few Vietnamese
were present. The second night (of course I had to go back)
was more packed than the first night with expatriates—
mainly French. Clearly the social event of the year. A trip
to the Saigon market café for coffee afterwards brought
us abruptly back to Vietnam, but still humming tunes
of the swing era played throughout the performance.

US politicians kept coming in droves. In November, I met with Senator Abraham Ribicoff (D-CT) and Senator Charles Percy (R-IL) at the IVS house. Most of these visitors stayed close to Saigon, but Senator Edward Kennedy was the exception. Kennedy's staff arranged for him to venture out of Saigon to meet with IVS volunteer Dave Gitelson and others in Cần Thơ, to hear reports of villagers killed by South Vietnamese military. IVS volunteer William Seraile later reported:

> A meeting with Senator Kennedy, scheduled for January 12, 1968, was abruptly cancelled when our jeep was blown up. We all rushed out and Hintze [IVS volunteer] jumped in our Land Rover to take injured Vietnamese to the hospital but quickly jumped out when a Vietnamese man yelled "NO!" A dog walked too close to the front tire and the vehicle (Land Rover) was blown up with a mine. [50]

There was speculation that the South Vietnamese military had directed the attack, targeting either Kennedy, because his brother Robert had become the leading anti-war candidate for president in the US, or Gitelson, because he lived in a remote village near Cambodia and was a principal bearer of information about atrocities committed

---

[50] Sagnier, *The Fortunate Few*, 138.

by the South Vietnamese military against Vietnamese civilians. The bombs used in the attack turned out to be low grade and might have been just a warning. But Gitelson was killed in an ambush just two weeks later near his home village.[51] His death furthered speculation that he had been personally targeted, as notices blaming his death on the Việt Cộng surfaced before his body was found or his death confirmed.[52]

Politicians visiting from the US on "fact-finding" missions became ubiquitous. We got word that over 160 VIPs, including fifty members of Congress, were planning visits during the first three weeks of January. Willie Meyers and others at the Vietnam Education Project were certainly doing their job of raising awareness in Washington. While I was encouraged that Vietnam was getting so much attention on the home front, I began to see these visits as counterproductive. They consumed an enormous amount of time and resources for US government and military officials, diverting them from their primary missions. The visits essentially became photo ops, enhancing politicians' credibility when they talked about Vietnam back in their home districts, but seemingly doing little to change their preconceived notions about the war.

Still, IVS volunteers responded whenever we were asked to present our view of the war and to expose the politicians and other dignitaries to Vietnamese who were opposed to the US presence in their country. One group included prominent religious leaders who were strong advocates for peace. They had stopped off in Saigon after attending a conference in New Delhi and were on their way to a meeting in Japan to lay the groundwork for the first World Conference for Religion and Peace, to be held in Kyoto in 1970. The group included Rev.

---

[51] *Time* magazine published a short article about Gitelson, describing his work with IVS and noting that at about the same time he died in Vietnam, a friend was accepting on his behalf the distinguished service award from Macalester College, recognizing Gitelson's contribution to "international understanding." "Youth: The Poor American," *Time*, February 9, 1968.

[52] John Balaban, *Remembering Heaven's Face: A Moral Witness in Vietnam* (Poseidon Press, 1991), 76–80.

Herschel Halbert, an Episcopal priest; Rev. Homer Jack, a Unitarian Universalist who helped found the Congress of Racial Equality and the National Committee for a SANE Nuclear Policy; United Methodist Bishop James K. Matthews; Harold Stassen, a participant in the US Inter-Religious Committee on Peace and former governor of Minnesota and president of the American Baptist Convention; and Rev. Ralph Abernathy, a respected civil rights leader and an associate of Dr. Martin Luther King, Jr. Rev. Abernathy was the best known in the group and attracted the most attention from US media and Vietnamese officials. But it was Stassen, a former Republican governor of Minnesota and unsuccessful candidate for president in 1948, who asked the most penetrating questions during the four days of meetings with Vietnamese religious leaders.

More reporters from the US also visited Vietnam during this time, including a reporter I had known previously from *The Washington Daily News*. My father had worked at *The News* for many years as a political reporter and music critic and had recently expanded his portfolio to include movie reviews. I hoped that *The News* would send him to Saigon to gather background for a review of *The Green Berets*, which was soon to premiere at the Tân Sân Nhật Airport. But no such luck. I doubt he ever reviewed the movie or, if he had, whether my letters from Vietnam might have influenced his assessment.

The US military and South Vietnamese government spokespersons continued to give visitors to Saigon glowing reports of American and South Vietnamese progress in the war. But reports from the countryside told a different story, highlighting the deterioration of security and waning support for the US war effort because of the actions of the US military.

(Letter home: January 14, 1968)
Almost every IVSer I talked with recently reports the worsening of security in his area and has a tale of another mishap on the part of the Americans that takes a toll in

lives, money, and hearts and minds. Roger Montgomery
witnessed a group of copters firing machine gun rounds
into a nearby pond to pass the time. Apparently one round
skipped over half the pond into a nearby rice field, burning
much of the crop that had been set out to dry in the sun.
Compensation is questionable. In Vĩnh Long two jeeps of
Americans were ambushed. Five were killed, including the
top provincial advisor whom I met when I studied language
there; when the (Vietnamese) province chief and one of
his assistants went out to see what happened, they were
wounded by rounds from an American helicopter. Some
peasants chopping wood in the hills near Đà Nẵng were
cut down when a spotter plane pilot thought their water
canisters were rocket shells. All of these things repeated over
and over have the effect of prolonging this war. It's difficult
to rally peasants getting chopped up from both sides.

While reports from the countryside revealed increasing unrest and anti-Americanism among the South Vietnamese, life in Saigon continued. Everyone began preparations for Tết, the Vietnamese celebration of the lunar New Year, which usually occurs around the end of January. This meant that the pace of work for us at IVS slowed, and I agreed to join Roger Montgomery on a quick two-day trip to Tây Ninh, a mid-sized city near the Cambodian border.

The Holy See of the Cao Đài religion sits outside of Tây Ninh. Cao Đài is an amalgam of many religions, incorporating elements of Taoism, Confucianism, and Buddhism. Organized like the Roman Catholic church, the religion counts both Jesus Christ and Victor Hugo among its patron saints. There were at that time about 1.5 million followers of Cao Đài in Vietnam and another 1.5 million in other countries. In the middle of the Holy See is an elaborate temple—part cathedral, part pagoda—with many intricate architectural features. At the foot of the altar is a large throne reserved for the Cao Đài pope.

A focal point of the building is the painting of a large eye, referred to as the Divine Eye, which symbolizes the religion's belief that God is a witness to everything.

The temple in the Holy See was worth the ninety-kilometer trip from Saigon via Vespa scooter, but we were conscious of dwindling security as we ventured farther from Saigon. A good rule of thumb for judging security was the number of vehicles on the road. For the first thirty kilometers we encountered numerous trucks and buses and ox carts. Then the traffic began to change, and for the last sixty kilometers we saw only US military convoys. The road was full of holes from exploded mines, and heavy military vehicles kicked up lots of dust and belched dirty smoke as they passed. Helicopters fired rockets far beyond the rice fields on our right, encouraging us to try to go faster. But Vespa scooters were not built for speed, and we were greatly relieved when we finally reached Tây Ninh unharmed.

Despite our blackened faces from the dust of the road, Roger wanted to stop at a high school on the outskirts of town to visit some colleagues from his teaching days in Tây Ninh. School was just letting out at about 6 p.m. Roger was immediately embraced by some former students and met with the giggles of small girls as well as several teachers, who invited us to join them for beer in a small shop behind the school.

We learned quickly that Tây Ninh was a city in stress. Although there was not a large American presence in the city, three recent incidents had set off a wave of anti-Americanism. The first was the strafing and killing of twenty-nine woodcutters who were chopping wood in a "free fire zone." These were zones declared off-limits by the military, but the boundaries were never easily identified. In the second incident a US soldier struck a match and lit an ox cart on fire, burning the rice and straw in the cart and injuring a woman riding on top. The third incident involved a drunken American soldier who dragged the wife of the deputy district chief into the cab of a truck after she refused to show him an ID card. He did not have the authority to ask for the card, and fortunately another US soldier intervened to end the incident.

We were not surprised when our teacher hosts said plans were underway for demonstrations against the American presence. Such incidents would not have caused a significant stir in some northern cities like Quy Nhơn, where the inhabitants had become numbed to the bad behavior of GIs stationed in the area. The more intense reaction in Tây Ninh showed how little the town had been impacted by the war up until that point. It did not bode well for the continuing US presence in the area.

We were delayed on our return trip to Saigon when a helicopter landed in the middle of the road. It had come to pick up the lead driver of a long US military convoy who had been injured when his truck veered into a ditch. The driver had headed into a turn too fast and lost control of the truck. Fortunately, he was the only one injured. When the road cleared, we resumed our journey. Morning traffic was steady, which was reassuring, but we were conscious of rockets firing off in the distance. They seemed to be landing much closer to us than from where they originated. But the latter part of the trip was on smooth roads, and we eventually made our way safely into Saigon, a bit weary from the tensions of the day but glad we had made the journey.

There were now over 500,000 US troops in Vietnam, and the best thing anyone could say about the war's progress was that it was a stalemate. As my IVS colleague Gerry Liles observed, "We are simply fighting the birth rate." The major battles were still being fought in remote areas, including a battle that began January 21, 1968, in Khe Sanh. The Việt Cộng surrounded and attacked a US Marine garrison and ultimately kept reinforcements at bay for over five months before the US could drive them away. This battle was reminiscent of the 1954 battle of Điện Biên Phủ, when the Việt Minh—the army of the Vietnamese insurgency against the French—surrounded a remote outpost that the French had set up in order to halt the flow of men and weapons between Vietnam and Laos. The Viet Minh surrounded the outpost with 40,000 men and cut off air access. Within two months the Viet Minh had overrun the base. In retrospect, the collapse of Điện Biên Phủ marked the end of France's effort to subdue its former colony.[53]

While the similarities between the battle of Điện Biên Phủ and the Việt Cộng's siege on Khe Sanh are intriguing, it is doubtful that the North Vietnamese believed the Battle of Khe Sanh would be the *coup de grâce* of the war. More likely it was part of the larger strategy to get the US military bogged down in meaningless battles, while the North set the stage for taking over all of South Vietnam. Unbeknownst to most Americans, the most significant attack of the war was just days away.

---

[53] Robert Cowley and Geoffrey Parker, eds., *The Reader's Companion to Military History* (Houghton Mifflin Company, 1996).

CHAPTER 13

War Comes to Saigon: Tết 1968!

Firecrackers woke me up at 3 a.m. Accustomed to night-long celebrations, I returned to sleep, but only for a few hours. I was due to take housemate Thọ to the airport before breakfast. By 7:15, we were up and on my Vespa heading to the Tân Sân Nhựt Airport. It was January 30, and Thọ was set to board a plane to Đà Nẵng to celebrate Tết 1968 with his family in Quy Nhơn. He never made it.

Suddenly, an unexpected roadblock forced me to brake hard, causing the Vespa's back wheel to slide almost out of control. We were on Hai Bà Trưng Street, the main road to the airport. Around us the city was just beginning to wake. Why were armed Vietnamese soldiers blocking our path?

"The airport is under attack!" the soldiers shouted. "Turn back!"

No argument on our part. We turned around.

Tết is traditionally a day of celebration, the first of three days when the whole country takes time off to celebrate the New Year and honor their ancestors. In 1968, as in previous years, the warring parties had again agreed to a truce during Tết. But the noise that had awakened me at 3 a.m. was not celebratory firecrackers; it was the sound of gunshots and mortar rounds that signaled the end of a truce barely begun.

Trần Hung Đạo's attack of the Chinese during Tết 1789 flashed through my mind.

We had no knowledge of the scope of the attack or how long the roads would be blocked, so Thọ and I headed back toward town, only to confront another roadblock stopping traffic from both directions. This roadblock was near the entrance to the alley access to our house. We pointed to the alley, and soldiers waved us through. But rather than turning into the alley, we headed to the Air Vietnam Office downtown to find out when Thọ could fly to Đà Nẵng. The streets were strangely deserted, and our progress was repeatedly halted by more roadblocks. Such roadblocks were often set up during student demonstrations, so I did not think they were particularly unusual. We passed within two blocks of the American Embassy, unaware that it, too, had been attacked and that nineteen Việt Cộng had penetrated the compound.

We finally reached the Air Vietnam office and encountered a large crowd as dozens of others, like Thọ, were seeking to reschedule flights out of the city. But we quickly got the message: no planes would be flying that day.

Still unaware of the nature of military activity in the city, we headed to the central market for a bowl of *hổ tiểu*—Chinese noodles. Thọ said he wasn't upset about the disruption in his plans. His parents had died some years earlier, and there was only one aunt in his hometown whom he knew well. But still he felt obligated to go home because it was Tết and that is what you do at Tết.

Some soup venders were open, but otherwise the market was empty. Something felt very different. We heard the sound of small arms, which we still thought were firecrackers. But we also heard and saw helicopters overhead. Something was definitely wrong.

We finished our soup quickly and headed toward the outskirts of town to the IVS headquarters. There we found much confusion and a large sign on the bulletin board: "No one allowed on the streets until further notice." The IVS house complex was bounded on two sides by clumps of trees. The other two sides were exposed to the roads. After two hours, Thọ thought better about hanging out in an American complex and said he would hitchhike to town. I did not offer to take him back downtown.

News of the attacks across South Vietnam began to trickle in, just as a parade of Vietnamese people, fleeing the fighting and the bombing, began streaming by our complex.

(Letter home: March 6, 1968)

At 2 p.m. a Vietnamese cleaning woman at the IVS house heard planes flying low and broadcasting to everyone to leave an area not far from IVS, by 6 p.m. Less than an hour later people started streaming by the house, heading for Saigon. Most were on foot but some rode on motorcycles, Lambros (3-wheeled vehicles) and scooters—some with four to five people per vehicle—in their flight to security. Some told us they were heading to a relative's home. Others did not know where they would end up. They only knew that they had to leave or face the fury of air strikes that were certain to come that night. They loaded as many goods as possible onto bicycles, on their backs or on top of their heads, and carried young children too small to walk. One woman carried only a large, framed picture of an ancestor.

Some families set up a water station across the street from our house. Tom Fox and I tried to figure out how we could help and discovered boxes of chewing gum left by Care, Inc., in the IVS warehouse. We gave the chewing gum to the families to pass out to the refugees.

IVS volunteers working in and around Saigon, or visiting the city for Tết, poured into the compound, and two things became clear. There were not enough beds available and the compound itself might not be safe from stray US air strikes, particularly because of the trees on two sides.

IVS chief Dan Whitfield sent IVS volunteer Mark Lynch off to find more secure lodging. Lynch finally returned about 5:15 p.m. with news that there were twenty or more rooms available in a USAID guest house near the town center, each with two beds. We piled into five or

South Vietnamese families fleeing into Saigon to escape US bombing on outskirts of city in wake of 1968 Tết Offensive. (Saigon, 1968)

Family fleeing into Saigon to escape US bombing following the Tết Offensive. (Saigon, 1968)

South Vietnamese families fleeing into Saigon to escape US bombing on outskirts of city in wake of 1968 Tết Offensive. (Saigon, 1968)

six cars with whatever possessions we could easily carry and headed out, wondering if we would ever see this peaceful compound again.

The city immediately came under martial law, and the authorities imposed a 5 p.m. curfew. We stayed at our safe haven for three nights, waiting for the fighting to end and watching the nighttime actions. After dark we went to the sixth-floor balcony to watch the war, a bizarre form of entertainment. The eerie silence that came over the city each evening was broken up by helicopter gunships firing tracer bullets and the sound of trucks, jeeps, and occasionally tanks roaring down the city's wide boulevards. Fighting at the American Embassy ended nine hours after the initial attack, but fires still burned near the main airbase.

We had little to do during the day but observe the war from our windows.

(Letter home: written February 2, 1968,
8:15 a.m.; mailed March 6, 1968)

*Still sporadic fighting in the streets as people gather
below our building in a small alley trying to buy bread
from a bake shop. From up here (second floor) it looks like
people are trying to buy large quantities. The storekeeper
cracks open a large iron door to hand out the bread and then
quickly pulls the door shut to keep people from stampeding
the shop. Voices are heard, fast and shrill; bitter faces appear
on those being left out. The smell of bread is enticing.*

(Letter home: February 3, 1968, 11:05 p.m.)

*After a quiet third day in the guest house, sniper fire just
crackled outside the fourth-floor window. A number of us were
in one room making light of our stay. "Sgt. Pepper" played on
a tape recorder; the atmosphere was party-like. Then a tracer
came sailing across the window, a flare was dropped, and
more shooting was heard. Also heard a high, anguished voice,
yelling "MEDIC!" from an officer's building across the street.*

*One of many South Vietnamese tanks on routine patrol of outlying areas of
Saigon in response to 1968 Tết Offensive.* (Saigon, 1968)

The next day, as the streets seemed a bit calmer, we returned to the IVS house. We were relieved to find it had remained intact.

My only contact with my family in sixteen months had been through letters and one phone call at Christmas. I could only imagine what my father was thinking when he walked into *The Washington Daily News* newsroom on the first day of Tết, to be greeted by the afternoon paper's first edition. Blazoned across the front page was this headline:

WAR HITS SAIGON
Parts of Embattled City Evacuated to Permit Bombing VC
Strongholds: GI Clerks, Patients Join the Fight[54]

The news story picked up on pages 2 and 3 while the rest of the front page was devoted to an editorial entitled "Where Were We? Where Are We?" and displayed a cartoon entitled "US Embassy." The cartoon depicted General Westmoreland dropping his gun as a Việt Cộng soldier jammed his weapon into Westmoreland's stomach. The caption read, "We have turned the corner – General Westmoreland."[55]

The Washington Daily News was never known for harboring anti-war sentiment, but the surprise Tết attacks were certainly a wake-up call.

On February 4, four days after the January 31 attack, IVS CEO Arthur Gardiner sent a letter to "Parents and Friends of IVS Volunteers in Vietnam":

> The following message was received this morning from the State Department:

> AS OF MONDAY NOON SAIGON TIME NO REPEAT NO IVS CASUALTIES REPORTED EXCEPT JOHN BALABAN SLIGHTLY WOUNDED IN CAN THO NO CAUSE FOR CONCERN ... [Ellsworth] BUNKER [US Ambassador to Vietnam]

---

[54] "War Hits Saigon," *The Washington Daily News*, January 31, 1968.
[55] Cartoon entitled "US Embassy," *The Washington Daily News*, January 31, 1968.

This I hope will be reassuring to you although it is not clear at the time that I write whether Saigon has been in touch with the IVS team in Huế, and perhaps in other northern towns of [South] Vietnam..." Arthur Gardiner, Chief Executive Officer, IVS.

On February 9 Gardiner wrote again:

IVS was able to resume direct communication with the office in Saigon on February 8th in the afternoon. Aside from the group of volunteers who are unaccounted for in Huế, six altogether, all others are safe as of that time. I am glad that we can assure you in this fashion about son or daughter. We are communicating separately with the parents of those in Huế.

While the Tết Offensive, coming on the traditional day of peace and celebration, had taken most of us in Saigon by surprise, we later learned that some IVSers in the field had received at least general warnings of a pending attack. Jay Worrall was providing refugee relief and teaching English near An Khê, close to the Central Highlands. The area around An Khê was almost entirely controlled by the NLF, and Worrell often relied on Vietnamese villagers to let him know when it was safe to travel to a particular village that he was assisting. Shortly before Tết, one of his students told him he expected a large attack on An Khê and instructed Worrall to stay in his home until the attack was over. "You will be safe there," his student told him.

Len Ackland, who was teaching English in Huế, received a more direct warning some months before the Tet Offensive. Huế had a long history of political activism in opposition to the government and was the center of the uprising that had led to the overthrow of Ngô Đình Diệm in 1963. It was also a focal point of a similar uprising led by the Buddhist Thích Trí Quảng against Nguyễn Cao Kỳ in 1966, during which a significant

US information office was burned to the ground. That protest failed to achieve change and only intensified the anti-American sentiment in the city.

Ackland shared the IVS letter to President Johnson with some of his students, which led to several long conversations with them about the war. In late 1967, just a few months before Tết, his students told him:

> During the French war, French civilians were often assassinated; in this war it hasn't happened yet but could begin happening. We know how you feel about the war, but when Vietnamese people see you riding your bicycle down the street, they think of you as just another American. The revolution is coming, and we don't know if we can save you. [November 16, 1967][56]

Ackland's students did not disclose the pending attacks on Huế, but their warning, coupled with his growing dissatisfaction with IVS's role in Vietnam, led him to leave Huế in December and return to Saigon.

Most IVSers, and presumably the US military, received no warnings of the attack. IVS volunteer Mark Lynch was invited to a friend's house in Biên Hoâ fifteen miles outside of Saigon. He recounted:

> After dinner, I rode my Vespa scooter back to Saigon. As I later learned, the rice paddies on either side of the highway were teeming with Việt Cộng troops in place for their attack a few hours later on Saigon. I have always admired — and been thankful for — the discipline of those troops in resisting the temptation to pick off a stray American that night.[57]

---

[56] Len Ackland, excerpt from draft of *A Life Shaped by Suicide and Vietnam* (working title), expected publication date 2026.

[57] Mark Lynch, "Viet Nam: An IVS Perspective," *Yale '66 at 50* (Reunion Press, June 2016): 265.

Five other IVS volunteers were not so fortunate. In Huế, the NLF captured one IVS woman and two IVS men. After two months they released the woman, Sandra Johnson, along with a Quaker nurse captured elsewhere. The two men, Marc Cayer and Gary Daves, were led on a treacherous journey on foot for one month and then by truck over the Hồ Chí Minh Trail to Hanoi, some 400 miles from Huế. The trucks, which could only travel at night to avoid US bombs, took three days to arrive in North Vietnam. Cayer and Daves languished in North Vietnam for five years until finally being released by the Vietnamese government after the peace accord was signed in 1973.[58]

Two other IVSers, Chris Jenkins and Steve Erhart, were visiting Vietnamese friends and, while they were not captured, they did have a harrowing few days. Erhart hid out a few days with friends until they told him it was too dangerous for them for him to stay. He spent the last few days of the battle for Huế in an old French fort held by ARVN soldiers.

Jenkins's friends hid him in a back room of their home in the Imperial City for three weeks until the US military drove out the NLF and recaptured the city. During the three weeks, the NLF held propaganda sessions at night and went door to door recruiting volunteers and asking about any Americans that might still be in the city.[59] They came to the house where Jenkins was staying, and he recognized the voice of one of the NLF cadre as that of one of his students. Jenkins was about to pop out of hiding to say hello when concern for the well-being of the family that was sheltering him held him back. He eluded discovery throughout the attack.

---

[58] Marc Cayer, from Quebec, Canada, had arrived in Vietnam just before the Tết Offensive and spoke no Vietnamese and little English but was able to communicate somewhat in his native French language. Cayer wrote a compelling story of his trip north and time spent in North Vietnam, translated from French to English by IVS volunteer Stuart Rawlings. (Marc Cayer, "Prisoner in Vietnam," Asia Resource Center, Washington, D.C., 1990.)

[59] Don Oberdorfer, Tet!: The Turning Point in the Vietnam War (Johns Hopkins University Press, 1971), 199-235.

Jenkins was fortunate. Given the anti-American and anti-government feeling in Huế, he might well have become one of 2,800 people the Việt Cộng executed in Huế during the three-week battle. Their bodies were thrown into mass graves.

Those executed included some US government employees as well as French and German nationals, but most were Vietnamese "collaborators" whom the Việt Cộng had systematically sought out and identified for execution long before the battle began.[60] These included South Vietnamese officials and anyone who had worked with or for the US.

The mass executions were perhaps the darkest event of the war for the Việt Cộng. While the Tết Offensive was generally seen as a defeat for the US, the mass killings fueled the belief that a communist takeover would mean the slaughter of millions. Documents and newspaper reports revealed that the mass graves were filled with the bodies of Vietnamese killed out of revenge by the retreating Viet Cong troops.[61]

Though I had not received any warning of the pending Tết Offensive, I did know that things were getting worse for the US.

(Letter to friend: January 15, 1968)
The war is not going well for ol' USA, the situation [is] in no way similar to the rosy picture Westmoreland and Bunker tried to present this last fall. Security is worsening in almost every corner, and we are now running a tight race between successes in the fields and Vietnamese attitudes.... The general insurrection (strikes are occurring with more frequency) may still be a long way off, but the roots are there. Continuation of the same with still no end in sight is going to lose it all together.

---

[60] Oberdorfer, *Tet!*, 199-235.
[61] Oberdorfer, *Tet!*, 199-235.

The Tết Offensive was very costly to the war effort of the Việt Cộng because of the thousands of lives lost and the significant depletion of supplies. US military command believed the US could readily capitalize on the weakness of the Việt Cộng with more troops—250,000 more troops—which would have increased troop strength at the time by 50 percent.

But Washington was exhausted, and Johnson said "No." The Tết Offensive proved to be prime-time TV viewing. The simultaneous attacks across the country and the nine-hour takeover of the US embassy in Saigon by nineteen Việt Cộng showed the world that North Vietnam and the Việt Cộng were not going away. American opposition at home was on the rise.

The US, however, was not ready to give up either. The Tết Offensive failed to spark a national uprising in Vietnam against the US as the North had apparently hoped.[62] The North Vietnamese and the NLF were not capable of a military victory. At best, they could keep the US at bay while controlling much of the countryside.

Stalemate.

History should have taught us that the Vietnamese would never give up. The war would continue, not unlike the "thousand-year war" with the Chinese, the hundred-year war with the French, and now a twenty-year civil war, with support from the USSR on one side and from the United States on the other. Vietnamese had always held a long perspective. This was no better exemplified than when the US and North Vietnam agreed to begin meeting for peace talks in Paris. The US delegation rented hotel rooms. The Vietnamese rented apartments.

---

[62] Oberdorfer, *Tet!*, 199-235.

CHAPTER 14

Turmoil and Transition

Twenty thousand villagers—now officially referred to as refugees—streamed into Saigon on the first day of the Tết Offensive. Fighting in the city subsided within twenty-four hours of the first attack, but the refugees kept coming. The future of IVS in Vietnam was very much up in the air. But for the immediate present there was urgent work for IVS volunteers.

(Letter home: February 11, 1968)

Today, more than 3,000 [refugees] came from one area alone, Gò Vấp, about five kilometers outside the city. Tomorrow, who knows. The pattern has become fairly obvious. A group of Việt Cộng will go into an area, start rousing the people and then attack a police station or government office. The American or GVN response follows very closely, with massive fire power from the ground and air. Fires begin and the people start flowing out with whatever they can bring along. If they are lucky, a few vehicles, like today, will soon be on hand to take them to a refugee center. There they sit, not knowing what happened to their homes and possessions or if they will have enough to eat in the days that follow.

Students at the Saigon Student Union immediately sprang up to help. They have shown amazing tenacity

in discerning the needs at the various centers and getting
commodities quickly and efficiently (from government
sources) to the sites—mostly under the leadership of
Nguyễn Văn Thuế (student at the National Institute of
Administration) and Hà Thương Cát (an old hand at youth
work, now a teacher in Gia Định). The students are living
in the refugee center, spending literally twenty-four hours a
day on the premises. Some look like they face exhaustion.

Some fifty-five centers sprang up around Saigon to provide shelter and essential services to the refugees. Students with whom I worked accepted responsibility for running four of these. Others were handled by teachers and members of the Rural Development Cadre—an arm of the Saigon government. IVSers drove students and supplies around town, picking up rice, straw mats, and *nước mắm* from the Ministry of Social Welfare and distributing them to the various centers. We also drove roving teams of medical students to the centers and work crews into the countryside, to begin shuffling through the debris in the burnt-out areas that had so recently been dotted with thriving villages.

My work took me to a hospital in the Chợ Lớn area of Saigon, referred to as China Town. The hospital was full of patients, and refugees packed the grounds outside the hospital. They flooded the area because they believed that hospitals offered security. Members of a USAID sanitation team did not share their view, however. Fearing for their own safety, the USAID team abandoned the hospital, even as the chief medical officer of the hospital expressed his fear that the lack of sanitation would lead to a breakout of cholera. Dr. Samuel Epstein, a Boston physician who had recently arrived in Vietnam, and I pounded on a few doors at USAID, at last succeeding in bringing attention to the problem. I was also able to find the right contacts for students to get medical supplies, lime, and DDT, essential supplies for their centers.

(Letter home: February 11, 1968, continued)

Today I have been on my scooter, trying to coordinate IVSers with vehicles to make sure they were at the right place where they were needed the most. I went out to the Gia Định center about noon just as the flow of refugees was reaching its peak from the Gò Vấp area. As refugees poured in we could see US bombers strafing the area. There was no end in sight.

It soon became clear that the center at Gia Định could not hold all the refugees needing shelter. Many would need to be moved into the city, but the effort to move them ran into two problems. First, the refugees themselves resisted any relocation. They wanted to stay as close to their homes as possible, no matter what the conditions, and the trauma of moving again was almost as great as the trauma they had experienced in the initial removal from their bombed-out villages.

The second problem was the challenge of selecting the centers to house them. Student leaders wanted to minimize their contact with the South Vietnamese government and sought to help the refugees move to the four student-run centers. But it wasn't clear if those centers had enough capacity to handle the move. The students' desire to maintain independence from the government flared up when a government official asked some of their leaders to make a statement condemning the communists for the plight of the refugees. They refused. It seemed clear that the deluge of refugees flooding into Saigon was the result not of communist-inspired guerilla warfare, but of the widespread bombing of the countryside that was the US's principal response to the Tết Offensive. The students did allow some propaganda at their centers, as well as the placement of televisions that were tuned to the government-run channel, but they made it clear when asked that they were not working for the government.

We transported as many refugees as we could each day before the 7 p.m. curfew. Then we had to get off the streets. While we, the IVSers, went back to our compound for a meal, hot showers, and a bed, the students stayed on at the centers, working into the night.

As the flow of new refugees finally showed signs of slowing, Saigon began to return to normal. The refugees who had flooded the Nước Chợ Lớn hospital were moved to other spots before cholera could break out. Government services were restored, and IVS began to assess its future in Vietnam. It became clear to me that much of what IVS had hoped to accomplish as agents of change could not continue under the conditions that prevailed after the Tết Offensive.

This was particularly true for my work with youth leadership, as I sensed a growing distance between us. The students were becoming increasingly suspicious of any Americans working in Vietnam—even those tied to IVS. And their suspicions could not be completely faulted. At least one IVS volunteer went to work with the CIA directly after leaving IVS, though I didn't know if knowledge of this was widespread among the Vietnamese who had known him.[63]

As I felt the distance growing between my regular Vietnamese colleagues and me, I began to question whether my presence in a small house in a run-down section of Saigon put all of us who lived there in danger. Although the Tết Offensive did not spark a wide uprising across the South, it did make it clear that there were many NLF sympathizers and cadre members living in Saigon.[64] I did not want to leave Vietnam. But I knew I had to leave IVS.

---

[63] My IVS predecessor, Charlie Sweet, left IVS mid-assignment and joined the CIA.

[64] In January 2000, on my first trip back to Vietnam, I met Ngô Thoi at his *phở* restaurant, from which he helped organize the Tết Offensive in Saigon. I had passed by his shop many times while living in the city and had eaten there on occasion. I knew nothing of his NLF connections.

CHAPTER 15

Echoes from Home

It was during this time of uncertainty that word reached us in Saigon of violence hitting hard back home. On April 4, 1968, we and the rest of the world heard the startling news: "Dr. Martin Luther King has been assassinated." For me it was a stark reminder that Vietnam was not the only place where violence threatened to strike unexpectedly. Learning the news, I wrote:

(Letter home: April 6, 1968)
The death of Martin Luther King (April 4) and the ensuing violence has come as a shock to us here, though not a surprise. Violence has become so much a part of our life in Vietnam that we have come to expect it, not only here but at home as well. The soldier returning to civilian life does not lose easily instinctive use of violence, which he has been exposed to for two or three years—and taught the necessity to survive. Violence is an instrument of national policy, while nonviolence is only an illusion, a dream of a King or a Gandhi. It is not taught to children in elementary school.

Yet the shock is real, perhaps as another reminder of the vulnerability of our society to the reign of irrationality. For us also a reminder that even when we leave Vietnam we will not be withdrawing from the stage of human suffering, needless and indiscriminate. Only the characters will change.

As wrong as it may sound, our ability to empathize with the Vietnamese, to expose ourselves unrelenting to their sufferings, was based on the knowledge that at almost a moment's notice we could leave Vietnam and take ourselves out of the picture. We would never forget our experiences here, but they would soon fade in importance and Vietnam may even be written off as a rather unfortunate place that got the wrong end of historical determination. Perhaps now that my own country and my own family are threatened by this same historical trend, I can understand better the people of Vietnam and the uncertainty of their existence. The rays of hope that exist here will certainly emerge in the US, yet it is now necessary to take a longer view of things and not to expect the sun in a few months or even a few years.

PART II

The Children

Những Đứa Trẻ

"My pain is like a river of tears,
so full it fills up the four oceans."

Thích Nhất Hạnh

CHAPTER 16

Coming to America— Casualties of War

The odor hits you first. And stays with you forever. When I remember my time in Vietnam, the smell that returns most vividly is not the reek of garbage in the stagnant creeks in Saigon. That, I got used to. But I never got used to the smell of rotting flesh, blood-soaked bandages, unwashed bed sheets. This was the smell of most of the hospitals I went to in my new job: field agent for The Committee on Responsibility to Save War-Burned and War-Injured Vietnamese Children (COR).

Strange name for an organization. COR had come to Vietnam to help war-wounded children, and it needed my skills: the ability to communicate in Vietnamese, knowledge of how to travel safely throughout the country, and a comfort level working with the Vietnamese people. It was also just the right time for me. I was ready to see visible results of my work. My job with IVS—"to promote economic development by supporting youth engagement"—was always amorphous at best, and it was now no longer possible. The Tết Offensive put a damper on my work in support of youth engagement in rural development. The South Vietnamese military was now drafting students into civilian guard units to assist in securing the city during their spare time.

My Vietnamese counterparts began to believe that the US would use the Tết Offensive as a reason to abandon the country. They worried about what would happen to them if the US left and Vietnam fell to the communists. As Vietnamese closely associated with Americans, how would the new regime treat them?[65]

Even worse, some of the groups with whom I worked were operating as if the war did not even exist. Yes, all families were impacted, but the fighting was happening in the countryside, not in Saigon. Even after the Tết Offensive. Life in a time of endless war had its own rhythm. Everyone went about their business as usual, seemingly limited only by the mandate to be off the streets by the 10:00 p.m. curfew. It was even possible to drive the hundred miles to the resort beach town of Vũng Tàu on weekends—as long as there were no unusual reports of fighting on the route. But Tết had changed all that for me. The war in the country was too present, and I could no longer be a mere spectator.

COR was either a political organization with a service component or a service organization set on making a political impact. The distinction might have mattered to the IRS, but not to me. Both were legitimate, and both were badly needed. COR's primary mission was to bring war-wounded children to the United States, where they would receive intensive medical care not available to them in Vietnam. It didn't matter which side caused the injuries. Some were horribly burned by the flaming napalm that US planes poured down indiscriminately on jungles and rice paddies and children alike. Others were hit by Việt Cộng rocket fragments or maimed by exploding landmines.

In addition to providing medical care, COR's founders had a political objective—to bring the war home to people in the US. The children ended up in hospitals around the US, and wherever COR doctors treated Vietnamese children, they made sure that the local community was aware of the work. Reporters and TV news crews were notified, and invariably stories appeared on air and in the local papers. The Vietnam War was now a local story.

---

[65] After the war ended, many South Vietnamese were placed in "re-education camps" for as long as five years, some in squalid conditions. An unknown number died in the camps. I learned on my first trip back to Vietnam in 2000 that, even twenty-five years after the war, anyone who had worked for the US military or government before 1975 was still being shut out from government jobs.

COR sent US doctors to Vietnam to identify children who needed tertiary medical treatment to repair the wounds of war, usually reconstructive surgery. But these doctors, skilled in their medical work, knew neither the country nor the language. Thanks to IVS, I was reasonably fluent in Vietnamese, so it fell to me to accompany the doctors to the hospitals, serve as interpreter, and seek the approval of family members to let COR take their war-wounded child halfway around the world for medical care that was unavailable in Vietnam.

John Balaban and the author preparing to take a child to the US for medical treatment; reported in The Saigon Daily News. *(Saigon, 1968)*

Usually at least one family member would stay close to the child in the hospital, giving us an opportunity to explain what the doctors were proposing and what it would mean for their child to travel to the US for what might well be a six-month stay for treatment and recuperation. Once I had to go into a prison in Quảng Ngãi to get permission from an NLF soldier, the father of a boy who had been wounded. With cold, steely eyes, the father gave his approval.

In most cases, families gave permission freely. US bombs might have caused the injuries, but the families were more than ready to let their children go to the US if it meant the children could get better. As long as we promised to bring them back home. I could only imagine the inner turmoil family members were experiencing as they prepared to entrust their children to COR's care.

After the family gave permission, I arranged to bring the child to Saigon, obtained a passport and visa for the child, and then secured a spot on a US military medical transport plane. COR hired Vietnamese women with some English language ability to help care for the children while they were waiting in Saigon for departure and then to accompany the children to the United States. These women, known as *convoyeuses*, were critical to our efforts.

COR was the brainchild of Dr. Herbert Needleman, pediatrician and professor of psychiatry in the University of Pittsburg's School of Medicine. Dr. Needleman was well-known for his research on neuro-developmental changes caused by lead poisoning in children. Supporting Dr. Needleman's initiative were several very prominent doctors, including Dr. Albert B. Saben, Dr. Benjamin Spock, and Dr. Helen Brook Taussig, who served as honorary chairpersons. Joining them were Methodist Bishop John C. Wesley Lord and the Rt. Rev. Paul Moore, Jr., a highly decorated Marine veteran who in 1972 would become bishop of the Episcopal Diocese of New York. COR chapters formed around the US to raise money and to provide support for the children when they arrived in their new communities. Families hosted the children in their homes while they were recuperating.

The US government, the US military, and the South Vietnamese government each gave their blessing to the endeavor. All the wheels were in motion.

When I joined COR in March 1968, the program had been going for about four months. Thirteen children had already arrived in the US for care, and more children were waiting in Saigon for their flights. But the program hit a snag.

COR's Saigon office was designed for two field agents and one Vietnamese social worker-assistant. But when I began, I was the lone field agent. John Balaban, a fellow IVS worker, had been in discussion with COR about coming on board full-time, but while working in the hospital in Cần Thơ, south of Saigon, during the Tết Offensive, he was hit with a piece of shrapnel and had to return to the United States to recover.

By this time, Balaban, like me, no longer believed that he could serve effectively with IVS in Vietnam. Like other IVSers, he had come to believe that our work was counterproductive. "IVS personnel can continue to do individual services for the Vietnamese," he wrote, "but I believe that in doing so they're doing Vietnam a disservice, for, willingly or not, IVS workers serve American propaganda and programs of pacification."[66] Once back home, however, Balaban felt a strong pull to return to Vietnam and sought to gain his draft board's approval of his change in assignment as a conscientious objector. "Working at the Cần Thơ hospital that week of the Offensive, I saw a depth of misery that I had never guessed," he told me at the time. "I had to come back to help ease that suffering, whatever way I could."

I was hired to carry on in John's absence, but fortunately not entirely on my own. COR had also hired a very able Vietnamese woman, Miss Nhung, to help with the program, particularly by providing care for the children in our charge. The children had been lodged in local Saigon hospitals with the assurance that they would only be there for

---

[66] Balaban, *Remembering Heaven's Face*, 70.

two to three weeks while the paperwork was completed and transport was arranged to take them to hospitals in the US.

When I started my work, things seemed to be in good order. COR had already obtained passports for the children who were waiting in Saigon. The South Vietnamese government had issued the necessary travel passes. COR had received general authorization from the US government to transport the children on military aircraft at no charge. But there was one significant caveat: the children could travel only on a standby basis.

Large planes carrying wounded American soldiers flew out of Vietnam every day. We did not think there would be any problem finding room for two or three children at a time. I expected to get the necessary approvals for the child to travel to the US without difficulty.

Then I hit a major roadblock. To my dismay, I was told that, although the travel had been approved, the children could not leave for the US. There was no room on the plane.

As the weeks went by, this scenario happened so often that I began to suspect the US government's cooperation was a ruse and that we would never get the children out. After all, why would the US government want war-wounded Vietnamese children showing up in Boston or Nyack, New York, or San Francisco, or any of the other cities where COR formed chapters to receive the children?

I asked the COR office back home to investigate and soon got a response. The planes each day were indeed full. Because of the Tết Offensive, American casualties were on the increase—not from the battles that took place the first few days of the Offensive, but from the ensuing campaigns. In response to Tết, the US military stepped up its patrols and forays into Việt Cộng territory, and the result was inevitable: increased deaths and casualties and more and more wounded US soldiers returning to the US for medical care.

The shortage of available air transport was grounded in the grim realities of war. The children now waited in limbo with no idea when they would be leaving Vietnam. But my focus was already on the next batch of children and the maze of everyday bureaucracy.

Each application had to pass through numerous hands before receiving final approval. My first step was delivering the necessary paperwork to the first office, assuming it would be processed quickly. When I returned the next day, however, I was usually told that the application was "in process." After persistent questioning, I eventually learned what the second step was. And then the third step. And so it went on, until I realized to my dismay that the application for a Vietnamese passport had to go through thirteen steps before it could be approved and a passport issued.

As I became a familiar face within this part of the South Vietnamese bureaucracy, I was allowed to follow the trail of the application and talk to the next person in charge of approvals. Eventually, beleaguered officials allowed me to hand-carry the passport applications from one desk to another, sometimes getting immediate approval. But the process still seemed endless.

Balaban, who had returned to Vietnam in April, came up with a way to speed the paperwork. Instead of submitting applications one-at-a-time, we waited until we could bundle several applications and submit them together. Clipped at the top of each application was the child's photograph, often with the wounds of war visible on their faces. We shamelessly began putting the picture with the most severe-looking facial scars on top of the stack. Applications travelled more quickly through the bureaucracy after that.

Despite the inevitable frustrations of dealing with governmental red tape, we did encounter one positive note. Even though we were in a country where corruption and bribery were commonplace, we never received a request for a bribe. Of course, we never felt tempted to offer one; there would have been far too many people to satisfy.

CHAPTER 17

Children in Limbo

COR's Dr. Peter Wolfe was an imposing man, tall and stout, with a temper that matched his physique. Fortunately for me, his temper was usually aimed not at me, but at the Vietnamese policy-makers who frustrated him at every turn when he tried to gain their support for the COR program. Fortunately for the survival of COR, his anger and frustration erupted not in the office of the civil servants but back at our office and living quarters. The twenty-minute trip from the passport office to our house should have been long enough for him to cool down, even on the hottest days, but apparently it just turned up the intensity. Upon arrival, he typically slammed down his satchel and proceeded to blast away with a verbal assault. I passively listened and endured.[67]

Wolfe, a child psychiatrist from the Judge Baker Guidance Center in Boston, arrived in Vietnam in early April 1968. His role was to help identify children who might benefit from receiving treatment in the US. I had been with COR for a month when he and I made our first trip to a provincial hospital in Đà Nẵng, north of the Central Highlands.

Đà Nẵng was a pleasant surprise. The city was off limits to the thousands of US soldiers stationed in nearby bases and had therefore

---

[67] My generally "laid-back" nature, which I often considered to be a hindrance, was sometimes seen by others as an advantage. My COR colleague John Balaban wrote: "With his sandy hair, already thinning, and slow deep voice, Berliner had a positive effect on the families and bureaucrats that we dealt with. I was far more on edge, far angrier." Balaban, *Remembering Heaven's Face,* 138.

retained much of its small-town atmosphere, despite a population of 250,000 people. Bordered by a river and mountain on two sides, Đà Nẵng sat on the edge of the South China Sea. The recent rainy season had left trees lush and healthy, in contrast to the withering trees in Saigon that contended constantly with exhaust from large trucks and three-wheeled cyclos. Đà Nẵng was also one of the cities least impacted by the Tết Offensive, and it maintained a casual atmosphere despite an 8 p.m. curfew. Only the continual roar of F-4 fighter planes landing at the nearby air base and the occasional sound of mortar blasts off in the distance reminded us of the war close at hand.

A trip to the Đà Nẵng hospital across the street from the IVS house quickly brought the reality of the war into perspective. We were shocked. The hospital was one of South Vietnam's busiest, a sprawling complex of wards, operating rooms, and half-built facilities. The men's orthopedic ward was a temporary wooden building with a cement floor. It was built to house the overflow of patients who were no longer in critical condition but still needed the constant care of a physician. When all the beds were occupied, immobile patients were placed on stretchers in the corridors. Flies were their constant companions. Family members hovered nearby, adding to the overcrowding and blocking the paths of nurses scurrying back and forth.

Upon entering the hospital, we were struck by typical hospital smells plus the stench from soiled patients, a debilitating combination. The sudden noise and dust from a medivac helicopter heightened the chaos.

(Letter home: April 16, 1968)
In contrast to our findings in Saigon, the hospital is crowded with war victims with no sign of a let-up. Medivac helicopters land three or four times a day with wounded from the countryside. With great assistance from the chief of medicine, Dr. Thuong, we have selected 10 children to go to the United States for treatment... Children from four to eighteen suffered a variety of

*wounds, mostly caused by gunshots or mortar fragments.
One boy, about 11, was burned by gasoline; the others are
paraplegic for the most part, caused by the severing of
nerves. One young girl will need reconstructive surgery
on her nose, which will help her breathing a great deal.*

I knew from my time with COR in Saigon the frustration of dealing
with both the Vietnamese bureaucracy and the US military. Now
I learned the most important and difficult part of my job—getting
permission from a parent or relative to send the child to the United
States. For families who had lived their entire lives in remote villages,
Đà Nẵng might have been the farthest they had ever traveled from
home. They might never have had direct contact with any foreigners
and knew Americans only by the airplanes and helicopters flying near
their villages, dropping bombs and napalm, or from armed soldiers at
military outposts. Suddenly they were confronted with the knowledge
that their child needed extensive medical treatment that was simply
not available in Vietnam.

(Letter home: April 14, 1968)
    *One woman, the mother of a four-year-old paraplegic
boy, reacted violently against the idea, becoming quite
emotional in the process. The girl we used as an interpreter,
a secretary of the hospital, had no real sense of delicacy
and seemed to upset the woman more than soothe her. We
explained that we were not forcing her child to go, and
she decided she would talk to her husband and let us know
in two weeks. Then as we were leaving the ward, I saw
her again, putting clean clothes on her child as if she was
preparing for a quick departure. I went back and tried to
explain again that the decision was completely up to her,
that perhaps treatment could be done in Đà Nẵng. I was
afraid she would take the child out, depriving him of any
medical treatment at all. It seemed to calm her. The next*

morning when we came back, she completely changed her
mind, perhaps a result of seeing other parents giving their
consent or from the persuasion of others in the ward.

Although some families readily gave their consent, they often insisted that a family member travel with the child, apparently out of fear that the child would not return to Vietnam. Of course, it was impossible to accommodate this request, much to their dismay.[68] Once we got the family's permission for the child to go to the United States, we took a family member to get his or her signature notarized at the local police station, no doubt another strange ordeal for them. Then we went back to Saigon to tackle the next arduous paper chase through Vietnamese officialdom. More hours spent in government offices, watching thirty-five different forms being shuffled across at least eleven desks. On the wall in one office was a sign: "Civil servants are the soldiers to fight on the political front." All we wanted was approval to send a child to America.

We received assistance in the hospitals from American doctors sent to Vietnam by the American Medical Association, as well as from Swiss and US military doctors. One physician in Cần Thơ seemed anxious to help but only if the children had fine minds and are "worth saving and can contribute" when they return. He said he was forced to select patients on this basis since there were so many. "If the others die," he said, "then it is God's will." We were unable to determine if he gave an IQ test before providing medical treatment.

After spending three days in the hospital in Đà Nẵng, Dr. Wolfe and I had some much-needed time to ourselves on Sunday, before returning to Saigon. We arranged for a car to drive us north toward Huế to look at the refugee camps. After following the road out of the city and around the bay, we could see in the distance the road winding

---

[68] One child, Châu Quỳnh, stayed in the United States because her paralysis could not be cared for in her home village. She was adopted by her host parents and currently lives in California. I was heartened to learn later that very few of the more than one hundred children sent to the US did not return to Vietnam.

its way up to the Hải Vân Pass, which we were told afforded spectacular views of the mountains and the South China Sea. But just outside of Đà Nẵng the view was an endless string of refugee settlements — old, new, and some in-between.

(Letter home: April 14, 1968)

Almost all the refugees come from areas within a thirty-nine-mile radius of Đà Nẵng. The houses are of wood and cardboard, and many with tin roofing, are built on sand that yields nothing but a few onions if the sand is prepared properly. But there is scarcely enough room between the houses to raise anything except for a few chickens. Somehow the people manage because there are few signs of malnutrition. But on the tip of their tongues is the same question one heard in Saigon after the Tết Offensive. "When is the government going to give what it promised?" In the middle of the area are two rows of half-completed cement houses, stopped when materials were cut. The remains of a few public latrines are a monument to American stupidity. They were built by a Marine Civic Action team with goose-necked bowls but no running water. They stopped up quickly. Open wells have become garbage pits; people feared the coming of the hot season. Improper protection from the heat would surely mean the death of some small children. A deathwatch was taking place in one house for an older woman, a result of natural causes. "When will you go back to your village?" I asked. "When there is peace," they said.

The war had a persistent way of raising its ugly head unexpectedly. Just as we had all but forgotten the Tết Offensive in February, a new attack interrupted the flow of life in Saigon. Called the May Offensive, the new round of hostilities started much the way the Tết attacks had, on a seemingly ordinary Saturday night. The Việt Cộng attacked the Tân Sơn Nhất Airport and other military targets in the city with mortars, and we woke up Sunday morning to the sounds of gunfire seemingly from just down the street. Saigon officials imposed a twenty-four-hour curfew. When I first heard the gunshots, I became fearful because my bedroom was on the first floor, with a large open window near the ceiling and a not-very-secure lock on the door. I decided to lie under my bed to protect myself from stray bullets or even an intruder. After twenty-minutes, however, the mosquitoes became unbearable, and I crawled back into bed.

(Letter home: May 9, 1968)

Yet the rest of the city apparently was not troubled. Several friends came over not aware of any restrictions, and others called on the phone, surprised to learn that anything was going on at all in our area. By mid-afternoon we were able to venture out to find the city quiet and not overly affected. By Monday, however, fighting again spread to other parts of the city, leaving our area quiet for the time being. The same areas hit at Tết (by US bombers) were being hit again but not with the same intensity. It even seemed at the beginning that Vietnam and US air forces had learned something from the havoc created by bombing during Tết and were using more restraint. As the fighting continued, however, this impression disintegrated. US helicopter gunships and South Vietnamese Sky Raiders have been bombing continuously around the edge of Saigon and in Gia Định. The area beyond the IVS house near Tân Sơn Nhất Airport was hard hit (the IVSers have evacuated the quarters again to the same hotel); the only real difference is that the fighting and air strikes have not come as close to the heart of Saigon. (Our house is in District Two and is probably safer than most areas because of the number of soldiers and Vietnamese and US military police scattered nearby in small compounds.)

After we talked with some colleagues at the IVS house, Balaban and I became concerned that the Bửu family's house, where we were living while working with COR, might not remain safe, at least for Americans, so we made a mad dash on our motor bikes back to the house to pick up our go-bags with our passports and other essentials.

When we arrived at the entrance to the alley leading to the Bửu house, we found two Saigon police officers at the entrance with rifles drawn. "VC down alley around corner!" they shouted. It seemed unlikely because we, unlike the police, knew the alley dead-ended at the Bửu house, and there was no other point of entry.

We ignored their warning and sped by them, relieved not to see VC outside the house. Members of the Bửu family were huddled around a television, watching scenes of shooting in Saigon—some within blocks. Despite the sound of gunshots in the neighborhood, the TV coverage made it seem like a far-off adventure.

Some of the family members protested that we were abandoning them in the middle of the attack. We told them we thought they would be safer without Americans in the house and left quickly. We returned to the Bửu house the next day.

(Letter home: May 9, 1968)

So far today (Thursday) no new developments have occurred to give any indication whether the fighting will spread or die away. The areas under strict curfew have not been attacked, and the fires are staying well out on the edge of the city. Still the Bửu family, with whom I live, are not taking any chances. They have already stocked up on a good supply of food not only for them but for us as well. Right now, we can still go out to restaurants to eat. I don't expect the fighting to increase, the whole thing having been an attempt to harass rather than take over the city. I will stay in this house unless it becomes obvious that is not a good idea. The family here would prefer that we stay and does not feel any

*personal threat due to our presence. By the time you get this
letter things no doubt will have quieted down considerably.*

On May 14, I wrote again to report on the changing situation in
Saigon.

(Letter home: May 14, 1968)

*Saigon is quiet again. Barbed wire still stretches across
some streets in different parts of town, but the bombing on
the outskirts, morning and night, seems to have stopped. It
appears that the press may have blown up the attacks, giving
them more importance and greater intensity than they
deserved. It's important to remember that Saigon is a very
large city and sprawls for miles from the center. Life in the
center of town goes on almost as normal although fighting
may be going on in one of the outlying districts. Today we
had lunch at the Majestic Hotel, six floors above the Saigon
River. The whole scene was very placid and relaxing.*

I don't know when my parents got my letters, but for the second
time, they received notice about my situation. A telegram from the
head of COR reached them on May 15:

Message from Saigon. Dear Mrs. Berliner: Yesterday
we received a message that 'SAIGON IS QUIET, TELL
FAMILIES SAFE'. This Message was sent by John Balaban.
I am sorry this message is delayed, but I have been unable
to reach you by phone yesterday or today. Sincerely, Mrs.
Warren Goodrich.

CHAPTER 18

Paperwork Breakthrough
and a Brief Respite

The process of obtaining permission for COR children to leave the country continued to be frustratingly cumbersome until, after what seemed like endless weeks of wringing our hands, we experienced a breakthrough. On May 13, we received passports for five children, and word came that we could expect eight additional passports within a week. At almost the same time we received news that another child, Lê Văn Cử, had been cleared to board a military plane to the US. Cử was fourteen at the time and had severe facial injuries that required reconstructive surgery. His clearance to leave was particularly significant for me, as Lê Văn Cử had threatened to be a nightmare case for COR.

This was the second time we had received clearance for Cử. The first time, on the day of his scheduled departure, he disappeared from the hospital on his own. All of our hard work seemed to be going down the drain. We believed either he or his family had gotten cold feet when we shared his departure plans the night before. Fortunately, we located him later that day and were able to confirm his family's willingness for him to leave for the US. Having learned our lesson, we kept him under watchful eye at the Bửu house until the next flight could be arranged some days later.

What a relief, finally, to see some results of our labors! Balaban and I had not realized the pressures we were feeling in those weeks of working and waiting. Cử's presence in the Bửu house had been a daily, if subliminal, reminder that we had not done our job.

John and I celebrated Cử's departure by treating ourselves to dinner at our favorite French restaurant—Galois, one of the few still operating in Saigon that we could afford. Our favorite menu item was *osso buco*, an Italian veal dish cooked with onion and carrots and a variety of spices. After a constant diet of rice and greens, with occasional small pieces of chicken or beef, it was nice to be able to sink our teeth into the rich pieces of meat. Our monthly pay of $500 made such a meal a luxury.

May 26 was another banner day. Three children and their escort, Bùi Thị Khuy, also called Mary Khuy, left Vietnam for Boston's Children's Hospital. The children were in good spirits and ready to start the journey. Miss Khuy was perhaps more nervous. But she spoke passable English and carried herself with the utmost dignity, as well as a degree of confidence that made her invaluable. This was true of most of the women we hired to be *convoyeuses* for the children. Their job in Saigon was to help care for the children during the long waiting game and then travel with them to the host cities in the US. There they visited the children on a regular basis to give them comfort and help with communication with their families.

Mary Khuy was in Boston when I visited there later in the year. When I saw her again, I realized that I had developed strong feelings for her, somewhere between infatuation and "I can't live without you." But her proper Catholic upbringing prevented her from entering into a casual relationship, and I was not in any position to offer anything more. I reluctantly held my feelings to myself.

Tragically, soon after returning to Vietnam in the spring, Miss Khuy was struck by a military vehicle on the streets of Saigon while riding her moped home after work. She died on impact. Another gut-wrenching funeral.

John Balaban and the author with hospital personnel, preparing to take children to US for medical care. (Saigon, 1968)

(Letter home: July 17, 1969)

This has been a very trying and sad week. It started with literally pulling a child from his hospital bed to take him back to Đà Nẵng.... It ended with news of the death of Mary Khuy, our employee and friend, struck by a military vehicle while driving home after work on her moped.

I felt I was mourning for a whole generation, but mostly felt a very personal loss.

In the wake of the Tết Offensive and the subsequent attack on Saigon in May, the South Vietnamese took additional if somewhat ineffectual steps to beef up security in the city. Lower echelon government officers spent as many as three evenings a week staying up all night to guard office buildings. This made them too sleepy the next day to do much work, although it was rumored that they had also slept on duty the night before. The South Vietnamese government conscripted students into a special military unit charged with guarding the banks of the Saigon River. The conscripts received only two or three weeks of training for this task. A Vietnamese acquaintance told me the unwilling recruits were placed there to draw fire from the Việt Cộng, or as a way of making them more loyal to the government. The buzz phrase in those days was "civil defense," as the government tried to organize the population, neighborhood by neighborhood. There were no signs of such organizing in my neighborhood.

Meanwhile, the heads of COR urged us to keep identifying more children for treatment in the US, saying they wanted to send fifty children at a time. They gave us no explanation for that daunting aspiration. Doubtless they thought the arrival of a large number of war-wounded children all at once would attract major press attention and expose more Americans to the horrors of this war. But their reasoning scarcely mattered; we had a hard enough time finding hospital beds in Saigon for even eight or ten children to stay while awaiting departure papers. And while hospital administrators and doctors were very supportive of COR's efforts, they also made it clear that using hospital beds to house patients awaiting transfer was putting a strain on their resources.

Although the number of children receiving care in the US never met its lofty goals, COR made good use of the press to highlight the urgency of taking care of children wounded in the war. Balaban and I met with *New York Times* reporter Bernard Weinrab, who submitted a superb story about COR's work. Although that story did not make it to press, the *Times* subsequently printed a long piece that vividly described the challenges faced by families in the US who took the COR children into their homes as they recuperated from medical care.[69] Nan Ickeringill wrote that shoes and underwear were as alien to some of the

---

[69] Nan Ickeringill, "In US Homes, Wounds of Vietnamese Children Are Healing," *The New York Times,* December 11, 1968.

children as were the strange language, television, and fire alarms that triggered vivid memories of bombs and gunshots. The author noted that, at the time of the article, seven of forty-seven COR children had completed their medical care and returned to their homes. In retrospect, the number seems small, but at the time each success felt like a great victory in the midst of all the turmoil and destruction.

Some of the challenges faced by COR gained visibility when *The New Republic* ran an article in June of 1968, describing the tremendous obstacles COR faced because of red tape. In addition to obtaining appropriate approvals from medical personnel, COR had to get approval from the ministries of health, interior, and finance, as well as the police, before bringing the child to the US. If the child was a male, the ministry of defense had to screen and approve the application to ensure it was not a ploy for evading the draft. At least one child died while his application moved through the bureaucratic maze. Seeking a rationale for the hierarchy of approvals required, *The New Republic* noted that the South Vietnamese government was "not anxious" to help COR because of concerns that the children's presence in the US might provide fuel to the growing anti-war sentiment in the States.[70]

Good Housekeeping magazine, one of America's most iconic publications, ran a feature entitled "One Family's Pledge." It covered four full pages in the magazine and included pictures of the Moore family in Newton, Massachusetts, who cared for numerous COR children, one to two at a time.[71]

Our efforts to help a handful of Vietnamese children thrust us into what seemed a theater of the absurd—one-on-one medical care in the midst of raging warfare. The contrast struck me hard on one occasion when I spent time with Donald Duncan, a correspondent for *Ramparts* magazine, on a visit to Saigon. Duncan, a former member of the US Army Special Forces, had made headlines three years earlier when he

---

[70]"Caring for the Wounded," *The New Republic*, June 8, 1968, 11.
[71]Elizabeth Keiffer, "One Family's Pledge," *Good Housekeeping*, December 1968.

publicly resigned from his position in protest of the war.[72] He thrilled us with his tales of fighting off leeches in the jungles of central Vietnam while training South Vietnamese irregulars in guerilla warfare. During the May Offensive, we were sitting together in the Bửu house when we learned that street fighting had broken out. Duncan bounced up and rushed toward the area where we heard shots. I followed a few blocks behind him but felt no need to get closer to the action.

The reports of fighting and sounds of gunfire that had drawn this former soldier into the streets had become, for us, just a routine part of daily life in Saigon. One eager college graduate visiting Vietnam on a fact-finding mission accused us of accepting the grimness of war, because we didn't cry out at every injury to humanity. But our seeming inaction was not due to insensitivity; it was just part of surviving in the surreal world that was Saigon in the midst of war.

Nature seemed to conspire to enhance the sense of unreality, for the rainy season came, as usual, making no allowance for the war.

> (Letter home: June 7, 1968)
> *The city is now being drenched daily with the initial rains of the monsoon season. The clouds begin to form, and the skies darken about 4 p.m.; rain begins an hour or two later. After a half hour of steady pouring some of the streets accumulate up to a foot of water—stalling cars and forcing many on bicycles to get off and walk. The garbage that has accumulated along the side of the streets and around the markets sets loose, coming to a halt blocks away. But the soothing sound of rain dulls the burst of mortars in the distance. In the morning the air is fresh.*

With continuing pressure from COR in the US, a shakeup in the Thiệu government, and considerable pleading on Balaban's part, the

---

[72] Duncan was the author of *The New Legions* (Random House, 1967). He appeared on the cover of the February 1966 issue of *Ramparts*, where he announced, "I quit."

average time required to get a passport for a wounded child to travel to the US shrank from four weeks to one week. As things began to run relatively smoothly, I seized the opportunity to take a long-overdue vacation, choosing once again to travel to Cambodia. Although the flight from Saigon to Phnom Penh took less than an hour, making the transition from the chaos of Vietnam to the apparent calm of Cambodia took much longer.

How could so much wanton killing in one country be almost nonexistent in the country on its border? As we abruptly learned just seven years later, the difference was leadership. Under Prince Sihanouk, Cambodia enjoyed relative peace, but in 1970 a coup drove him out of the country, and Cambodia fell under the rule first of Lon Nol and ultimately Pol Pot, who proved to be a ruthless dictator. His rule became a tyranny of genocide, with the number of deaths he inflicted on his own people rivaling those suffered in Vietnam during the war. Pol Pot's demonic reign lasted four years before opposition forces, with the help of Vietnam, succeeded in ousting him in 1979.

But in this visit Cambodia was, as before, a place of respite and wonder. I spent the week swimming in the sea along the coast at Sihanoukville, eating in French restaurants in Phnom Penh, and again visiting the ancient temples of Angkor Thom.

After a week of rest, enhanced by evening meals at a cheap café in Siem Reap with the travel bum set that included Danes, Germans, Indians, and Americans, I was ready to go back to work.

CHAPTER 19

Võ Nam and Nguyen Độ

Sometimes the children we selected for transport to the US ended up staying in Saigon for medical treatment. Like some of the homecomings for children who had made it to the US, such cases did not always have happy endings. Ten-year-old Nguyễn Độ suffered from severe burns, caused by "gasoline from the sky," he said. No doubt napalm. But his skin healed, and after about five months his doctors said he was ready to return to Đà Nẵng. Độ was eager to return to his family and was very playful in the Bửu house the night before we left.

Võ Nam was a different story. Also ten, he was paralyzed from the waist down, wounded by artillery shells during an attack that had killed his parents. He had learned to walk with crutches and braces but had no control over his bladder, so was bound to a catheter that he did not know how to empty. The doctors at the National Institute of Rehabilitation asked us to take him home, saying they had done all they could for him and needed his bed. But there was no "home" and Nam spoke only of an aunt who "lived far away." Our only option was to return him to the hospital in Đà Nẵng.

A torrential rain was pelting the streets and hospital windows when I arrived at the institute to take Nam back to Đà Nẵng. Miss Nhung, a woman of about fifty and a part-time COR *convoyeuse*, was assigned to accompany Nam from the institute to the Bửu house, where he would spend the night. When he saw Miss Nhung approach him, Nam burst into tears. Miss Nhung had a calm, matter-of-fact nature that seemed typical of mature Vietnamese women. But she was also very businesslike. When she tried to coax him into dressing, Nam became hysterical. I left Miss Nhung to deal with the child and went to find a taxi, often a laborious task but even harder when a rain-soaked passenger threatened to soak the taxi's interior—no matter that the taxi was a 1945 Renault in ragged condition. I eventually flagged one down and asked the driver to wait while I returned to get Nam and Miss Nhung.

Nam was now partially dressed but no more reconciled to leaving than he had been earlier. I wrote, *"by force, pulling on his pants and breaking his grip from the bedpost, we got him into the taxi along with Miss Nhung and another woman we had hired to take care of him in the hospital. I rode back to the house in the rain on my scooter, already contemplating R&R in Penang to get rid of pneumonia."*[73]

When we finally arrived at the Bửu house, Nam met Độ for the first time, and soon his outbursts were reduced to sniffles. By 9 p.m. he had begun taking a moderate interest in life, getting caught up in watching *Mission Impossible* on the US Armed Forces Network. I slept in the same room with Nam and Độ and worried most of the night that Nam's urine bag would overflow. I was up well before the alarm went off at 6 a.m. and soon was out the door, carrying Nam in one arm, my bag and Nam and Độ's bundles in the other, while Độ carried Nam's crutches and braces to a waiting taxi. Thanks to a new COR colleague and former IVSer, Jerry Liles, a taxi waited for us at the mouth of the alley.

The taxi took us to the airport shuttle service, courtesy of Air America (commonly known as the CIA airline). With the help of IVS volunteer Hugh Manke, whom we encountered by chance at the airport and who was also going to Đà Nẵng, we boarded a C46 cargo plane, fitted out with fold-down passenger seats along the sides. Nam showed great curiosity in the plane and the ground below when not covered by clouds, and for the first time in fifteen hours he seemed like a normal kid. Once in Đà Nẵng, Manke located another IVS volunteer,

---

[73] Letter home, July 17, 1969.

Phil Yang, who picked us up in his jeep and took us to the Đà Nẵng hospital.

Although it had been some months since I had left IVS, it seemed a strange serendipity that whenever I found myself stranded or in need of aid, a former IVS colleague or other humanitarian volunteer appeared out of the blue to offer rescue. This was yet another of those times.

(Letter home: July 17, 1969)

Nam was taken to his old upstairs ward in the orthopedic section, and I left him there while trying to discover the whereabouts of his aunt. My only contact was a nurse in the hospital, now on leave to have a baby. Finally locating her at her home, I learned the aunt had not been in contact with her for three months. There seemed no alternative except to leave Nam in Đà Nẵng. Even if his aunt were there, it seemed he would need to be close to a medical facility and a nurse who could take care of his bladder problems. But convincing him of this was beyond the limits of reason. He was not particularly anxious to see his aunt, but the prospect of continued hospitalization in strange hands was frightening. In the short twenty-four hours that I was with him I'd become the symbol of security and protection that he had come to expect in the Saigon facility. When I prepared to leave him, the tears of the day before repeated and he clung to my shirt. When I pried his tight grip from one spot, he latched on to the camera strap. The cycle was continued for a grueling period until I was finally free (at least physically) and could leave. A Vietnamese technician held on to Nam as I descended the stairs. I could hear his crying the total distance of the hallway and out through the front of the hospital. Sometimes I still hear it.

I now needed to catch a flight with Độ to Quảng Ngãi, and the 5 p.m. departure time for the ten-seater Beechcraft plane was rapidly approaching. Độ was waiting for me at the IVS house, extremely agitated by the delay in getting him home. His excitement had intensified at the thought of meeting his family, so it was with much relief that I could tell him we would leave that day. We had already had one falling out when he thought I had left his bundle in Saigon. I hadn't. A flight attendant had taken it to the baggage section without our knowing it.

> (Letter home: July 17, 1969)
>
> *A trip to Quảng Ngãi is less than an hour, almost*
> *straight south, a hundred kilometers along the coast.*
> *The land in between is hilly and battle scarred, up until*
> *the valley that surrounds the city. Here it is green with*
> *scattered villages, solid dikes, and signs of normalcy. It*
> *is deceptive. Quảng Ngãi province has taken one of the*
> *worst beatings of any province, 70% destroyed according*
> *to Jonathan Schell.[74] The province town, also called Quảng*
> *Ngãi, is mortared frequently and excursions into the city*
> *at night by NLF troops are not rare. One travels the road*
> *to the main district towns with healthy skepticism.*

As we approached the air strip, Độ looked with concern at the ground. He said he did not recognize the area. Not surprising, since the only other time he had flown over the area he had been flat on his back on a stretcher, heading to Saigon. His mood perked up considerably as we drove toward town, courtesy of Keith Britton who worked at the Quaker orthopedic clinic in Quảng Ngãi and just happened to be at the air strip. But when Britton pulled into the Quaker compound, Độ again became quite agitated. He suddenly thought he was going to be left there, just as Nam had been left at the hospital in Đà Nẵng. But we stopped there only momentarily, while Britton unloaded his van. Then

---

[74] Jonathan Schell, *The Military Half: An Account of Destruction in Quang Ngai and Quang Tin* (Vintage Books, 1968).

we were off to find Độ's home. Britton recognized the approximate address of the refugee camp, just down the road. We pulled over at a Buddhist orphanage to ask for help in finding the camp, but Độ was already heading through the orphanage and out the back door across a field to a small village, not quite sure if this was the right place. We asked the first person we met if he knew where Độ's home was. The man pointed to the next group of refugee housing.

As we approached the first house, Độ's pace quickened. He had been burned on the legs and still could not place his right foot squarely on the ground when walking, but the injury did not slow him down. As he darted under the extended tent-like roofs up one row of houses, we had to trot to keep up, stepping over ropes and past food stalls. He turned abruptly into one house only to turn back just as abruptly, confused and distraught, then remembering and walking past three more entrances before turning in again. Finally, the right house. Độ was home.

A family member offered Britton and me a warm beer, Salem cigarettes, and lots of gratitude. Độ explored the house, greeted his cousins, ran out into the neighborhood. A slight sprinkle started, and we excused ourselves.

By 6:30 p.m. we were back at the Quaker house in Quảng Nai, sitting down to dinner.

CHAPTER 20

Đoàn Quang Trung

Not all reunions are happy ones, and not all of the children taken into COR's care faced their homecomings with delight. So it was with Đoàn Quang Trung, a fourteen-year-old boy who had nearly lost his life in an explosion that left his face almost unrecognizable, and his chest crisscrossed with deep scars. Those injuries landed him in a Vietnam hospital near Quảng Ngãi, where we met him six months later. COR doctors determined that Trung's medical condition was stable, and that he could benefit from one or more surgeries to rebuild his face. But those surgeries would need to be done in the US.

After twelve months in Denver, Trung returned to Vietnam, physically stronger, more mature, but still with very visible scars on his face.

(Letter home: August 30, 1969)

Monday morning, August 26, I woke up at 6:30 a.m. and went to the airport with Đoàn Quang Trung, a fourteen-year-old boy who had been living in Denver for the past year getting plastic [surgery] procedures. His face and chest are still left with unsightly scars, but it is clear he is a healthier human being. Whether he will be able to readjust to Vietnam or not is another question. In some ways he seems more American than me, from slouching at the dinner table to asking disarming questions seemingly out of the blue. He had become a Christian while in the United States. [Most Vietnamese are Buddhists.] He spent the first day back talking with credible English about the birth of Christ—the large star that shone like a flashlight leading the way for kings with gifts. While his English was excellent, his Vietnamese was sorely lacking. The first day he could hardly speak a word, and only with the coaching of Miss Hảo, our next escort, was he able to acclimate back into his language.

The first full day back in Vietnam was difficult for Trung.

(Letter home: August 30, 1969, continued)

When Trung wasn't questioning our religious convictions, he was sulking and crying by himself from a heavy case of homesickness for his Denver foster family. He would constantly look at his watch and remark upon the things he would be doing in Denver at that moment—mostly playing it seems.... Clearly his interest was just going back to his village for a visit and then returning to the US....

The trip to Đà Nẵng was long with stops in Nha Trang and Quy Nhơn. Trung had spent most of the time looking at pictures of American friends, except for a short period when he wrote a letter to his girlfriend—Suzie. Arriving in Đà Nẵng about 1:30 p.m., we were downtown by 2 p.m. and able to get a 5 p.m. flight to Quảng Ngãi.

The time in between was spent eating lunch—Trung wouldn't eat much rice, only the meat and vegetables on top—and resting at Phil's house. [Phil was an IVS volunteer working with shoeshine boys.] Trung kept his distance from the shoeshine boys, and in fact avoided most Vietnamese with whom we came into contact. He refused to answer their questions until I commented sharply on this, and then he answered with great circumspection. For example, when asked where he was coming from by a Vietnamese man in Đà Nẵng

*he replied, "from Quy Nhơn, no from Nha Trang. Actually,
from Saigon." He never did say he had been to America.*

We spent the night at the American Friends Service Committee
compound. AFSC had established a rehabilitation center in Quảng
Ngãi that made artificial limbs. Demand for limbs was high during the
war, and no doubt long after the war ended, due to tons of unexploded
bombs remaining in the dirt. The two of us left the next morning, in
an AFSC jeep, to meet Trung's mother.

By 9 a.m. we were on the newly paved road to Chủ Lai, north of
Quảng Ngãi. Some IVS volunteers had traveled south on this road
just the week before. They ran into a firefight—small-arms fire—and
drove by a burning village, but that kind of activity was the exception.
Tuesday was sunny and friendly and the road full of traffic.

We stopped briefly at a US air base, where Trung had spent part of his
time after being wounded. He wanted to see some of the people who had
treated him. None were still there. We drove off the sprawling air base
and turned left on the road through the town of Chủ Lai. It consisted
mostly of wooden shacks, where Vietnamese were selling cold drinks
and PX goods. We missed the Catholic church that was a landmark for
getting to the local dispensary where Trung's mother would meet us and
drove across the river into Quảng Tín province. Realizing our mistake,
I turned around and, upon more careful inspection the second time, I
found the turn leading to the church and the orphanage. A few more
wrong turns and backtracking got us to the small hospital.

Trung waited in the car while I went to see if our appointed
rendezvous would take place. We had left a message at the hospital
a week before with directions that it be delivered to Trung's mother,
letting her know that Trung would arrive either Monday, Tuesday, or
Wednesday. It was with some surprise and great relief that I found his
mother sitting there, as she apparently had done the whole day before.
I called Trung over to present himself, as his mother went scurrying
off to gather up siblings and cousins and perhaps take a deep breath
before the reunion.

(Letter home: August 30, 1967, continued)

As some pictures I have indicate, the whole scene was quite tender, with no embraces but distinct sighs and a few tears. Trung's younger sister was the most expressive with a broad smile for her brother and the camera. Trung told her, "You look very thin."

With a crowd of medical personnel and patients gathered around, Trung asked about the communists. On the way up on the airplane we had talked about the VC in his area. Trung said they were quite present, although they didn't seem to bother him or his family. But he knew someone who had his throat cut for apparently informing on their presence in the village. For that reason, he thought it would be impossible for me to go to his village without "a large army."

To the crowd in front of the medical unit his questions about the communists seemed out of place. As one person muttered, "He has gone to America and now he is worried about communism." The response of the people to Trung's concern led me to believe that they were much more accommodating to the Việt Cộng than he. I told his mother I wanted to visit their house and asked if she thought it was all right; she readily agreed. Trung asked with concern if the communists would come into the house after I left. She effectively squashed his fears.

So, with Trung and his mother, younger sister, and one cousin, the five of us drove down the road towards Tam Kỳ, north from Chu Lai, for about 3 kilometers and then turned left, on the opposite side of the street from the South Vietnamese district headquarters. The dirt road soon turned to sand and began to narrow at a bend, making it impossible to drive further. This was disappointing to Trung's sister and cousins... because they assured me that we were quite far from their home.... With new vigor

from the country air, I hoisted Trung's duffle bag on my
back and followed his mother down the path. Trung had
returned to Vietnam with numerous smaller bags, one for
every member of the family to carry. His mother led the
way, carrying her load on a flat straw tray supported on
the top of her head. The sun was bright as we started a
few minutes before noon, and there was a small breeze.

The walk to the top of a small ridge, on a path eroded
by rain, was the most difficult part of the journey but
also the most rewarding. At the top, we could see a large
valley below with bristling rice fields and clusters of trees
that surrounded small villages. I asked Trung's mother
to point out her village, but she said it was hidden from
view, my first indication of the length of the trip ahead.

At the bottom of the first hill, we came to the edge of
a village that included some well-built houses—one with
stucco walls and a large multicolored-tiled patio in front.
Setting down her parcels, Trung's mother consulted with
some people who had appeared to see the American and
then she raced away down the path. I was disconcerted at
her sudden departure, but she came back soon with two
hot bottles of Coca-Cola. As thirsty as I had become, hot
Coke did not seem like the answer, but of course I could
not refuse. My stomach slightly bloated, we set off again
for the final and longer leg through two rice fields and
several wooded areas, crossing a small stream on a bridge
made of old metal slats used to construct helicopter pads.
I stopped to listen to the frogs and the sound of wind
moving through the rice. Saigon was never further away.

Trung's duffle bag felt like it weighed forty pounds as I shifted it
constantly from one shoulder to the other, and then finally to the back
of my neck, supported by both my arms. It was with a great thud that

the bag finally landed on the coarse cement floor of Trung's house. I stumbled to a bench and sat down, forty-five minutes after we had begun to walk.

A small crowd gathered to greet Trung. I didn't really know what they expected to be the result of procedures like plastic surgeries. I had seen before the shocked looks on the faces of family members when a child returned, still with prominent scars. While Trung's looks were much improved from when he left Vietnam, he was still left with deep scars and excess cartilage from the series of reconstructive surgeries. I sensed some disappointment with his looks, but the excitement of having Trung home prevailed.

(Letter home: August 30, 1969, continued)

Driving in the car towards Trung's village, he had asked his mother if the house were clean. Arriving home, he decided that three younger half-brothers were not, and he marched them out to the well and gave them a bath—sans soap. The second thing he did upon arriving home was reach in his bag of goodies and pulled out candy for the neighboring children, which he distributed away from his house in an attempt to disperse them. Eventually the children migrated back to his house and crowded inside, much to Trung's distraction. Nevertheless, he unpacked some of his belongings and distributed gifts.... Not much was said during this process even when, almost exhausted, he sat down as the family and friends fondled their new possessions. An older man asked Trung if he liked being home, addressing him by "Cu," a name I took to be one used by the family in the home.... "My name is Trung," he replied, suggesting that he was no longer the little boy that had lived there 18 months before.

After some hot tea (I begged off a second bottle of Coke this time), I gathered my camera, briefcase, and a pineapple that Trung's mother had presented to me and started for the door. Trung's mother was concerned that I would lose my way. Trung offered to walk me back. I felt bad about Trung having to make the long trek to the jeep and then back home, but I also felt vulnerable walking by myself in such an isolated area. So, I readily accepted his offer.

Trung's mother sent along his little sister, perhaps wanting to make sure that Trung had, in fact, come back home to stay. Together we walked quietly, except at times when Trung and his sister broke out in common laughter. We stopped once at a house along the way to get some water for Trung. His sister gave me some tea as well. I could not drink tap or well water for the entire time I lived in Vietnam because of the risk of catching malaria. Tea, either hot or warm, was the drink of choice any time of day. The Vietnamese believed that hot tea on a hot day was more refreshing than a cold drink. Although the path was more familiar than I had anticipated, Trung still walked me all the way back to the Quaker jeep, still parked where I had left it—to my great relief. We said goodbye and Trung turned around with his sister and headed back to their home. I felt elated to be heading out and overpaid the Vietnamese boy whom I had recruited to watch the jeep, a vigil he had kept for more than two hours.

Trung had developed a strong attachment to his American hosts, as had they to him. They were particularly fearful that they would lose all contact with him once he returned to his village. They were thus delighted one day when a letter showed up from him with an APO (Army Post Office) return address. Trung, in his diligence, had found a US Marine outpost and asked a soldier there to mail his letter.

CHAPTER 21

A Very Bad Day

The USAID jeep slowed as we approached the small roadside village. Suddenly, without warning, a toddler stepped off the sidewalk—colliding with our front fender. My driver, Nam, veered to the left, too late to avoid impact, and stopped the vehicle. He hopped out and went to the boy, now sprawled out on the road. Quickly a crowd gathered. I hung back near the jeep, knowing how volatile a crowd can be when aroused. Suddenly, Nam started running up the road, chased by a man waving a rifle. Shots rang out as Nam rounded the bend. My mind was a blur.

Someone in the crowd shouted, *"Người Mỹ ở đây!"* ("There is an American here!")

The crowd turned toward me. Panic set in.

"Hey buddy. Do you need some help?" A voice out of the blue, in English.

Two American soldiers were driving by on their way to the nearby helicopter base. I felt a huge relief and then suddenly remembered the child. I quickly explained what had happened. We crossed the street, picked up the boy, and with his mother headed up the road where Nam had been chased. He had run off into the brush and was nowhere in sight, but there was no time to stop. This had suddenly turned into the worst day of my life.

The American helicopter base was less than two miles up the hill on the left. The child who had been struck by our jeep was taken inside a canvas-clad structure. I told the American soldier—I never knew his name—about what had happened, and without hesitation he said we needed to go back to the village and find my driver. As much as I wanted to help Nam, I dreaded heading back to the village where we might face an angry mob. But halfway down the hill we encountered two men pulling a wagon with Nam lying prone on the bed. He was alive, but obviously hurting. As we pulled up, he shouted at me, "You leave me down there. You forgot about me." But there was no time to explain. We put him in the jeep and headed back up the hill. A helicopter sat on the paddock. The soldiers placed Nam on a stretcher and carried him onto the helicopter. I hopped on and landed in one of the two passenger seats in the middle of the chopper. The pilot took off, not with a gentle rise as we often equate with helicopters, but at a sharp angle, turning while he was climbing. Later I was told that the abrupt take-off was necessary to avoid sniper fire. I held on to whatever I could grab because there had been no time to fasten the seat belt designed to keep me inside the open air transport.

Almost as suddenly as we had taken off, we descended and landed on a wide patch of the road about ten minutes outside the village. The copilot told me that there was a very sick baby inside the house that needed to get to the US medical facility at the Cam Ranh air base. "Are you okay with holding the baby?" he asked. I nodded, not knowing what the alternative was.

He went into the house, and I fastened my seat belt—very securely. Nam lay still on the stretcher. For what seemed like an interminably long time I waited for a baby to hold on a lifesaving flight, no longer thinking about what had transpired in the village. Finally, the co-pilot emerged from the house, without the baby.

"Where's the child?" I asked as he hopped into the front of the copter.

"Didn't make it," he said and up we went. I wondered how many times he had said that before.

We soon arrived at the sprawling Cam Ranh base and landed next to another canvas-clad structure with a big red cross on top. Nam was rushed inside, and I followed along. Although I was the only person not in army garb, no one paid any attention to me. The doctors went to work patching up Nam's side where a bullet had pierced his body. John Denver's voice drifted through the air, "Leaving on a jet plane, don't know when I'll be back again."

I thought of the woman whom I had met nine months earlier while in Washington D.C. As we were getting to know each other, one of us always seemed to be getting on an airplane, travelling around the US. I was sent to talk about Vietnam to civic clubs and newspaper editors. She was sent by The United Methodist Church to educate voters about the Equal Rights Amendment. The other was left at the airport waving goodbye.

Laughter jarred me back into the present. The doctors working on Nam were making jokes. I wanted to scream, "Hey there, someone's life is at stake! Pay attention!"

It was only several years later, while watching the TV program *M*A*S*H,* that I realized humor was a necessary survival mechanism for doctors in a war zone.

The operation was completed, and Nam slept. I needed to get back to Quảng Ngãi where I had started the day. But I wasn't sure how to go about it. The Cam Ranh air base was huge. I didn't know how long it would take to arrange a ride to the city thirty miles south. So I did what seemed most efficient: I walked to the front gate and put out my thumb.

I had hitchhiked once before in Vietnam, during a less stressful time, near Phan Rang. My first ride there was a Vietnamese produce truck. It had dropped me off in a small town in what seemed like the middle of nowhere. My second ride was provided by some Korean soldiers. They were heading to Phan Rang but needed to stop at their base on the way. They sensed I was hungry and left me in a hut while going off for some food. After explaining that the mess hall was closed, they produced two raw eggs and a piece of bread. Not the most appetizing lunch, but edible.

This time, after about thirty minutes waiting in this isolated village, I grabbed the first ride offered—on the back of a motorcycle driven by a Vietnamese soldier. I got dropped off near the USAID office and went inside to let them know what had happened. They seemed particularly concerned about the USAID vehicle that had been left in the village. Before I knew it, I was being escorted to another vehicle and with two USAID workers headed back to the village where the accident had occurred. This was the last thing I wanted to do that day, but fortunately the trip went well, and we were able to retrieve the USAID Scout without incident. I finally made it back to the Quaker compound in time for dinner. When I tried to tell my dinner companions about what had happened that day, I must have sounded very confused, because their attention drifted elsewhere. I spent the rest of the meal in silence.

I visited Nam a month or so later at his home. He was still recovering and asked about compensation for his injuries. Vietnamese were often compensated by the US military when they could establish that they had been injured by US warcraft. I wrote to COR suggesting we do the same, but I never heard back. And I never went to see Nam again.

CHAPTER 22

A Night on the
Cambodian Border

"Find children for treatment and get them to the US, then take the children back to their villages when they return to Vietnam." That should have defined our job, each step with its own set of challenges. But that was not enough. COR also asked us to help Vietnamese families keep in touch with their children while they were in the US, to check up on the children after they returned to Vietnam, and to visit the children's homes to see if they needed ongoing medical care. No doubt these seemed like reasonable requests to COR's directors back in the States, but it was these tasks that often put us most at risk. "Finding children" happened in hospitals in major urban centers. Returning children to their homes and making follow-up visits took us to remote villages, through uncertain territory.

This was especially the case with Châu Quýnh, a beautiful Cambodian girl who lived near the Cambodian border in southwest Vietnam. A 9-millimeter bullet had struck her in the back and paralyzed her from the waist down. COR met her in the hospital in Cần Thơ and selected her for treatment in the US, a decision that gained the approval of the Vietnamese hospital medical director. But on the day COR came to pick her up, she was not in the hospital. A US Air Force surgeon had ordered her to be discharged and taken back to her village, because he saw COR as "a communist organization." While doctors from the US worked in the local hospitals, they had no

The author (upper right) with villagers gathered to welcome a COR child home after receiving medical care in US. (South Vietnam, 1969)

specific authority over hospital decisions. But they still tried to assert their authority as Americans.

In Quỳnh's case, one of these doctors told Balaban that it would be a waste of money to send her to the US for treatment, and that, in any event, he said "no left wing organization is going to get propaganda out of this hospital."[75] He was aware that Dr. Benjamin Spock, a pediatrician and well-known anti-war activist, was on COR's Board of Directors. There was no question that COR's work had political overtones. But that did not discount the need to take care of the children, many of whom had been injured by US actions.

After much pounding on the table up through the ranks, both American and Vietnamese, Balaban was able to reverse the doctor's actions, and the child was brought back to Cần Thơ. She eventually ended up in Portland, Oregon, where she received treatment. Her

---

[75] Balaban, *Remembering Heaven's Face*, 164.

paralysis was deemed to be permanent, and her condition suggested that she would be plagued with medical problems for the rest of her life. Before returning her to Vietnam, COR wanted us to confirm that she would be able to return to her home in Po Tu village, northwest of Cần Thơ, and, if so, if she would be able to get the physical support that she would continue to need.

Reaching Po Tu required a flight from Saigon to the US Special Forces camp in southwestern Vietnam, near the Cambodian border and several kilometers from the village. A COR staff member, Tô Kim Hoa, accompanied me to the camp, but once there, we found our plan to visit Po Tu stymied. The road from the camp to the village was not safe. "Charlie" was laying mines regularly, enough to make Americans think twice about taking a truck on the roads.[76] But Honda motorbikes traveled the distance frequently. When a Cambodian interpreter for the US troops offered to take one of us on the back of his motorcycle, Hoa did not hesitate to volunteer, and I did not object. It made sense for her to go, but no doubt I felt a little guilty sending her off to the unknown.

With nothing to do except wait for Hoa's return, I decided to take stock of my surroundings. What I saw and what I experienced in the camp were vivid reminders of a country at war.

(Letter home: December 2, 1969)
The camp is built right at the western base of a
small hill, and well dug in. The main team house had
thick stone walls and large wooden beams holding up a
ceiling of board and sandbags. Nestled behind the house
is another solid structure, the main command bunker.
Other bunkers spread outward from the two-house

---

[76] "Charlie" was the term US soldiers adopted to refer to the Viet Cong. It was a truncation of "Victor-Charlie," terms used in the NATO phonetic alphabet to refer to "V" and "C."

*complex, made of cement and sandbags. A larger
perimeter was constructed around the whole hill and
was lined by shack dwellings occupied by families of
the CIDG soldiers.[77] The special forces commander lets
the families stay there because he thinks it will make
the Cambodian and Vietnamese soldiers fight better. I
climbed the rocky hill with Lt. Lilly, a bulky man with
thick glasses and a blond crew cut. He was from Arkansas.
I spent much of my time at the base with Lt. Lilly. He
had been there for two weeks but had learned what to
expect from six months of duty along the Cambodian
border north of Ba Xoài. He was expecting the worst.*

*"Charlie is really getting his shit together," he said
while we stood on the flat top of the hill, a covered ledge
thirty feet long. Lilly pointed toward the Cambodian
border, a mountainous range six kilometers away. "NLF
territory," he said. "That mountain is in Cambodia, and
it is occupied by the NLF." He pointed to the left to two
small mountains, dubbed Death Valley and Happy Valley.
They had a common characteristic. "They are occupied
by Charlie. We haven't sent a helicopter in there for two
months. Charlie has big guns and a whole fortress carved
into the mountain. We used to send patrols around the base,
but we have been ordered not to take any more casualties."*

*I turned to the small hill on the east. "At least
that's yours," I said. "Nope. It's Charlie's," he said. I
took an involuntary step backwards and must have
looked startled. "Don't worry. A rifle shot can't carry
this far. But they can sure put in those mortars."*

---

[77] The Civilian Irregular Defense Group, while technically an arm of the South Vietnamese government, consisted primarily of South Vietnamese who were of Cambodian descent. The US military had more confidence in ethnic Cambodian recruits and preferred to work with them rather than with the Vietnamese.

Just below the ridge on the hill were some gun
emplacements and small camps set up by the
Cambodian "hires," the Special Forces' private army.
As Lilly looked over the camp, he turned reflective.
"Most of the Special Forces camps that were overrun
were overrun from within.... It is going to be a hard
decision whether we let any of them up here," again
referring to an impending attack. "But the top of
the hill is the last place you want to go. When they
attack this place, they will take a lot of casualties."

Lilly expected an attack anytime but most likely in
February around Tết. "But this time they will come to stay.
Last year they overran the province but then they fled."

Lilly seemed to be prototype Green Beret, always
wanting to be in the action. He said he was tired of the
"paperwork war" taking up his time in the command
building and wanted to get back into the field. His respect
for the NLF was also apparent. Just two weeks ago,
while a US admiral was visiting the navy contingent
at the camp, while his helicopter was parked on the
pad, two 107 rockets were fired into the compound. "We
had four Cobra gunships circling the area waiting for
something to happen. Charlie sure has a lot of balls."

A while later, out in front of the team house,
he reflected for a moment when the subject of the
NLF came up. "Shit, I hate those damned hippies
back home and I am here fighting Charlie."

Hoa was now back in the camp. She reported what we had already expected—Po Ti village was no place for a paraplegic. Châu Quỳnh's family was very poor. They lived with a few animals in a house with a dirt floor and not much furniture. They had to walk a long way each day for water, so sanitation would be a challenge, posing a threat to Quỳnh's skin grafts and potentially bringing on a urinary tract infection. We would need to advise COR that Chao Quỳnh could not return to her home.[78]

Back home it was Thanksgiving Day, and our hope had been to come to Ba Xoài and then return to Saigon in time to share in a Thanksgiving meal. But it was already midafternoon, and no plans had been made for our return. We asked the radio operator to call Châu Đốc and see if we could be picked up.

(Letter home: December 2, 1969)

Three American soldiers were also waiting to get off the base, and we were all provided with some spaghetti and meatballs while we waited. As the afternoon shadows crept in, I came to accept that there would be no turkey for me on this day. Occasionally a helicopter appeared over the mountain and landed briefly in the compound, only to depart quickly after dropping off supplies. "They didn't want to stay on the pad too long," said Lilly. "Too big a target."

I spent the time waiting reading a Herman Hesse novel and learning more about the operations of the camp. It did not fit in the Special Forces manual. It was too stationary. There were 800 CIDG soldiers under the command of the camp commander. They were essentially mercenaries. Their base pay, paid directly by the SF command, was twice the pay of regular Vietnamese soldiers. They also benefited from combat pay, which increased their pay by 30 percent. Many of the Cambodian soldiers are also members of an off-shoot of the Free Cambodia movement that opposed Prince Sihanouk. It also strongly opposed the Việt Cộng, not because they were communists but because they were Vietnamese. There was a long history of Vietnamese

---

[78] Châu Quỳnh was adopted by her American family in California and remained in the US.

expansionism that usurped Cambodian territory, and
most of the people living in the area were Cambodian.

One thing became clear. Cambodian soldiers' loyalty was to the Americans and only to the Americans. These private armies were doing nothing to further the cause of the South Vietnamese government. There was speculation that they hoped the Americans would turn their attention to Cambodia and help them with their cause.

This apparently was not in the US game plan. The US did expand the war to Cambodia, but mainly further north in an attempt to shut down the Hồ Chí Minh Trail through air strikes.

December 2, 1969, continued)

By 5 p.m. I was beginning to doubt that we would get a
ride out of the camp. Hoa, a very attractive slender young
lady with long silky black hair, was also showing concern
and found herself in an awkward position. There were no
Vietnamese women on the base to provide comfort and
protection. But her strong Catholic upbringing gave her
the inner strength to face the possibility that we would
be spending the night in the camp. Perhaps her saving
feature is her remarkable composure, one that could carry
her through a night in camp with twelve Special Forces
soldiers, about eight navy men, and 800 CIDG cadre.

We solicited a dinner of hamburger and rice. No
turkey for us, even though a turkey dinner was prepared
for the US soldiers. Afterwards I wandered the camp and
talked with some of the American troops. A few ominous
signs kept cropping up. Mysteriously all four Vietnamese
cooks had disappeared from the camp that morning. That
usually meant that they knew something that others
didn't and thought it best not to be there. As I sat looking
over the rice fields, I saw a lanky Cambodian wearing

*a sarong walking among the gun emplacements. No
one seemed concerned. As dark enveloped us, a number
of tracer bullets flew overhead. I didn't learn if this
was normal or unusual. A Special Forces sergeant came
bustling through and announced loudly, "There is going
to be a lot of sandbag filling tonight," as he disappeared
around the corner. I quietly asked another soldier what
he meant. He said they expected an attack in the next
day or so. "There is a war going on out here," he said
looking at me as if I was totally oblivious. "We don't
want Charlie taking this camp looking the way it does."*

*With an attempt to be upbeat I asked another soldier
what they did when the mortars start flying. "We all
have our battle stations," he said. His was located in the
stone bunker next to the team house. "It's a good place
to be if they are coming with air. But I wouldn't like
to be stuck in there if they are coming on the ground.
But what can I do? That is my station." Another soldier
chimed in. "The place to be is on top of the hill. But I will
never make it. I will take my chances somewhere down
here." Hoa was not present during this conversation.*

*A warrant officer gave Hoa his room for the night and led
me to a bunk in the team room. I left her alone finally about
8 p.m. Walking back to that room, I bumped into Lilly.*

*"Did Captain MacDonald give you a station in case we are
attacked?"*

"No."

*"Well, you are pretty safe here," he said with a broad smile.
"It will get lonely unless something happens. And then you will
hear everyone rushing by. You probably will want to follow."*

*He told me he was standing watch from 3 a.m. and
he would try and get a helicopter out of Chi Lăng to
come early in the morning. I thanked him profusely.*

Suddenly I felt exhausted and decided to sleep.
Despite the tensions of the day and the uncertainty of
what was to come, I slept soundly the rest of the night.
When I crawled out of my mosquito net about 6 a.m. I
saw Captain McDonald. He had been up all night.[79]

With morning, the waiting began all over again, until finally a chopper came in to drop off mail on its way to Chi Lăng, the main Special Forces support base for the Mekong Delta. It was only eighteen miles away, but trucks could no longer travel the road safely. Hoa and I decided to hitch a ride and try our luck at Chi Lăng.

The information officer at Chi Lăng asked us what kind of travel credentials we were carrying. Rather than try and explain what COR was, I told him I had press credentials—which I had recently acquired. Within five minutes the place was buzzing. Apparently, the press was not very welcome at Chi Lăng. I quickly tried to explain our medical mission of mercy, but it fell on deaf ears as he started counting off all the priority classes of travelers that came ahead of the press.

Eventually I had to see the commanding officer of the camp himself to explain my presence. Colonel Peters was not convinced. "We are not trying to interfere with the freedom of the press," he said. "That's one of the reasons we're here, but we've had a lot of bad press lately. Who gave you permission to come to my base, anyway?" I explained I was coming from Ba Xoài and that Military Assistance Command-Vietnam

---

[79] I did not fully appreciate how dangerous Ba Xoài was until some years later when a COR colleague sent me an article that had appeared in the *Far Eastern Economic Review* just a month before my visit. (Arnold Abrams, "My Friend, The Double Agent," *Far Eastern Economic Review*, November 13, 1969, 358–360.) In that article, Abrams reported that a nearby sister Special Forces camp, Camp Kate, some ten kilometers from Ba Xoài had been overrun by North Vietnamese soldiers. The Green Berets at Kate had been forced to spike their guns and flee. Abrams gave as his source for the article Captain Brian McDonald, commander of the Ba Xoài camp, the same commander whom Lilly had referenced when he asked me, "Did Captain MacDonald give you a station in case we are attacked?" In retrospect, I'm glad I had not read the article before departing for Châu Quỳnh's village.

in Châu Đốc had given me a ride there. That made it even worse. "Those are my men out there, not MAC-V's. Anyone who goes there needs my permission."

Finally Colonel Peters tired of this banter and agreed to give us transportation to Cần Thơ. I don't know what the alternative was, but he acted like he could have turned us off the base, out into the enemy's hands, if he had felt like it.

It was still another two hours of waiting and a lot of driving around the sprawling complex before Hoa and I arrived at the runway, a mile from traffic control. There we boarded a troop-carrying helicopter and headed for Cần Thơ. The machine gunners were all high on marijuana.

We landed safely in Cần Thơ, and I helped Hoa get on a flight to Saigon. I stayed in Cần Thơ, in hopes of spending a restful night away from Saigon. I also needed the time to gear up for what I knew awaited me upon my return—exuberant preparations for the wedding of an American friend and his Vietnamese fiancée. The disconnect between a mountain Special Forces outpost and the normalcy of life in Saigon was too much to transcend in a single day.

And I also knew that I needed one more night away from Saigon. My second six-month commitment to work with COR was coming to an end. I was exhausted from long days of hopping on airplanes, sleeping in different beds each week, and knowing that for each child I rescued, there were hundreds more that would never get a chance. It was hard to keep in focus the potential political impact of my work, and I became less content with the role of humanitarian. I wanted to end the war.

And so, I had decided to leave COR. When I returned to Saigon I would be starting my new life, as a full-time reporter for Dispatch News Service International. The following Monday, I was set to visit the site of the Mỹ Lai Massacre.

PART III

Words Take Flight

Lời nói Cất Cánh

"Words can travel across thousands of miles.
May my words create mutual understanding and love."

Thích Nhất Hạnh

CHAPTER 23

Dispatch News
Service International

When I first encountered Dispatch News Service International, it was a fledgling Saigon-based news service that focused not on US military strategy and achievements but on the impact of the war on the Vietnamese people. Its founders were people my own age, and most of those involved with Dispatch had, like me, gained experience in Southeast Asia before beginning to report on developments there. Because it lacked the technology that allowed television networks and major newspapers to bring immediate news to the doorsteps of the American people, Dispatch concentrated on stories that would resonate weeks or months after initial publication. In this endeavor, Dispatch had a key resource, a cadre of freelance writers who had worked in Vietnam in other capacities, including with IVS, and so had knowledge of the country and language skills. The latter were especially critical, as it meant that Dispatch, unlike the major media outlets, did not have to rely on the English language press releases that flew daily out of US military and civilian offices in Vietnam. Equipped with a unique set of resources, Dispatch set out to report the war in a very different manner than did the mainstream media.

Without a great deal of reflection, I decided to leave COR at the end of December 1969 and stay in Vietnam with Dispatch. I had reported on high school basketball games since tenth grade, worked on my high school newspaper, served as editor of my college paper, and spent a summer as beat reporter on a big city daily. So this was a natural step—on one of the biggest news stages in the world. But it came with significant challenges, particularly because there was no salary and no guaranteed income. I had some meager savings from the eighty dollars a month IVS had paid into my savings account, supposedly to cover the cost of reentry to the US after our tour. COR paid me just enough to live on. I figured I had about six months.

A letter home shortly before I joined Dispatch described my final days with COR, which looked more like the life of a combat reporter than a humanitarian worker.

> (Letter home: October 13, 1969)
> *My latest trip involved a helicopter ride from the*
> *Quảng Nam Province town of Hội An to the district*
> *headquarters at Đức Đức, with intermittent stops. One*
> *night was spent at the Đức Đức MAC-V compound, and*
> *meals were taken at the Fifth Marine Regiment. With*
> *artillery rounds fired about every fifteen minutes, it was*
> *all another stark reminder that the war continues.*

This might have been good preparation for reporting on the war in Vietnam, but Dispatch had no interest in covering battles or attending the "Five O'Clock Follies,"[80] relaying questionable statistics from US military information officers on the number of VC killed or reporting on the lives of American soldiers. We left that to the mainline press. Dispatch found its stories not in the trenches but in the refugee camps, in the hospitals, in the villages, and on the streets.

Dispatch began in 1967 as the brainchild of Mike Morrow and others with the idea of focusing on the human cost of the war, particularly from the Vietnamese perspective.[81] Many of its reporters

---

[80] A label reporters gave the weekly press conference in Saigon when the US military relayed all the vital statistics of the week.

[81] Mike Morrow graduated from Dartmouth and then went to Taiwan to learn Chinese. From there he travelled to Vietnam and became a freelance reporter and stringer, while at the same time fleeing from the draft. In 1967 he formed Dispatch News Service International with the help of a Philippine friend, Emer Manawis. John Steinbeck, IV, was a signatory on the incorporation papers.

came to South Vietnam in a humanitarian capacity and lived among Vietnamese people—learning the language and culture—before focusing on reporting. This gave them a unique perspective and an edge over most of the war correspondents from traditional media.

During its first two years of operation, Dispatch placed articles in *The Seattle Times*, the *San Francisco Chronicle*, the *National Catholic Reporter*, alternative weekly papers, and numerous college publications through the College Press Service. It also published a newsletter that was distributed directly to individuals.

Soon after I joined Morrow at Dispatch, he left the country, and I was thrust into the role of Saigon bureau chief. This was not a role I wanted, fearing that it would limit my writing opportunities. But Dispatch's effectiveness depended on some coordination, and I became the obvious choice. I never regretted this decision until my last days with Dispatch three years later, when I realized how little I had actually written myself.

Dispatch sent out articles, either through its Washington office or directly from Saigon, to publications in the US and other countries. The articles were not earth-shattering, but together they painted a graphic picture, showing the enormous physical and psychological impact the war was having on the people in South Vietnam—from military maneuvers to dumb bureaucratic decisions. Some articles were even whimsical. One described the impact on the economy when the US decided to stop subsidizing the importation of sugar to Vietnam. Speculators immediately began hoarding sugar and the minister of economics sent out an order banning the baking of Moon Cakes—a staple of Tết celebration—which caused a great uproar. This became known as the "Moon Cake Affair."

Dispatch also sought out prominent Vietnamese to elicit their personal reflections on the war. Among them were singer-songwriter Trịnh Công Sơn and Professor Lý Chánh Trung. In an article entitled "Oh, Huế, I Wish Safe Days Could Return...," written after the 1968 Tết Offensive, Sơn waxed eloquently about the Huế he knew and the Huế it had become.

This month every year I go to Huế. To go there means to return to something insignificant but good: a narrow house, the bowl of "*bún bò*,"[82] unhusked rice, my friends at the small coffee shop Me Tun. It is also to spend the summer holding her hand.

The essence of Huế lies in her little dimensions. The city is not noisy or busy. The sidewalks are intimate. On one street of the city one can wave to friends all day long. Strangers who come here have the impression that everyone here is related...

There never will be an old Huế again. Here, people had never had an opportunity to be rich in a month or a day. It took four generations—grandfather, father, son, and grandson—to build a house; this house was handed down from generation to generation and people, though they may go far from their home, would always remember exactly the places the house's columns touched every beam, every step.

Therefore, it will take a long time before one can look at Huế without seeing her damaged face. The Huế of the past vanished when the high roofs of Thượng Tứ gate and Dổng Bò gate were shattered and spotted with holes.[83]

Dr. Lý Chánh Trung, a professor of philosophy at Saigon University, was known for his staunch advocacy for peace and often appeared at student rallies. Because he was a Catholic, he received more latitude from the government than did most Vietnamese critics of the war. Dispatch distributed a translation of his speech, "Why Do I Want Peace," delivered on August 9, 1968, at a meeting held at the student offices of the Saigon University Student Union, from which the following are excerpted:

---

[82] A Vietnamese soup enjoyed primarily in the central part of Vietnam.

[83] Trình Công Sơn, "Oh, Huế, I Wish Safe Days Could Return...," Dispatch News Service International, March 5, 1969. (Published in the *National Catholic Reporter*.)

As I am Vietnamese, I cannot endure seeing foreigners indifferently devastate our country by the most modern and terrible means and speak of the so-called "protection of freedom" for the people of South Vietnam,...

...And I advise Americans who really want to protect freedom to protect the freedoms in their own country:

—freedom for Negroes who are restless in their ghettos.

—freedom for the Indians who are living dead lives in limited zones.

....That's better than "protecting freedom" for the yellow-people who live far away by using fantastic destructive means....

I want peace because I am a teacher. The mission of a teacher is to form Man. But how is man formed in an entirely corrupt society?... How can Man be formed when so many human beings are destroyed every day that human souls become insensitive and unmoved by any kind of horror?... "Nothing is more opposed to education than violence, devastation, carnage, delinquency, and corruption caused by war." [quoting a public appeal signed by 65 university professors about six months earlier]

...A teacher's career is a peaceful career because teaching is using the human voice and human words to convert man, and nobody can speak or hear above the noise of these bombs. Teachers in Vietnam today are only selling words and meanings, knowledge, degrees. Socrates, the first eternal teacher of the West 2,500 years ago, compared these men who sell their knowledge with prostitutes. I don't want to be a prostitute. I want peace.

Lastly, I want peace because I am a Catholic. My religion is a peaceful religion; my God died on the cross 1,968 years ago to teach mankind a lesson of love, i.e., a lesson of peace...

...I wish to see my career become again a mission, not only a source of intellectual occupation, and to see my Church become great in belief and charity among people who will once more live in friendship.[84]

One of Dispatch's Vietnamese contributors was Trần Koi Phúc, who wrote an article addressing the plight of two million ethnic Cambodians who lived in Vietnam. He wrote that the Khmers, as they were called, were beginning to mount protests against the South Vietnamese government because President Thiệu had denied them special status as an ethnic minority, despite overwhelming support from the State Assembly.

> Saigon's monsoon season grows to a close, but the storm clouds of popular dissent keep building over the capital city. Latest in an increasing number of confrontations with the government has been the quietist of Vietnam's ethnic minorities, the Khmers, or Cambodian residents in Vietnam.[85]

Like many protests at this time, the Khmers' pleas failed to gain traction.

Steve Erhart wrote an article entitled "US Declares War on Rubber Trees."

> In Tây Ninh Province the Americans can't see the Việt Cộng for the trees. So, they're cutting down the trees— the rubber trees. And rubber, according to the chief of American civil assistance in the area, is the "only viable industry left to the province—the only one." After five years in Vietnam George Wood, an American with USAID, is leaving this month with feelings of bitterness about the

---

[84] Lý Chánh Trung, "Why Do I Want Peace?" Crystal Erhart, trans., Dispatch [Newsletter] 1, no. 5, (February 25, 1969): 1, 6.

[85] Trần Koi Phúc, "The Betrayed Vietnamese," Dispatch News Service International, November 1969.

latest example of American short-sightedness solving Vietnamese problems.[86]

Don Luce wrote of a US military "sweep" of a fertile peninsula north of Saigon that forced 12,000 Vietnamese into a refugee camp outside the coastal city of Quảng Ngãi.[87] The sign at the entrance read, "Refugees are not allowed to leave the camp," which suggested that it was more akin to a prison than a haven for refugees fleeing from the fighting. The process of removing peasants from villages that were under Việt Cộng control was one of the many flawed tactics of the war. Rather than depriving the Việt Cộng of support, the strategy just spread that support to other areas, and poor living conditions following forced relocation hardened refugees' opposition to the South Vietnamese government.

One of the most dramatic news stories of the war involved Luce and another regular contributor to Dispatch, Stephen Erhart. While working for a US engineering firm in Saigon, Erhart discovered plans for the Côn Đảo prison camp on Côn Sơn Island. France had built the camp during its fight to maintain colonial control, and South Vietnam, with US support, expanded it to support the war against North Vietnam. The plans indicated the possible existence of below-ground prison cells, later called "tiger cages" by the US media.

Erhart gave the plans to Luce, just in time for the arrival of a US congressional delegation, including staffer and future congressman and senator from Iowa, Tom Harkin. The delegation arranged a

---

[86] Stephen Erhart, "US Declares War on Rubber Trees," Dispatch News Service International, March 3, 1969. Most Dispatch articles and photographs are housed at the Swarthmore College Peace Collection, 500 College Ave., Swarthmore, PA 19081.

[87] After resigning as chief of party for IVS in protest of the war, Luce returned to Vietnam frequently and filed numerous news articles with Dispatch. He subsequently formed the Indochina Mobile Education Project and from June 1971 served as co-director, with David Marr, of the Vietnam Resource Center.

visit to the prison and invited Luce to accompany them. While touring the prison, Luce slipped away from the delegation. With a hand-drawn map, he found a secret door to an area where over 500 starving and tortured men and women were shackled under grates in a walkway. The prisoners were neglected, sitting in diarrhea and with sores around their ankles cut by their shackles. Harkin took photos of the prisoners, which were published in *Life* magazine in the July 17, 1970, issue. The photos caused global condemnation.

Don Ronk drew attention to "Black Minh," the name other street children gave a boy who roamed the streets of Saigon. "Minh at sixteen is almost a caricature of humanity, with his unwashed body, filthy clothing, scars, body parasites, and cynicism," Ronk wrote.[88] Minh was one of many Afro-Asian children, now in their teens, left behind by French soldiers and ostracized by the Vietnamese. Their treatment served as a harbinger of what was to become of Amerasian children, children of American soldiers, who no doubt numbered in the thousands by the time the US withdrew from Vietnam.

Tom Fox wrote a stream of stories from 1969 to 1972, from light fare such as "Still Golf on Sundays," to significant pieces such as "Bình Định Province Nears Collapse," to editorials. One published in 1969 was "Period of Grace Over; US Must Quit Vietnam."[89]

In an article entitled "Vietnam Refugees Settled—By Decree," I reported on a new method that the South Vietnamese government had come up with for handling the refugee problem. A USAID spokesman explained that, under South Vietnam's recently announced "Normalization" policy, persons removed from their homes by the war would be "settled in place—and no longer called 'refugees.'" In reality, the new "policy" was merely a linguistic conjuring trick, giving a new name to an ongoing human tragedy. "In place" simply meant that families fleeing the fighting would be assigned to camps built on barren wasteland, using any materials that were readily available,

---

[88] D.E. Ronk, "Vietnam's Haunted Eyes," Dispatch News Service International, 1969.

[89] Dispatch News Service International, 1969.

DISPATCH SAIGON BUREAU
JUSPAO / DISPATCH
APO SAN FRANCISCO 96243

CAPTION   VIETNAM'S HAUNTED EYES

                                 Photo by D.E. Ronk

© 1969 DISPATCH NEWS SERVICE INTERNATIONAL

"Black Minh" is the name the other urchins have
given him to carry through the streets of Saigon. Minh
at sixteen is almost a cariacature of humanity with his
unwashed body, filthy clothing, scars, body parsites
and cynicism. He is an Afroasian left behind by the French
army like the thousands of mixed blood children the Americans
are leaving in a society that doesn't want them. (Photo D.
Ronk)

"Black Minh" article and photo. (Saigon, 1969)

camps that could best be described as slums. Refugee families were given the equivalent of forty dollars to patch up what they would now call home. And they would no longer be "refugees."[90]

Dispatch articles shed light on the peace talks in Paris, including an interview with one of the official South Vietnamese negotiators in Paris and a lengthy profile of Madame Nguyễn Thị Bình—the high-ranking official of the National Liberation Front and newly-appointed chief delegate on the NLF's negotiating team in Paris. Vietnam scholar David Marr chronicled Nguyễn Thị Bình's long involvement in opposing the US-backed governments in Vietnam and her rise

---

[90] Richard A. Berliner, "Vietnam Refugees Settled—By Decree," *American Report*, November 26, 1969, 7.

```
                                                    JU.PA
                                                    APO SAN FRANCISCO
"RESETTLED IN PLACE" FOR VIETNAM'S REFUGEES

                        ©  1969  DISPATCH NEWS SERVICE INTERNATION

PHOTO CAPTION


        Built on barren wastelands that are unwanted by anyone
   else and of any available material, Vietnam's refugee camps
   are nothing more than vast slums.  Under the latest government
   directive on refugees, which would deprive them of the name
   but not necessarily the life and assistance, the "refugee problem"
   will be done away with by fiat.  (Photo by G.L. Liles)
```

"Resettled in place" refugee camp, article and photo (opposite) (Da Nang, 1969)

through the ranks of the NLF, as well as her support for the role of women in shaping the future of Vietnam.

It is this combination of political tenacity and femininity that makes Bình so effective, and so unique, among political figures at the international level. It is this unusual combination of characteristics which Ambassador Lodge will be dealing with in the months to come as he faces Madame Bình across the Paris negotiating table.[91]

The growing number of high-level political prisoners in South Vietnam also attracted the attention of Dispatch contributors. The most famous prisoner was Trung Định Dzu, who had lost his bid for the presidency of South Vietnam in 1967. Dzu was arrested in 1968 for advocating the formation of a coalition government that could negotiate with North Vietnam; he was convicted and sentenced to five years in prison. His son David, who was studying in the US at

---

[91] David Marr, untitled article, Dispatch News Service International, June 24, 1969.

the time, was subsequently expelled from the US on unproven charges of passing on secrets to the North Vietnamese. Another well-known prisoner was the Venerable Thích Thiện Minh, head of the Buddhist Youth Center. He said his only offense was that he believed in peace.

Dispatch contributors wrote about corruption among the South Vietnamese police and the criminal underworld of the large Chinese section of Saigon, Chợ Lớn, home to over one million people and the center of most business activities in the city. Gambling and prostitution were two of Saigon's biggest businesses. The enormous flow of money into the South Vietnamese economy from the American presence no doubt added flames to the underworld cauldron.

From Saigon, we sent Dispatch's articles to David Obst, a colleague of Morrow based in Washington, D.C., who then distributed the articles to media outlets around the country. But Obst wanted to make a bigger splash by circulating articles with more dramatic impact, rather than focusing on the ongoing problems created by the US presence in Vietnam. His opportunity came along with the discovery of US military actions in a collection of villages north of Quảng Ngãi, soon to be known to the world as Mỹ Lai.

CHAPTER 24

Mỹ Lai Massacre

Dispatch had no shortage of stories and was sending out three or four articles a week—all from free-lance writers who received a flat $25 or 60 percent of monies paid per article. Payments rarely exceeded $50. The challenge was expanding the market for Dispatch articles, which had much to do with convincing newspapers that Dispatch was a legitimate news service. This task was left to David Obst, who was managing the Washington office.

Obst also began recruiting local talent in the US and attracted the interest of Seymour Hersh, a relatively unknown thirty-two-year-old newspaper reporter with experience at United Press International and The Associated Press.[92] It turned out that Hersh was working on what would become one of the biggest stories to come out of the Vietnam War—the Mỹ Lai Massacre.

In March 1968, *The New York Times* published an article from The Associated Press reporting that US forces had fought with communist forces threatening the northern city of Quảng Ngãi. A US spokesperson announced that 128 guerrillas had been killed but gave few details of the fighting. There was no mention of civilians being fired upon by American soldiers.

---

[92] Seymour Hersh joined *The New York Times* staff in 1972. He was the author of a number of books, including *The Price of Power: Kissinger in the Nixon White House* (1983), which won the National Book Critics Circle Award.

Eighteen months later, on September 6, 1969, AP circulated a short article from its office in Fort Benning, Georgia, noting that a US Army officer had been charged with murder in the deaths of a number of civilians in Vietnam during a battle near Quảng Ngãi in March of 1968. According to Col. Douglas Tucker, a US Army information officer, the charge had been brought against First Lt. William Calley Jr., twenty-six years old, of Miami, the squad leader of the Charlie Company. Colonel Tucker announced that more than one civilian had died but provided no further details.

Hersh saw the story and became curious. Presumably Hersh wondered why it had taken eighteen months for the details of the event to emerge. After considerable research and direct talks with First Lt. Calley and men under his command, Hersh learned that the soldiers had been told that the cluster of villages known collectively as Mỹ Lai were Việt Cộng strongholds, that villagers were warned by fliers dropped from airplanes to leave the villages, and that soldiers were ordered to shoot anyone who remained in the village.

Hersh also learned that, in fact, information about the incident had been widely circulated—but not to the press.

The military had successfully covered up the event, and the story might have ended then but for Ronald Ridenhour, a military veteran and a journalist. Ridenhour began hearing about the event from soldiers in Vietnam and started gathering evidence. He then wrote letters to the Pentagon, the White House, members of the US Congress and the US State Department. With much prodding, Ridenhour's letters led to a military investigation. Finally, charges followed.

After learning the details of the massacre, Hersh set out to market the story, going first to *Life* magazine and then *Look* magazine. Both turned it down. The *New York Review of Books* asked him to turn it into a lengthy piece on the history of US war crimes. Hersh declined to do so. Finally, he turned to Obst. Obst convinced him that the best strategy was to approach daily newspapers. He asked Hersh to make the story a five-part series to be marketed through Dispatch. When Hersh delivered the series, Obst got on the telephone and called one newspaper in every major market in the US to offer the story for sale. Before he had finished, he had lined up thirty newspapers to publish the story the next day.

The five-part series took the United States by storm. Mỹ Lai became a significant subject of debate by members of the US Congress and fodder for the growing anti-war movement.

Here is what Hersh reported for Dispatch:

> Lt. William Calley Jr., 26 years old, is a mild-mannered boyish-looking Vietnam combat veteran with the nickname 'Rusty.' The army is completing an investigation of charges that he deliberately murdered at least 109 Vietnamese civilians in a search-and-destroy mission in March 1968 in a Việt Cộng stronghold known as "Pinkville.
>
> Calley has formally been charged with six specifications of mass murder. Each specification cites a number of dead, adding up to the 109 total, and charges that Calley did "with premeditation murder... Oriental human beings, whose names and sex are unknown, by shooting them with a rifle."
>
> The Army calls it murder; Calley, his counsel and others associated with the incident describe it as a case of carrying out orders.[93]

Years later, in a 2015 retrospective piece for *The New Yorker*, Hersh shared an interview with Sgt. Paul Meadlo, who had been at the center of the event. Meadlo described a scene of US soldiers raping Vietnamese and burning down houses to force people out in the open. He said that Calley had told his squad to round up all the people in the village and watch them. Ten minutes later, Calley ordered the soldiers to shoot the villagers. When some soldiers hesitated, Calley started shooting the villagers himself. Meadlo followed suit.[94]

---

[93] Seymour Hersh, "Lieutenant Accused of Murdering 109 Civilians," Dispatch News Service International, November 12, 1969.

[94] Seymour Hersh, "The Scene of the Crime," *The New Yorker*, March 23, 2015.

The massacre ended because of the heroic actions of a US Army helicopter pilot, Hugh Thompson.[95] Thompson, along with two co-pilots, was flying around the Mỹ Lai villages when he noticed a lot of commotion at the Sơn Mỹ village. His first instinct was to land and assist the soldiers on the ground in getting the children out of the village. What he saw as he moved in closer horrified him—dead Vietnamese on the ground and soldiers shooting point-blank into ditches where civilians had been led. As it became clearer to him what was happening, he maneuvered the helicopter down low between the Charlie Company soldiers and the women and children. He told his crew to face the US soldiers and if any of them started shooting at them to shoot back. Fortunately the shooting stopped, and Thompson was able to evacuate twelve Vietnamese via helicopter. Later, when awarded a medal for his actions, he tossed it aside. The citation said in part that Thompson was "caught in a crossfire" rescuing the civilians. Thompson knew that was a lie. Although Thompson reported the event to his immediate supervisors, using words like "murder" and "massacre," no investigation followed. At least, not at that time. Years later, in 1998, Thompson and his co-pilots each received the Soldier's Medal for their actions, with no mention of any crossfire.[96]

Release of the news about Mỹ Lai stirred up the military in South Vietnam and roused the US press and a top Vietnamese general, Trần Văn Đôn, who announced a fact-finding trip to the site. The US's press corps in Saigon wanted in on the story and demanded that the Joint US Public Affairs Office provide the press with transportation to the site; JUSPAO agreed. ABC News sent a film crew and asked me to assist with their coverage.

The visiting delegation included General Đôn, three South Vietnamese senators, and nine Vietnamese assemblymen. More than

---

[95] Thompson's story, along with others about Mỹ Lai, is described in detail on the walls of the War Remnants Museum in Hồ Chí Minh City, Vietnam.

[96] "Hugh Thompson, Jr., My Lai Rescuer, Dies at 62," *New York Times*, Jan. 6, 2006; https://warrantofficerhistory.org/PDF/Forgotten_Hero_of_My_Lai-WO_Hugh_Thompson.pdf.

twenty US reporters, photographers, camera operators, and soundmen clamored to cover the event. JUSPAO arranged to have a small twin-engine passenger plane fly the group to Quảng Ngãi, where military jeeps met them and transported the group to the Mỹ Lai area.

The visit turned out to be something of a circus.

The Vietnamese general and members of the National Assembly, as well as my press colleagues and I, met with the Quảng Ngãi province chief, who said that rumors of high fatalities at Sơn Mỹ around March 15, 1968, were off base. He told us perhaps a hundred people were killed, but most of them were Việt Cong. Only twenty-five could have been women and children.

The former Vietnamese district chief of one of the villages, Sơn Tịnh, also spoke. He said that he had never heard anything about what happened in Sơn Mỹ until the story broke in the news.

Vietnamese officials and press alike began moving on foot toward the cluster of villages that had been attacked. But we were quickly stopped by US military officials. They told us we needed to wait until the shelling stopped. US troops were doing the shelling.

We waited on the outskirts of Mỹ Lai and attempted to talk with villagers who might have been there at the time of the massacre. One woman claimed she had been there, triggering a rush by photographers trying to get her picture. None of the other villagers we spoke with claimed to have been present when the massacre took place.

Two hours later, we learned that it would not be possible for us to visit the area that day. It was already mid-afternoon, and there was no indication that the shelling would stop. Rumors quickly spread that the shelling had been completely staged by the US military to keep the press away from the village. Apparently, the last thing the military wanted was more media coverage of Mỹ Lai.

With obvious disappointment, the group of writers and photographers returned to the jeeps and headed back to the landing strip in Quảng Ngãi. We boarded the same plane that had brought us to Quảng Ngãi that morning. No one anticipated the excitement that followed.

Approximately twenty minutes into the flight, the single engine on the left side of the plane burst into flames. My side. Before panic set in, the flames went out. A few minutes later the flames came back. Every time the pilot cut off the engine, the flames went out. When he turned the engine on, the flames came back. One of the network reporters walked up to the cockpit as the excitement built in the cabin. He emerged from the cockpit, looked around, and then stuck out his hand, pointing his thumb—down.

The message was all too clear. The plane was going down. But cooler heads than mine began to pass around a more encouraging message. The plane was going to land with the help of one engine on the right side of the plane. The pilot proceeded to turn the plane in wide circles—all the time descending toward a base camp that was unknown, at least to me, miles ahead. The plane circled to the left, heading a little lower at each 360-degree turn. The ride was bumpy, but not overwhelming. Darkness had long since set in and, fortunately for me, it was impossible to see the ground.

All that remained was for the pilot to find a runway and straighten out the plane before it hit the ground. And he did. The stoic press erupted with applause. With legs shaking, I stepped off the plane and followed the crowd to an officer's mess and the promise of food and drink. But we were doomed to be disappointed. The mess had closed for the night, and there was no food to be had. After another two hours, a second plane arrived to take us back to Saigon for a 2 a.m. landing. Three days later, ABC sent me a check for $25.

If the plane had crashed, no doubt rumors would have circulated that the US military had deliberately disabled the plane in order to keep the press from reporting on the story. But because we ultimately landed safely, the subject never came up.

On March 29, 1971, a US court martial convicted Lt. Calley of twenty-two murders during the Mỹ Lai Massacre, sentencing him to life in prison. President Richard Nixon shortened his sentence and switched it to house arrest. Calley appealed his conviction, and in November 1974, a federal district judge ordered Cally's release, ruling that the pre-trial publicity surrounding his case had precluded a fair trial.

Hersh wrote that eleven others were charged with murder or assault, but each was acquitted, or their cases never went to trial. He also reported that thirteen army officers were charged for involvement in a cover-up of the event, including the man soon to become superintendent of the United States Military Academy at West Point. All charges against him were dismissed without a court martial.[97]

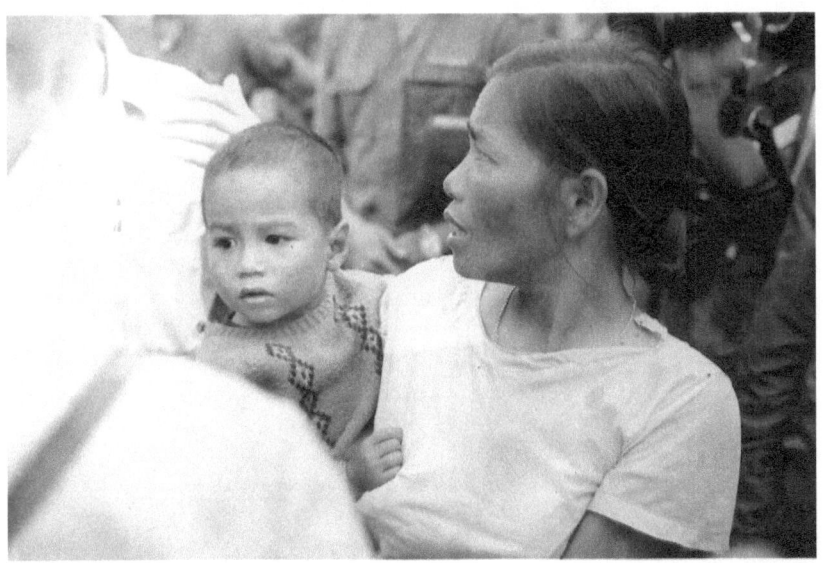

Mỹ Lai survivor and child during press visit some eighteen months after the Massacre. (My Lai, 1969)

---

[97] Seymour Hersh, "The Scene of the Crime," *The New Yorker,* March 23, 2015.

CHAPTER 25

A Shaky Future for Dispatch

Soon after leaving COR and starting with Dispatch, I returned to Washington, D.C., for the Christmas holidays. I had been back in Vietnam for seven months and was anxious to see a woman with whom I had become close during my previous stay in D.C. She was going to be in Washington for the month of January. My brother was also getting married during the holidays. I had missed my older sister's wedding and didn't want to miss another. And I wanted to get to know the folks in the Dispatch Washington office. Our view from Saigon was that the sudden success of Dispatch had led the Washington office to have more interest in distributing hot news rather than the human interest features we were sending from Saigon, and I was looking forward to discussing the concern with my US-based colleagues.

I had intended to stay two weeks; I ended up staying for six. Hersh put me to work checking out some wild claims about other massacres that turned out to be false. Obst was still running on the adrenalin of the Mỹ Lai story and another Dispatch release involving the use of hollow-point bullets by various police forces.[98] The story brought enormous criticism of the police and got wide coverage. It also reinforced Obst's conviction that Dispatch should be a vehicle for

---

[98] Hollow-point bullets were designed not only to stop an assailant but also to maim and are considered by many as inhumane. They were banned in international warfare under the Hague Convention of 1899, although the US never ratified the agreement.

breaking hot news rather than focusing on the human consequences of the war in Vietnam.

Obst also began recruiting articles and commentary from political figures with national reputations. He persuaded Senator Jacob Javitz (D-NY) and Senator Bob Dole (R-KN) to submit essays on the significance of the Mỹ Lai Massacre. Senator Javits wrote that the Mỹ Lai Massacre was really a wake-up call for the United States because it made clear that we were fighting a war where we had no ability to distinguish between our supporters and our enemies, between civilian and military. Javitz wrote:

> The press accounts of the brutal killings at Mỹ Lai have assailed the conscience of the nation and have sent shock waves of protest reverberating throughout the world... The profound corruption which this war is capable of has now been exposed; not alone because of the alleged brutality — horrible as that is — but because of its evidence of the hopelessness of our remaining as the stand-ins of the South Vietnamese themselves in a fight for their self-determination.[99]

Senator Javitz went on to urge President Nixon to "lead the nation clearly, quickly, and unequivocally out of Vietnam."

In sharp contrast to Senator Javitz's assessment, Senator Dole called Mỹ Lai an isolated incident that should not be used as a catalyst for abandoning Vietnam. He asserted that 75 percent of the American people (in November 1969) supported President Nixon's conduct of the war, and that the US had used great restraint in protecting civilians in Vietnam. He then declared: "I for one cannot tolerate an attempt to associate the alleged American conduct at Mỹ Lai with Huế, Nanking, and Lidice, names forever symbolic of the barbarous policies

---

[99] Jacob Javitz, untitled article, Dispatch News Service International, November 1969.

of totalitarian states.... We should not let the horrors of Mỹ Lai distract us from our mission."[100]

I returned to Vietnam at the end of January 1970 with ten one-hundred-dollar bills, which my colleagues had asked me to bring them so they could get black market exchange rates. Not knowing what the legal limit was on bringing US currency into the country, I hid the bills in my shoes for the flight. I also came back with the news that Dispatch News Service International might have to go on without support from Washington, D.C.

Upon landing at the Tân Sân Nhất Airport, I immediately felt myself shrouded in olive drabness and dust and experienced an acute feeling of unease. For the first time, I wondered if coming back to Vietnam a third time was pushing my luck to the brink. This was immediately followed by an unpleasant encounter with a taxi driver. I greeted the driver with some Vietnamese patter and told him where I wanted to go. While the Vietnamese people were generally delighted, and perhaps amused, to hear an American speak Vietnamese, the taxi driver became irate when I spoke a few words of Vietnamese. He immediately jumped back into the cab and said what must have been unpleasant words and raced off. He knew that he could charge a much higher fare to a new American arrival than from one who obviously had been there before.

Not a great deal had happened in Vietnam during my absence, and Tết 1970 passed quietly, almost passively. There were some tensions over the possibility of an attack—a few plastic charges were set off in unoccupied buildings in Saigon—but generally people were able to use their holiday period for a time of emotional release. The black market continued to function freely, despite the absurdity of the South Vietnamese and American governments in announcing their intentions to cut it out. A spirit of buying was in the air.

---

[100] Robert Dole, untitled article, Dispatch News Service International, November 1969.

(Letter home: February 13, 1970)

Because there's little confidence in the economy,
Vietnamese prefer to put their money in hard goods or
send it out of the country. One effect of opening the black
market was to stabilize the piastre somewhat. But its value
is still slowly deteriorating. Vietnam always seems to be on
the verge of an economic crisis and now is no exception.
Still there is some feeling in Saigon that the war is over for
now—that the VC decided to lay back for a while—but it
is generally recognized as a temporary thing. I went to see
[the movie] Alice's Restaurant *today at the US air base.*
The scenes of Arlo Guthrie at the induction physical were
widely cheered by the raucous GI crowd in the theater.

Mike Morrow left the country soon after my return. I was now the bureau chief of Dispatch, which had $1,500 in the bank—enough to pay monthly expenses for two to three months but with nothing left over for salaries. I set about to build our network of reporters and get articles out the door.

Except for action on the political front, life in Saigon was calm and barely impacted by fighting in the countryside. The US military was pushing the South Vietnamese Army to take on the brunt of the fighting, and the US casualty rate was dropping. It appeared that nothing would change in Vietnam if the US maintained its current level of commitment. Peace talks between the US and North Vietnam had begun over eighteen months earlier in May 1968, but seemed to be going nowhere.[101]

---

[101] A peace agreement between the US and North Vietnam was finally executed on January 27, 1973, which called for the US to start withdrawing troops from Vietnam. The US nevertheless continued to conduct bombing raids in Cambodia and Laos and provide weapons to the South Vietnamese Army.

(Letter home: March 1, 1970)

I'm off to Đà Nẵng again tomorrow for three or four days and may visit Quy Nhơn. We get rumors that the military has issued an anti-nerve-gas injection device to all troops up there on the premise that the VC are using gas. No reports have been made to that effect, but you know that if it were true the US could certainly make a lot of noise about it, so there must be other reasons.

Meanwhile I have been doing a lot of editing of stories coming out of Laos and at a good time. Things are getting hot there again, as the North Vietnamese take back an area that they long controlled until last year. The assumption is that they will push beyond the line of division and threaten some US strongholds. If so, everyone can forget about Vietnam for a while.

Dispatch also had visions of expanding its coverage throughout Southeast Asia, particularly as it appeared that the Vietnam War was no longer a daily front-page story. With the war expanding west to Laos and Cambodia, there were rumors of growing unrest in the Philippines, a country where the US had a heavy presence. President Ferdinand Marcos was a democratically elected president, but he was coming under increasing opposition because of corruption in the government and his growing authoritarian moves.

Eager to see the situation up close, I flew to Manila without a plan or any contacts and checked into the cheapest hotel I could find in a sketchy part of town. Two years earlier I had spent two weeks in Los Baños, forty miles outside Manila, and I thought that Los Baños might be a good place to start. It was the home of a university and the International Rice Research Institute, where Americans and other foreign nationals were developing new varieties of disease-resistant rice.

As I wandered through the tiny downtown area, I struck gold. I ran into former IVSer Lou Wolf, who was then living in the Philippines. Wolf had a wealth of information about the political scene and particularly some growing protests at Clark Air Force Base, the major base of US operations for deploying US troops and staging operations in the region and the launch site for bombers heading to Vietnam. In the course of five days, he introduced me to some young activists organizing anti-government protests, some members of the Philippine Congress, and a representative of the recently formed New People's Army insurgency movement. Somewhat to my surprise, he also arranged for me to tour Clark AFB.

I wrote an article for *New World Outlook*, a publication of The United Methodist Church, about the growing unrest but concluded that there was no immediate threat to the current government.[102] The US was willing to tolerate a number of threats to democracy in the Philippines as long as the Philippines maintained its support for the war and continued to allow the US to use Clark Air Force Base to pursue the war. Marcos was forced out of office on February 26, 1985, sixteen years later.

When I returned to Vietnam, I turned my attention once again to the growing political protests in the nation's capital and the horrendous treatment of political prisoners—mostly college students—by the Saigon government. After meeting with ten students who had recently been released after a number of weeks in a Saigon jail, charged with protesting the previous arrest of other students, I described their experience in a letter home.

(Letter home: April 1970)
Ten students, each with his or her own tale of horror
at the hands of the Vietnamese national police, lie in a

---

[102] Richard Berliner, "Unrest in The Philippines," *New World Outlook* (August 1970), 22.

small, cluttered room at the Faculty of Agriculture where
they are recovering—slowly—from weeks in jail. They are
the lucky ones. Eleven others, brought to trial at the same
time with these students, are still in confinement. And still
exposed to sophisticated torture techniques refined by years
of war.... The released students were taken immediately to
a lab room at the agricultural school. White tile benches
line the walls and serve as beds. Three tables in the center
of the room are piled high with medicine, donated by
clinics or bought on the local market. "They should be at
a hospital," said Dr. Nguyễn Đình Mai, "but after what
they've gone through, they want to stay together. We
haven't found a ward with enough space yet." Dr. Mai, three
months out of medical school, is the attending physician.
He expects to be drafted into the army within a month.

During this same period, I wrote an article for Dispatch reporting on a statement by eight prominent Catholic priests who called upon the Vietnamese government to respect the civil liberties of arrested students and other political activists. At a press conference held by the Committee to Struggle Against Government Oppression of Students on April 3, 1970, the priests released the names of three students who had been beaten almost to death. Their plea appeared to fall on deaf ears.

In May 1970, I went to Cambodia with a young photojournalist, John Everingham, to look into reports of Cambodian disruption and resettlement of the Vietnamese communities in Cambodia amidst the general state of unrest that permeated Cambodia after the coup against Prince Sihanouk.

(Letter Home: May 1970)

*Outside of a Catholic church in a village near the
Tonle Sap River, just north of Phnom Penh, two women
sat on a wooden porch ... looking blankly at the ground.
One sobbed softly, her eyes red and raw. Children stood
about, playing listlessly in the hot afternoon sun. The air
was humid but the prospect of rain still a few days off,
when the monsoon would hit.... The sobbing woman looked
up, showing a face that was not old but already worn.*

*A red scarf held her grey hair close to her head. She was
wearing a multicolored sarong around her waist, part of
the Cambodian dress. But she was not Cambodian, she was
Vietnamese. "They took my husband and my son," she said.
"We were living off in the fields when they came. I was so
afraid. I moved here because I did not want to be alone."
Another woman called me over. "Please tell them for us,"
she said. "They have arrested hundreds of our men, some
only fourteen years old. Now we do not have enough food
and no one to take care of us. Can you tell them for us?"*

I did not know who the "them" were or whom to tell.

I learned in Cambodia that all Vietnamese there were feeling the
pressure.

(Letter home: May 1970)

*The Cambodian regime, in its struggle to establish
its authority, is using traditional Cambodian hatred for
Vietnamese as a rallying point. For some Vietnamese this
meant death; others have been pushed out of their jobs and
homes and gathered in detention centers. All are afraid.*[103]

---

[103] Much of the Mekong Delta region of southern Vietnam was the home of
Cambodians before Vietnam forcefully expanded its territory to the current
boundaries. This expansion resulted in long-lasting bitterness among the
Cambodian people.

In a related story, I conveyed the concern of South Vietnam's Minister of Social Welfare Tran Nguyễn Phieu that 100,000 or more Vietnamese would end up as refugees in Vietnam from Cambodia. "We hope the situation won't come to this, but we have to be ready," he said. He thought over 10,000 people were already assembled at the border and seeking refuge with Vietnamese relatives. The official count was 3,000. Approximately 600,000 Vietnamese lived in Cambodia at that time, making up 20 percent of the total population.

Little did we know that soon one of Dispatch's own would become the subject of the next big story to come out of Saigon.

CHAPTER 26

Morrow Is Missing!

First there were rumors. Then it became fact. Three journalists were reported missing in Cambodia. Dispatch's Mike Morrow was one of them. The other two were Elizabeth Pond, from *The Christian Science Monitor*, and Richard Dudman, from *The St. Louis Post Dispatch*. "What in the world were they doing in Cambodia?" we wondered. But we should not have been surprised. President Nixon had announced six days earlier that US forces had invaded Cambodia to attack North Vietnamese strongholds. The three reporters had gone to follow American soldiers in an expanding war.

Cambodia had long been an oasis of peace, ever since Prince Sihanouk expelled all Americans in 1963. The Khmer Rouge, Cambodian communists, continued to wage a low-level guerrilla movement against the government, but with little impact. Cambodia was also being used by the North Vietnamese as part of the Hồ Chí Minh Trail to bring troops and supplies to the South. But for the most part the population was not impacted.

Despite Cambodia's official political neutrality, the US increasingly maneuvered to expand the war across Vietnam's western border into the land of the Khmer. When Prince Sihanouk was forced out of Cambodia and replaced by General Lon Nol in early 1970, the door opened wide. The US role in the coup was not clear, but what was clear is that the new government was pro-US and was willing to accommodate the US military.

Morrow, who was 27 at the time, Pond, 33, and Dudman, 52, went to report on this dramatic turn in the war, driving across the border heading to Phnom Penh, assuming that they would be behind the US and South Vietnamese troops. But unbeknownst to them, they had somehow gotten ahead of the invading US column they thought they were following.[104]

Morrow later wrote of his capture:

> We had approached a blown bridge, realized we could not go forward and started back. Two men stepped out from behind a tree and motioned to us to stop. ....
>
> We got out of the car immediately and pushed our hands high in the air on the command of the Vietnamese, who had come forward with his AK-47 pointed toward us.
>
> He told us to drop all our belongings to the pavement and to turn around....
>
> "I'm afraid you're going to shoot us when we turn around," I said.
>
> "Don't worry, I'm not going to shoot you." he replied. "Turn around."...
>
> Quick action by a pro-communist guerrilla officer probably saved the lives of this reporter and two other correspondents while we were in the hands of an angry mob the first day of our capture by the Khmer (Cambodian) United National Front in Cambodia on May 7.
>
> The officer, a 34-year-old ethnic Vietnamese from Phnom Penh ... arrived on the scene with three of his men as a rabid, anti-American crowd was running Richard Dudman

---

[104] Richard Dudman, *40 Days with the Enemy: A Story of a Journalist Held Captive by Guerrillas in Cambodia* (Liveright, 1971).

… and me blindfolded through a village, pulled along by a motorbike.

The officer came too late to save Dudman and me from a hearty clout on the head and an uncomfortable few minutes on the ground, still blindfolded, with our hands bound painfully behind our backs.

The officer posted one of his men with Elizabeth Pond … and the other two between the crowd and Dudman and me. Meanwhile he went himself for help from higher authorities.…

I learned later the Vietnamese was a five-year veteran, originally from the Mekong Delta. He and the Cambodian were not bent on murdering us at all. They got Elizabeth a bicycle when she could no longer keep up and served us tea when we arrived at the site of their unit's headquarters.[105]

Morrow better understood the extent of the danger and the role played by the veteran officer when the latter explained to him: "'The people wanted to beat you to death. Some wanted to do harm to *"Chi"* ["elder sister," a reference to Elizabeth]' the officer said. 'It would not have been right for them to kill you not knowing whether you were good or bad people.'"[106]

Pond reported that there were several rough and uncertain moments on the first day, when she could sense the anger in the crowds that came to see the American captives—even as they sat blindfolded in a schoolhouse. But ultimately higher authorities within the North Vietnamese ranks made it clear to her captors that they should not be

---

[105] Mike Morrow, "Red Officer Saved Writers from Mob," Dispatch News Service International, June 22, 1970 (published in *The Washington Post*, A1.)
[106] Morrow, "Red Officer."

harmed.[107] After the first day, each reporter noted, the biggest danger came from US airstrikes.

All we knew in Saigon was that the three were missing. And needed help. After about a week of no news, some of us at Dispatch decided to go bring them out. Our plan was to drive into Cambodia and hope they might be hiding somewhere near the road and spot us coming. They would then hop into our jeep, and we would head back to Saigon. I am sure we realized at the time that this was a foolhardy plan, but we didn't want to sit in Saigon feeling helpless. What we didn't know or consider was how dangerous the situation had become for Americans in Cambodia.

When we arrived at the border there were no border guards telling us we could not enter another country, and no one demanded to see our passports. We drove about twenty miles into Cambodia and saw little sign of life. No people; few animals. As the miles passed, we began to feel a sense of dread and soon acknowledged the futility of our effort. So, we turned around and headed back to Saigon.

Just as we were turning back, a cow suddenly appeared and wandered onto the road before I had time to stop completely. The cow hit the front side of the jeep and did a 360-degree flip over the hood, landing on its feet on the other side. It walked away, seemingly unhurt and unrattled by the interruption. I was horrified. A cow is a significant asset for Cambodian farmers, and I had visions of several Cambodians emerging from the fields, angrily waving their pitchforks or guns. Without waiting to see if the cow was hurt or if a mob of angry villagers would appear, I hit the gas and sped away. We made it back to the border without further incident.

Over the next six weeks we continued attempts to obtain the captives' release, including a visit to the North Vietnamese consulate in Phnom Penh. We sent letters and telegrams to North Vietnamese leaders as well as to Prince Sihanouk, the former Cambodian leader

---

[107] Elizabeth Pond, "Out from Cambodian Captivity: 'Don't Shoot, We Are International Journalists,'" *The Christian Science Monitor*, June 20–22, 1970.

recently exiled to Beijing. "Help us find the missing reporters," we pleaded. Our pleas seemed to be of no avail.

Then, abruptly, something changed. The trio's Cambodian captors, apparently having concluded that the three journalists posed no threat, simply took them to a relatively safe area near the border with Vietnam and released them.

Morrow and his colleagues were the truly fortunate ones. In a few short months after Morrow, Dudman, and Pond went missing, at least seventeen more international journalists, including four Americans, disappeared in Cambodia. Of the twenty missing journalists, only Morrow, Dudman, and Pond were released and seen alive outside Cambodia again.

Mike Morrow, Dispatch reporter, following release from captivity in Cambodia in 1970. (Thailand, near the Cambodian border, 1970)

CHAPTER 27

Good-Bye, Vietnam; Hello, America

Morrow was still missing in Cambodia when I left Vietnam for the final time. I had already planned to return to D.C. to set up a new Dispatch Washington bureau, and I realized that there was little I could do for Morrow while in Saigon.[108] It also hit me that three years was long enough to live in what was still an alien and increasingly hostile land. In June 1970, the war was on cruise control and looked like it would last forever—as long as the US maintained its current level of troop commitment. I was anxious to reconnect with the woman I had dated between my first and second tours in Vietnam, and who had become increasingly important in my life. It was time to say *"Tạm biệt"* to Vietnam.

On the eve of my departure, I went to see Vân, the architecture student who had been my mentor and closest friend when I first arrived in

---

[108] David Obst, who had been managing Dispatch's Washington office, had begun focusing on current news stories in the US and moving away from the service's original focus on Southeast Asia. Ultimately he and Seymour Hersh left Dispatch to form a new service, leaving a vacancy in Dispatch's management in Washington, which I filled.

Vietnam. If I was expecting a warm embrace, a showing of gratitude for my years of service to Vietnam, or even a smile and a farewell promise to stay in touch, I was in for a rude awakening. Dressed in a white tee shirt and faded trousers, Vân looked like a bitter man.

Vân had pinned his hopes of becoming a professional architect on the Americans, expecting the US to help bring transformation of his country, with youth leading the charge. Vân, who greeted me on my first day at work at the National Youth Council, had shepherded me in my first few weeks as I was getting my feet planted in a new world. This was the man who had sent me off to work camps with Vietnamese youth groups and to a two-week International Asian Youth Hostel conference to represent Vietnam when the Vietnamese delegate could not get a visa. [109]

Now I saw that, to Vân, my farewell visit was yet another testament to broken promises. Instead of looking forward to a US-supported victory over communism and the replacement of a corrupt government with one that truly represented the people, he was now facing a future almost certain to be controlled by the North. He had told me once that he would have joined the National Liberation Front but the conditions were too harsh. I didn't know how strongly he felt, but it was a choice that weighed on all young men's minds,

We said goodbye on the doorstep, and I went back to my room to finish packing.[110]

---

[109] I was the only American with a group of thirty-five Asian youth leaders, which did not seem to bother anyone except a representative of the South Vietnamese Consulate who did not like the optics of an American representing Vietnam. I agreed to remove Vietnam from my name badge.

[110] Vân made it out of Vietnam after the fall of Saigon in 1975 and ultimately settled in Seattle. He is still bitter about the American betrayal.

Weeks passed with no word of Morrow's situation. Then one day, back in Washington, D.C., I received a telegram at our Dispatch office.

MR. RICHARD BERLINER
DISPATCH NEWS SERVICE INTERNATIONAL
WASHINGTON/D.C./USA

AVOUS DEMANDE A COMMANDEMENT
DE NOTRE ARME POPLAIRE
DESSAYER RETOURVER LA TRACE DES JOURNALISTES

DISPAURUS STOP MAIS INVASION AMERICAN REND
DIFFICILS NOS
RECHERCHES STOP DES NOUVELLES DE
CES JOURNALISTE NOUS PARVIENNENT
UN JOUR JE NE MANQUERAI
PAS NE VOUS NE INFORMER
STOP CONSIDERATION DISTINQUE
N, SIHANOUK DU CAMBODGE

(Translation: "Regarding your request to the Commander of the Populaire Army to try to regain the missing journalists STOP The American invasion makes it difficult for us to make searches STOP If any news of these missing journalists reaches us I will inform you STOP Distinguished consideration. N. Sihanouk of Cambodia")

After spending a week or so in Washington to set up the new Dispatch office, I headed to Birmingham, Alabama, taking a break from my whirlwind life of the past few months to reunite with the woman I had dated during my too-short furloughs in the States. The break lasted three days.

On the second night I received a call about ten o'clock in the evening from my father. "Mike Morrow is free," he announced. Morrow had called my parents' home, hoping to find me. He wanted my help to get the story of his release out to the world. He didn't realize that, when he told my father of his release, he was already setting the wheels in motion. My father, ever the consummate reporter, dictated a story to *The Washington Daily News*, either right before or right after calling me. The *News* announced the release of the three reporters in its first edition the next day with a banner headline.

REDS FREE 3
U.S. REPORTERS

All 'safe and well', correspondent
phones the News' Milton Berliner

Cambodian Reds Release 3 Reporters

Three American reporters held captive by the Reds in Cambodia have been released and are safe in Saigon today, *The Washington Daily News* learned. Mike Morrow, 24, Indochina correspondent for Dispatch International, phoned *Daily News* columnist Milton Berliner that he and Richard Dudman, 52, *St. Louis Post Dispatch* and Elizabeth Pond of *The Christian Science Monitor*, all were "safe and well."

They were taken May 7 by Cambodian forces near the Cambodian town of Svay Rieing.

Mr. Morrow was trying to contact Mr. Berliner's son, Richard, head of Dispatch News Service International's Washington Bureau who returned from Vietnam 10 days ago after trying to effect the release of the newsmen through an appeal to deposed Cambodian Prince Norodom Sihanouk.[111]

The father had scooped the son.

Of course, I was in no position while in Birmingham to get the word out immediately, and I was not able to talk with Mike directly until the next day, when I returned to D.C. Fortunately for Dispatch, Morrow and Dudman agreed with each other that they would say little until they had each written their own four-part series about their experience, and that they would then release their stories on the same day. *The St. Louis Post Dispatch* was an afternoon paper, so Dispatch agreed to market only to morning papers. Among these were *The Washington Post, The Boston Globe,* and *The San Francisco Chronicle.*

The author's father breaks news of Morrow's and others' release from Cambodian captivity. (Washington, D.C., 1970)

---

[111] *The Washington Daily News,* June 15, 1970.

Morrow said their lives were probably saved because they were taken completely under the control of the North Vietnamese. He believes all the other missing journalists were killed at the hands of the Khmer Rouge. Our brief foray into Cambodia looking for Mike could easily have placed us on the list of missing reporters, including Sean Flynn and Dana Stone, who never returned.[112]

---

[112] The story again put Dispatch on the map, but it also brought to light a dispute with two of its early reporters, Obst and Hersh. Although operating as a separate entity, the two were continuing to use the Dispatch name on their articles. This created confusion in the marketplace and led us to file a lawsuit regarding our claim to have exclusive right to the name. The suit eventually led to a settlement. We retained the exclusive right to use the name, and no money was exchanged. This freed us to begin actively marketing the regular flow of stories that began coming into our new Washington, D.C., office.

CHAPTER 28

A New Home for Dispatch

After my brief sojourn in Alabama, I returned to D.C. and promptly tackled the challenge of finding office space for Dispatch's new Washington office. I was fortunate and found an affordable space in the basement of a posh brownstone in the Dupont Circle neighborhood of Washington, D.C. The entrance was off the back and down the stairs, and the office was anything but posh, with its concrete floor and exposed ceiling. But it had all the essentials — a large open room for our desks, files and telex machine, a bathroom, and a storage closet large enough to convert to a dark room. The room also had a couch, convenient for late-night naps. It was our window to the world. It also became a magnet for anyone wanting to connect to the Vietnam War.

Fred Branfman, who gained notoriety when he exposed the genocidal bombing conducted by the US Air Force in Laos, flew from Bangkok to Washington and came straight to the Dispatch office from the airport. He was just back from Laos with a suitcase full of pictures, drawn by children, of the planes in the air and bombs falling on their homes. He was angry and determined. We went to an antiwar rally that night, and he jumped on stage between speakers to tell his story.

This began his long commitment to stop the war, establishing Project Air War and working tirelessly to educate Congress and the American public about US military actions in Laos.[113]

Poet Allen Ginsberg came by one day.[114] He acted just like a guy off the street, wanting to pick up information on Vietnam. Although I had read *"Howl"* in college and knew who he was, I was too dumbstruck even to engage in simple conversation. I gathered up some articles and he left. Noam Chomsky, a well-known professor of linguistics and important voice against the war in Vietnam, never came to our office, but he met with Dispatch reporters in Saigon and promptly sent us a check for $10,000 upon his return.

And then there was the man from the Russian consulate. He stopped in one day, and I gave him a handful of articles. He smiled graciously and promised to come back. And he did, twice. Each time bearing a gift. One was a replica of a wooden ship, with a small bottle of vodka concealed in the hull. He came a fourth time and invited me to lunch. During the course of the meal, he stopped our light chatter and said in a heavy accent, "Mr. Berliner, where do you stand?"

"What do you mean?" I asked, becoming somewhat leery.

"I mean, in politics. What do you believe? I have a right to know."

I told him about the six months I had spent in Scandinavia while in college and how much I admired the system of social democracy I found there. "From birth to the grave," I said, "the government takes care of its people. But they do it within a democratic framework that allows for freedom of choice when it comes to choosing their leaders. They have multiple parties, not just one or two."

Apparently, I was no longer a prospect for becoming a secret agent. He never showed up again.

---

[113] See Fred Branfman, ed., *Voices from The Plain of Jars: Life Under an Air War*, 2nd ed. (University of Wisconsin Press, 2013). For additional information about Branfman and his role in exposing the secret US air war in Laos, see "Fred Branfman, Who Exposed Bombing of Laos, Dies at 72," *New York Times*, October 6, 2014.

[114] Allen Ginsberg was a leading figure of the Beatnik era, best known for his poem "Howl." He also became a prominent voice within the antiwar movement.

The author at his desk at Dispatch's Washington, D.C. office. (Washington, D.C., 1971)

Although I rarely had time to write articles and see my name in print, I felt a real sense of accomplishment each time a mainstream media outlet picked up one of our articles for publication. Over the course of three years, the Dispatch office churned out more than four hundred articles, all generated by freelance writers who were paid an average $25 per article if they were picked up by a publication or appeared in our own newsletter. None of the writers depended on Dispatch for their livelihood, but many were consistent contributors because Dispatch was one of the few outlets for freelance human interest stories. Some articles arrived by telex, but most came by mail and were sent out by mail. So, they had to be somewhat timeless as well as universal in appeal.

We took pride in the diversity of our outlets, from major newspapers like *The Boston Globe, San Francisco Chronicle, Dagens Nyheter* (Stockholm), *The Washington Post* and the *Philadelphia Bulletin.* But we also went outside the mainstream. Liberation News Service and the College Press Service distributed our articles, and we were published in alternative weekly publications such as The *Great Speckled Bird* in Atlanta, *The Los Angeles Free Press, The Lancaster* (Pennsylvania) *Independent Press,* and *The North Carolina Anvil.* Religious-oriented publications like *American Report,* published by Clergy and Laity Concerned, and *New World Outlook,* a publication of the Board of Missions of The United Methodist Church, and *Catholic Reporter* also ran our articles.

Many reporters sent still film with their stories, which our erstwhile volunteer darkroom director and former IVS volunteer, Steve Nichols, turned into prints for distribution. Of course, we never knew ahead of time what would emerge from the acid bath, and sometimes the result was shocking. Like the photograph of the Cambodian soldier holding up two severed heads of Cambodian insurgents, one in each hand. We declined to send this picture out, but we did send out others of Cambodian soldiers.

One picture Dispatch sent out in 1972 ended up three years later in the hands of the editors of *HARBUS*, the newspaper of the Harvard Business School. *HARBUS* published the photograph next to a front-page article that I, by then a student in the MBA program, wrote for the publication the day that Saigon fell in 1975.[115] The article gave my take on why the US had lost the war in Vietnam; I never learned how the editors happened to find the then-three-year-old picture to publish with the article. Never mind that the soldiers depicted in the photograph were Cambodian, not Vietnamese. The picture grabbed the reader's attention. The article was cathartic and bitter with what

---

[115] Richard Berliner, "Vietnam Lives," *HARBUS*, April 29, 1975. The fall of Saigon is historically dated to April 30, 1975. The date discrepancy reflects the twelve-hour time difference between Boston and Saigon.

the US had done to Vietnam. Most of my classmates and some faculty applauded the article; many, I am sure, did not.

Dispatch also stuck its toe into the world of radio. A freelance writer, Ed Zuckerman, contacted us about doing daily reports from Harrisburg, Pennsylvania, about the trial of the Harrisburg Seven.[116] In addition to a series of articles, he suggested we do a radio feed. And we did. This was accomplished by his recording a story on a reel-to-reel tape, which he would play to us over the telephone. We received the report by unscrewing the cap off the phone and hooking the tape recorder directly to the phone. We in turn recorded the feed and then called radio stations with the report. We had perhaps only three stations taking the feed, so it was not a great money-maker. But we felt a part of history.

The news service attracted a variety of stories, many addressing the human suffering caused by war. Dispatch was not able to handle stories that required extensive fact-checking. We generally relied on the writers for accuracy, but when a claim seemed too outlandish, the story was not released. One writer sent a story about new atrocities committed by US soldiers. We rejected it for lack of credible evidence or verification. But he also sent it, using the Dispatch name without our authorization, directly to our outlet in Sweden, *Dagens Nyheter*, which published the article. When asked later by the paper why the story had not received attention in the US, we told them we could not vouch for it.

Over five years Dispatch filed stories from reporters on five continents and twenty-three countries. As Dispatch became better known, articles began flooding the basement office from the four corners of the earth. Here are a few of the stories from countries other than Vietnam and Laos.

---

[116] The Harrisburg Seven were a group of Catholics, led by Father Phillip Berrigan, who were arrested for protesting the war by plotting to kidnap Henry Kissinger. The trial ended in a hung jury.

"Pollution Proves Killer in Japanese Cities" by J. Unger, February 25, 1972

"Gambia—Trouble in Vacation Land" by J. Coyne, February 24, 1972

"Huks Still Active in the Philippines" by L. Rivera, May 17, 1971

"Chinese Village Struggles to Better People's Existence" by J. Unger, January 11, 1972

"South Yemen Charges Guerilla Attack from Saudi Arabia" by J. Stork, November, 6, 1972

"Unique Election from Chile is Test of Allende's Strength" by George Lawton, May 25, 1972

"Slave Labor Practices Continue in the Amazon" by J. Radford, September 29, 1972

"Mehendra Of Nepal" by T.D. Allman, February 9, 1972

In 1972 alone, Dispatch circulated over two hundred articles, an average of one per day (not counting holidays and weekends). The biggest expense, next to the telex machine and our assistant editor's salary, was postage.

Some articles focused on changes taking place in the world. In November 1972, Leon Howell wrote about changes in the sugar industry in the Philippines. "The good years are over," he quoted one sugar plantation owner. "I don't want my children to be sugar planters."[117] The change was coming in the form of strikes by workers in the sugar industry, demanding better working conditions and pay.

Jonathan Unger noticed that in 1971 Mao Tse-tung's picture was coming down all over China. "Not so long ago, especially during the Cultural Revolution, portraits and statues of Mao were everywhere. Now they are quietly being placed in storage ... numerous street-side billboards depict only rugged workers, handsome Vietnamese fighters,

---

[117] Leon Howell, "Changes Come to Philippines Sugar Industry," Dispatch News Service International, November 22, 1971.

serious students ... but no Chairman Mao," he wrote.[118] Mao remained chairman of the Chinese Communist Party until his death in 1976.

But the focus always came back to the Vietnam War, now being openly waged in Laos and Cambodia. Michael Morrow wrote about US bombing raids in Laos, which had been going on since 1966—unknown to most Americans. The difference in 1972, Morrow wrote, was that the bombings were becoming less discriminant and more devastating. He cited a change in the rules of engagement for US military actions in Laos, which provided that the US could use napalm and reduced the restricted area around non-targeted villages to five hundred meters.[119]

Edward Allen wrote that although US spokespersons in Vietnam claimed that the war was winding down, doctors in Vietnam said the rate of casualties had not changed. He also cited the study done by Senator Edward Kennedy through his Senate Subcommittee on Refugee Affairs, pointing out that the official statistics only measured casualties that come to a hospital, not the ones who never made it to the hospital. Dr. Trần Gi Khải, director of the Quảng Ngãi Hospital, told Allen that casualties did drop off when areas designated free-fire zones were reduced in mid-1969. "But children in the field are still getting blown up by unexploded bombs and burned by flares that didn't go off." [120]

In a little over two years, the number of freelance contributors to Dispatch more than doubled from twenty to more than forty. Approximately one hundred newspapers used Dispatch material, including twenty-five college papers. In August 1972, my last month as general manager, Dispatch articles from nineteen different writers appeared in twenty-one different publications.

---

[118] Jonathan Unger, "Mao's Picture comes down—Ideas Carry On," Dispatch News Service International, November 22, 1971.

[119] Michael Morrow, "US Bombing in Laos: An Inside Report," Dispatch News Service International, November 22, 1971.

[120] Edward Allen, "War Not Winding Down for Vietnamese," Dispatch New Service International, November 22, 1971.

Dispatch always struggled financially, depending as much on outright gifts of money as on the sales of articles, and never could fully support even a small portion of the writers who contributed articles or worked in the Washington, D.C., office. But for them, and for me, it was a labor of love and a chance to make our observations known to a wide audience. For many of us, it also became a stepping stone.

Dispatch writers and editors went on to become fixtures in the world of journalism. Mike Morrow became a reporter for the *Southeast Asian Petroleum News* and ended up owning the publication. Tom Fox, after kicking off his career with the *National Catholic Reporter* and Dispatch, became a stringer with *The New York Times* and *Time* magazine in Vietnam and then went back to the US to work with *The Detroit News* and *The Washington Star.* In 1980 he became editor of the *National Catholic Reporter,* moving up to publisher in 1996.

Yvonne Pearson, the editorial assistant who handled much of the logistics in getting articles out, came to Dispatch in response to a help wanted ad in a local weekly newspaper: "News services seek editorial assistant to edit and distribute articles from around the world. Compensation NOT commensurate with duties or skills."

Pearson went on to become an award-winning author of children's books, receiving the Loft Creative Non-Fiction Award and the Shabo Award in children's literature, as well as publishing poetry and books for adults.

Len Ackland became an acclaimed investigative reporter while working for the *Des Moines Register,* and then became editor of the *Bulletin of Atomic Scientists.* Ackland received two notable awards. The first was the George Polk Award for Investigative Journalism for his series on redlining for the *Des Moines Register.* The second was the National Magazine Award for the *Bulletin of Atomic Scientists'* reporting on Chernobyl. He finished his career as a professor of journalism at the University of Colorado in Boulder.

Joe Gatins had a long career with the *Richmond* (Virginia) *Times-Dispatch.* David Obst became an American literary and movie agent. He was an agent for Carl Bernstein and Bob Woodward and was involved in production of the films *Revenge of the Nerds, Fast Times at Ridgemont High*, and *All the President's Men.*

John Everingham became an accomplished photojournalist. His article and graphic photographs of villages destroyed by US bombing raids in Laos were published in the *Washington Monthly*. The pictures, with his accompanying story, vividly exposed the secrecy surrounding the war in Laos and the impact of US military activities on rural Hmong hill tribes. His work also appeared on the front cover of the July 1972 issue of *Harper's* magazine. Everingham gained notoriety when he smuggled his fiancée out of Laos by helping her swim across the Mekong River. His feat was immortalized in a fictional TV movie starring Michael Landon called *A True Love Story.*[121].

My life took a different turn.

Article written by the author and published in the Harvard Business School newspaper the week that Saigon fell. (Cambridge, Massachusetts, 1975)

---

[121] In 1982, Michael Landon co-produced an NBC "true story" television movie, *Love Is Forever*, starring himself and Laura Gemser (who was credited as Moira Chen), about Australian photojournalist John Everingham's successful attempt to rescue his lover from communist-ruled Laos in 1977 by swimming and scuba diving across the Mekong River. The real Everingham was cast as an extra in the film.

CHAPTER 29

A Different Journey

Two years after taking over the Dispatch's Washington office, I decided to go to Miami to cover the 1972 Democratic National Convention. The war in Vietnam was still my biggest concern and the biggest issue on the minds of many of the delegates. At stake was whether the party would select a moderate, more electable candidate like former Vice President Hubert Humphrey or go with a single-issue candidate as a way of sending a message that the war was still raging and people were needlessly dying. The delegates went with the latter and, after raucous debate that lasted until 2 a.m. on the final night of the convention, chose Senator George McGovern of South Dakota to be their presidential candidate.

The enthusiasm of McGovern supporters convinced me that with the right campaign McGovern could beat Nixon and end the war. As frustration with the war was still mounting, I was also sure that I could no longer sit on the sidelines, helping to report on the war. Although my life up to that point had been heading toward following in my father's footsteps, it was time to jump into the political fray headfirst.

While I firmly believed that accurate news stories about the war would further efforts to end it, I was frustrated by the slow progress. Returning to Washington after the convention, I passed on the management of Dispatch to Joe Gatins and joined the McGovern campaign full-time. I planned at the time to return to Dispatch after the campaign, but my body, mind, and soul had made a seismic shift.

The McGovern election campaign was an unmitigated disaster. Nixon's victory was interpreted as a mandate for him to continue prosecuting the war at full speed. But it was also a wake-up call for a lot of idealists new to the rigors of electoral politics.

Soon after Nixon's inauguration, a new organization emerged to keep the pressure on Nixon to exit Vietnam and to challenge Nixon on a long list of budget cuts he planned to seek impacting human services. Called the Coalition for Human Needs and Budget Priorities, the organization worked with more than a hundred partners, including the American Federation of Teachers, Common Cause, the League of Women Voters, the United Auto Workers, The United Methodist Board of Christian Social Concerns, the Friends Committee on National Legislation, and The Urban League.[122] I joined a small staff that provided partner organizations with information with which to lobby Congress and to organize town hall meetings in congressional districts where the representatives might be persuaded by grassroots lobbying.

Our lobbying efforts against the war, along with the work of many other peace organizations and individuals, led in 1973 to the reintroduction of the Case-Church Amendment to a funding bill for the US State Department. The amendment, which would require all funding for the Vietnam War to terminate no later than August 15, 1973, had originally failed when introduced in 1972. This time, the amendment passed.

The US Senate supported the amendment by a 73–16 vote, a margin well above that required to override an anticipated Nixon veto. Democrats controlled the House of Representatives, but the outcome of the vote in the House was still uncertain. I joined the packed gallery in the House the day the vote was called. One by one, members of

---

[122] The records of the Coalition are held at the Hesburgh Libraries, University of Notre Dame.

the House walked to the front of the hall to cast their votes. The big board behind the Speaker's chair posted each vote as it was cast, with a running tally of "Ayes" and "Nays." It soon became clear that the result would not be close; the amendment would pass. Watching from the House gallery, I could not help but be overcome when the affirmatives carried the day. Final vote: 325 votes for, 86 votes against.

It was a defining moment, the culmination of seven years of concern, pain, wonderment, fear, exhaustion, and finally pure relief. For all practical purposes, the Vietnam War, for me, was over.[123]

---

[123] The US continued to have a presence in Vietnam until the fall of Saigon in April 1975. More than five thousand US personnel were killed after the peace agreement was signed.

PART IV

Voices of the
People of Vietnam

Tiếng Nói của Nhân dân Việt Nam

"Please call me by my true names,
so I can hear all my cries and my laughs at once,
so I can see that my joy and pain are one."

Thích Nhất Hạnh

CHAPTER 30

Uncovering Treasure

"**H**ere, take these.

"Take them back to the States with you.

"Show them our lives.

"Let them see what is really happening here.

"Perhaps then they will hear us."

Were these the exact words spoken? Probably not. I don't remember the conversation like it was yesterday. At least, not the exact words.

It was a normal day in Saigon—warm, the streets filled with the sounds of everyday life. Or perhaps it was not. I don't remember that either. I was making plans to return home and was clearly preoccupied.

Here is what I know.

It was spring, 1970. A young Vietnamese acquaintance, Nguyễn Hữu Thái, handed me a sheaf of papers. There were almost 150 sheets, neatly typed in English on a manual typewriter, the kind I had grown up watching my journalist parents use at home and at work.

I glanced at the pages, unaware of the heights and depths of human life they depicted.

Thái urged me to take the collection to the US, to find a publisher who could share the papers' contents with the world, to show the pain being experienced. He wanted to share the pain being experienced by so many Vietnamese. I did not know Thái well, but his sister and I were acquainted. I heard from others that although he was a soldier in the ARVN, he might have had Việt Cộng connections. It was not something I felt free to ask.

I took the papers and put them with other things I would be taking back to the States.

I never found a publisher.

The papers sat, pretty much forgotten, stowed in one of the many boxes that had traveled with me from house to house through the years. They were in a brown file folder, carefully packed among other relics and souvenirs. But still, forgotten.

Until I began to write this book.

And began searching through those boxes for reminders of details I should include, details that—like the sheaves of paper—had receded into less than a distant memory.

And then I discovered the file folder. With the words. So many words—from soldiers, from sisters, from poets, from freedom fighters, from teachers, from people imprisoned for daring to speak words unacceptable to those in power. Some of the poems had been previously published, probably in Vietnamese, then later translated to English. Letters sent home from guerilla fighters risking everything for their vision of a free, peaceful Vietnam. Diaries taken from the bodies of soldiers fallen in a skirmish, or a bombing, or perhaps even friendly fire. A young teacher's agonizing explanation of why she had decided to set herself on fire in hopes of catching the attention of the world.

So many words, so many voices. Some anonymous. Some offered under a pseudonym. Some previously published. Some completely private.

Until the day that Thái handed me a sheaf of papers and said, in words I now remember only as a plea: "Take these to the US. Get them published. People in your country need to hear these voices."

There is a universality in warfare, as in the human experience. These writings emerged from a specific war, a specific conflict, a specific culture. But they continue to speak to us, across barriers of time and context, long after America's Vietnam War officially came to an end. Each of the poems and letters came with a forward written by someone who referred to himself only as N.V.M. Describing the material, N.V.M. observed that the most anguished writing came from those caught in the middle, not committed to one side or the other. He also wrote that the longer the war goes on, and the more the country has to endure the "increasing American oppression," the more the young people of Vietnam will have no choice but to join the "armed violent way of the Việt Cộng."

The material given to me was all in English, though the originals were almost certainly written in Vietnamese, and the translators are unknown. I have not attempted to "correct" or alter the punctuation or other elements of the translations. The material here appears as it did in the sheaf of documents Thái gave me.

In the course of writing this memoir, I have tried to track down the authors whose work Thái shared with me. In most cases that has proved to be impossible. Reading their words today, I wonder what became of them and how they would feel seeing their words in print these decades later. While much has changed in those decades, the stories they tell still speak to a world that seems always to have a war raging somewhere. If anyone reading this book can add to their stories or help shine a light on their identities, I hope they will get in touch.

CHAPTER 31

Selections from Thái's Sheaf

From Thích Nữ Nhất Chi Mai, the thirty-three-year-old teacher at the Faculty of Letters, University of Saigon, who set herself on fire in a plea for peace.

> *Humanity will bathe in the freshness of the mercy of Buddha and the love of Christ and the humanism of mankind. I voluntarily sacrifice myself in order to ask what? That my sacrifice be understood, that it is for the peace of the nation, that it is for the humanitarian cause of justice. Following the sacrifice of Morrison[124] and Venerable Quảng Đức[125] I pray that the flame which will burn my body will reduce the ambitions and hatred, which are throwing so many people into despair and cause so many mournful scenes to the people...*

Mai wrote many letters and poems before taking her life. One read in part:

> *...O Vietnam, Oh Vietnam*
> *Why do we always have hatred?*
> *Who enjoys killing?*

---

[124] Norman Morrison, a Baltimore Quaker, set himself on fire at the Pentagon in protest of the war on November 3, 1965.

[125] Quảng Đức was a Vietnamese Buddhist monk who immolated himself in 1963.

If one side wins which side will lose?
Who brings glory and who will be shamed?

...Why does an American immolate himself?
Why does the world demonstrate?
Why is Vietnam silent?
And dares not ask for Peace?
I see myself, weak
And suffer very much
In life we cannot speak.
By death can the words for the first time
Be spoken

...With joined hands I kneel down
Endure the pain in my body
I wish to make this agonizing speech
Please hold back the fighting hand, 'oh men.'
Please hold back the fighting hand, 'oh men.'
It is more than twenty years now.
Much blood has been spilled
Do not exterminate my people
With joined hands I kneel down
One who immolates herself for
Peace in Vietnam.

From Trần Đại. "A disillusioned student social worker wrote this poem after participating in several work camps sponsored by the Americans in Vietnam."[126]

---

[126] N.V.M.'s introduction to the Trần Đại poem.

I have to build a latrine
While the people starve
Begging impatiently
For a handful of corn
Enough to feed them

I have to build a maternity clinic
But there is no one to give birth to a child
Their husbands are drafted and far from home
There are only devastated gardens and bunkers and foxholes
Their wives at home
Wait to breathe in
The warmth of their husbands
Instead of the smell of blood
Instead of the iron smell of rusty bombs

I have to build schools
Where the children can study
But they don't come
Because they are all in the street
Begging for cigarettes
Speaking some English
Eh! O.K. Salem!
Poor miserable children
You must learn in the street
You children
Don't need to attend classes

I have to build hospitals
And spend my life distributing medications
The old men from the village
Tell us with tears
My son in the hospital
And they cut off his two legs
My son was hit by a bullet

And now sleeps forever in the cemetery
Why don't you add to this little wooden building?
A morgue
A hospital without a morgue cannot be called a hospital at all
I see in his eyes
A tired old man
That brings his sadness here
While we work

When I distribute clothes
All of them accept
They help dress each other
And look at each other in wonder
They forget their sorrow for a day
They laugh loudly
Overcoats, skirts, hats
Worn over their deeply tanned skin
O, these strange clothes
Where did they come from?
I open my eyes wide in wonder
The blue, the red, the red-blue
Dazzle my eyes, my heart
It seems I am turning to stone
I feel as sad
I can no longer understand
I cannot understand
I cannot understand
What shall I do
When next summer comes!

This poem really hit home. I had participated in work camps with Vietnamese youth on numerous occasions. I had thought we were doing good work and building relationships. I did not experience or understand the pain expressed by Đại.

From Nguyễn Vân Thanh, written after her release from a South Vietnamese jail cell:

This may be the last letter I send you because I must make the choice, the choice of my life. I am being pushed to the wall. To choose this side or the other side—and not the middle way!

I can no longer use my mouth, my voice, my heart, my hands for useful things. All the people here have to choose to manipulate guns—and they must point them straight at each other's faces. On one side the Vietnamese city people and Americans, on the other side Vietnamese rural people and Communists and leftists.

What have I to choose?

All things are relative now—I can't side with either Americans or Communists. But one has no choice. On this side or the other side—With the Americans, you are accused of being valets of Imperialism, of pure Colonialism; you are on the side of foreigners, of the people who kill your people who bomb your country, with the eternal foreigners who have wanted to subjugate you for thousands of years...

No, it's a desperate situation. I want so desperately to be still in jail—where one isn't posed with the terrible problem: to choose... I can't keep quiet. I can't have peace of mind these days.

I can't become a mercenary in this kind of puppet army. Americans in uniform are not my friends at all. They are just foreign troops in my country. Furthermore, I can't carry a gun and kill my people, Communist or not. They are all my compatriots that I have learned to love, to cherish.

No. I can't physically or mentally.

I have met many of our friends. They're so desperate.

Lust ... dropped by to see me. He said he could not
fire in the battlefield without bleeding in his heart;
he can't help crying for his own dilemma.

Tran said desperately, maybe he would side
with the VC against these militarists!

Many of my friends in Huế must have to choose—prison on this
side or some kind of "desperate collaboration" with the other side...

I want quietly to do my thing well—to build a
new environment for my country—but you can't do it
without the choice of a political system. Not with foreign
domination—Chinese, French, Japanese, or American ...

From Thái Nguyên, after learning of Stokely Carmichael's work with
the Black Panthers in the US. Vietnamese youth were keenly aware of
the struggles against racism in 1967 throughout the United States.

I just learned that you and your people rose up,
Your blackness brilliant with drops of sweat
The black that shouted, the color that demanded—
so many, you were a forest of coal.
The color that rose is like loud waves
Black power! Black Power!
From this side of the Pacific, we follow you each minute, each day,
We follow you march that destroys citadels and barriers.

Your demonstrations are like great woods, like mountains,
O students in tattered clothes,
in the sun that burns, that parches the throat
you must drink water from the fire truck pumps.

O weak, thin students
they push you out of their schools.
You are forbidden to play in parks where signs say:
Colored people and dogs forbidden!

Your demonstrations are like great waves and currents
o, old mothers who bring your children along,
where you go they shoot tear gas
and free their dogs to snatch at you.
For the sake of your children's future, mothers, you must
struggle for a decent life.
We are all sons of one Creator.
What crimes have we committed besides having colored skins!
No, diamond-bright Blacks will rise up in pride
to shout in common, thousands together,
Black Power! Black Power!

You demonstrate rain or shine.
O, young men whose eyes burn with hatred,
with our money they produce bombs and bullets.
When we are homeless
they discriminate.
Justice is for the rich, the powerful.
Rise up to smash them to pieces,
these narrow-minded people, these unjust ideas,
and building a future of reconciliation and harmony.

Carmichael, Carmichael, do you know
that the world follows your march, each step
towards justice, towards freedom,
towards peace, towards wealth,
up the rungs towards a brilliant promise.

Thousands of miles separate us
But we share hatred
Fires burn villages, burn our hearts.
Lack of medicine, of school, of rice, of clothes.
Our people must guard each grain of rice,
A simple patched cloth and a life full of sweat.
Our students don't look human.
They learn to hide before they learn to read.
Because of poverty our girls
by the thousand become prostitutes.
O torment great as seas and mountains,
We can't count high enough
to count our country's hardships.
Carmichael, Carmichael
Better to die than to live in slavery!

From Miên Đức Thắng, a well-known folk composer and singer, singing at a student protest rally in 1968. Thắng was later jailed by the South Vietnamese government and sentenced to five years of hard labor for writing songs "which weaken the Anti-Communist spirit of the Army and the Republic of Vietnam."[127]

From the poem, "The Bullet":

O, these copper bullets
  So brilliant and so red
Which our Allies offer
  To the people instead
Of food and clothing
  Our devoted Allies

---

[127] From N.V.M.'s introduction to the poem.

Increase their aid with
  Bullets red and bright,
These copper bullets
  While people of hunger are dying
And they cannot eat these
  Millions of bullets flying
O! in the name of peace
  We, your friendly Allies
Offer you, people of North and South
  These bullets so civilized.

A "normal" day in a rural village. (South Vietnam, 1967)

Classroom in a rural village. (South Vietnam, 1967)

Remains of house outside of Saigon, destroyed by US bombs following the Tết Offensive. (Saigon, 1968)

USA, 2024

"Am I a veteran?" The question still lingers. But after wrestling through this memoir, I can unequivocally answer: "No."

When they were serving in Vietnam, whether voluntarily or not, members of the military were totally subject to the orders of their commanders. They were taught to assume, for their own safety, that everyone they encountered was an enemy. Their travels in the country were, for the most part, limited to moving from one base to the next, from one patrol in enemy territory to the next. Few military personnel actually had the opportunity to develop relationships with Vietnamese people. They could not leave Vietnam on a whim without being called a deserter—a tag that would stay with them the rest of their lives. And for those who survived the war, including the more than 500,000 wounded, their homecoming too often came with verbal, and sometimes physical, attacks from fellow Americans, who blamed them for participating in what had become a very unpopular war.

My journey in Vietnam was, indeed, very different from theirs. Yes, it took me on helicopter flights over contested territory, the target of hostile gunfire. It took me to bombed out villages, abject refugee camps, and overcrowded hospitals. But it also took me into the schools, cafes, temples, and homes of the Vietnamese people. In those places I learned about the aspirations of Vietnamese who, despite a long history of suffering—from centuries of Chinese occupation, a hundred years of French colonization, and twenty years of civil war— still hoped for a time of peace and democratic governance.

Many of my Vietnamese colleagues felt trapped in a malaise of ambiguity. They had no control over their futures. They could not plan a career path. Most even put off serious relationships for fear that if they married, they would not be able to carry out the commitment to protect their spouses and children. The war was always there, playing like a funeral dirge in the background. Their greatest wish was for peace, ideally under some form of neutral government, not beholden to the US or to Russia.

But they also realized that this was not realistic. They knew that ultimately, they would have to choose: continue to protest the American military presence and the South Vietnamese government through hunger strikes and protest marches or join the National Liberation Front. The first choice meant risking jail, betting on the emergence of a Third Force that could negotiate a peace settlement with the North and bring an end to political imprisonment as well as military conflict. Many knew that this was a pipe dream. The second choice meant giving up the relative safety of their urban existence and accepting the hardships and dangers of the guerilla warrior.

I saw at first hand the toll the war was taking on families—mothers and fathers, children and elders, all seeking to live "normal" lives in the midst of political upheaval and military conflict. Yet I also learned of the resilience of the Vietnamese people and their capacity for experiencing joy and beauty. I saw this reality in Sunday visits to the zoo and workcamps in the mountains. I was introduced to their love of art, poetry, and music. While there was little opportunity for displaying art, artists were active behind the walls of their homes. An oil painting of a group of musicians, entitled "Three Sisters," came home with me and hung on my walls for years until a son purloined it for the foyer of his own home. Poetry was a common form of expression, evidenced by the poems found on dead Vietnamese soldiers or smuggled out of prisons from those who opposed the war. Music flourished, both in popular form and in the ancient tradition known as Ca Dao. The words of the songs were themselves poignant poems.

Little of what I experienced in Vietnam led directly to my hopscotch career, but all that I did in those years in Vietnam gave me critical tools and the confidence to take on responsibilities in a variety of settings, from the halls of Congress, working for a prominent US senator, to the poorest neighborhoods in Birmingham, Alabama, working as director of a community development organization. My commitment to service evolved into life-long engagement in organizations dealing with housing, food scarcity, homelessness, and neighborhood revitalization—always with the goal of empowering those with whom I worked to take on the challenges of daily living.

My years in Vietnam were not only a different journey. They were a road map for a life worth living.

Appendix

Letter to President Lyndon B. Johnson

September 19, 1967

Lyndon B. Johnson   AN OPEN LETTER
President
United States of America
The White House
Washington, D. C.

Dear Mr. President:

As volunteers with International Voluntary Services, working in agriculture, education, and community development, we have the unique opportunity of living closely with Vietnamese over extended periods of time. Thus we have been able to watch and share their suffering, one of us since as early as 1958. What we have seen and heard of the effects of the war in Vietnam compels us to make this statement. The problems which the Vietnamese face are too little understood and their voices have been too long muffled. It is not enough to rely on statistics to describe their daily concerns.

We present this statement not as spokesmen for International Voluntary Services, but as individuals.

We are finding it increasingly difficult to pursue quietly our main objective: helping the people of Vietnam. In assisting one family or one individual to make a better living or to get a better education it has become evident that our small successes only blind us to how little or negative the effect is, in the face of present realities in Vietnam. Thus to stay in Vietnam and remain silent is to fail to respond to the first need of the Vietnamese people--peace.

While working in Vietnam we have gained a genuine respect for the Vietnamese. They are strong. They are hard working. They endure. And they have proven over and over their ability to deal with foreign interference. But they suffer in the process, a suffering greatly intensified by today's American presence. This suffering will continue and increase until Americans act to ease their suffering. It is to you, Mr. President, that we address ourselves.

Our testimony:

The effects: We do not accuse anyone of deliberate cruelty. Perhaps if you accept the war, all can be justified--the free strike zones, the refugees, the spraying of herbicides on crops, the napalm. But the Vietnam war is in itself an overwhelming atrocity. Its every victim--the dead, the bereaved, the deprived--is a victim of this atrocity. We are usually far from the scenes of the worst brutality, however more than enough still comes to our attention. Viet Cong terrorism is real; so are the innocent victims of U.S. bombing, strafing, and shelling.

What we have seen: We have all seen or know about the human results of this war. Therefore we do not need to list an awful tally of atrocities. How Vietnamese react to these atrocities, however, is little known.

2

One week before the election Viet Cong indiscriminately sprayed mortars on the Delta city of Can Tho, hitting hospital wards, and demolishing poorly-constructed houses; the toll: thirty Vietnamese dead, three hundred wounded (the more solidly built houses of Americans prevented any American casualties). A small anti-Viet Cong rally was held the next day, but according to one resident, "Many of the people here place the ultimate blame on the Americans... If the Americans weren't here in the first place this wouldn't have happened."

One day after the elections a Saigon paper (Than Chung--banned the next day) ran two pictures of bomb destruction in North Vietnam with the following comment (translation): "We can never accept the one-party system in North Vietnam but neither are we able to forget our blood ties with our fellow Vietnamese there, just as we are unable to forget the Vietnamese caught in the mortar attacks on Can Tho and Thang Binh..."

For the Vietnamese, victory at any price is no longer acceptable.

We have flown at a safe height over the deserted villages, the sterile valleys, the forests with the huge swaths cut out, and the long-abandoned rice checks. We have had intimate contact with the refugees. Some of them get jobs at American military establishments and do fairly well. Others are forcibly resettled, landless, in isolated, desolate places which are turned into colonies of mendicants. Others go to the Saigon slums, secure but ridden with disease and the compulsion toward crime. These are refugees generated not by Viet Cong terrorism, but by a policy of the war, an American policy.

Wrote one volunteer, "Cai Be (in the Mekong Delta) has a very successful refugee program as measured by the criteria of the government, but when measured by any human criteria it stinks. We have neatly arranged hamlets, good canals, military security, elections and dozens of other assets which win points in Saigon, but we don't have people living decent lives...These refugees are with few exceptions farmers, but they have been settled on plots of land so small that only the ingenious manage anything like a decent life. I say that the most ingenious can do this without knowing a single person who is that ingenious...Not only do (refugee camps) force these people into an existence which is marginal at best, they do incalculable violence to the customs and traditions of the Vietnamese people... The government has not offered a new and better life, it has only exchanged one form of terrorism for another." This is a situation created by a policy of war. But as one ranking American officer has said, "Refugees are a GVN problem."

What we've heard: Just as in the United States, in Vietnam there is no consensus about how the war should be stopped. But there is consensus on one issue: it must be stopped. To relate what the Vietnamese think is difficult, but we can relate what they say.

3

In a refugee village one of us heard an old woman say these words (translation): "These days of sorrow are filled with napalm, hate, and death. The rice fields turn brown. The new year brings a cold, clutching fear."

A young Buddhist teacher, on the eve of her self-immolation, made her last attempt to express the anguish of the Vietnamese people: "You Americans come to help the Vietnamese people, but have brought only death and destruction. Most of us Vietnamese hate, from the bottom of our hearts, the Americans who have brought the suffering of this war...The tons of bombs and money you have poured on our people have shattered our bodies and sense of nation." A Saigon Catholic youth leader, active for over ten years in the youth movement, said: "We are caught in a struggle between two power blocs, and we can never forget that. Many people told me you cannot trust Americans, but I never accepted it. Now I am beginning to believe it. You come to help my people, but they will hate you for it." At the Ong Ich Khiem Pagoda in Danang, the broken heart of last year's Struggle movement, a Vietnamese friend paused at a shrine, by a wall covered with the photographs of young boys and girls. "Killed by Ky's Saigon troops during the Struggle," he explained in restrained English, soldiers brought up to Danang by hastily-loaned American C-130's in the interests of 'stability'. A Vietnamese who teaches English scribbled out a poem over beers in a tiny dirt-floor restaurant:

Monsoon laughters, peace for this shattered land
of troubled minds of corrupted men
of human pyramids of blood-soaked rice
of hungry faces of pitiless barb wire.

The tide of the war: As volunteers in Vietnam, we work with people, not statistics. War reported in statistics gives a false picture. We read the monthly totals of Hoi Chanh (Open-Arms returnees), and then ask who these people are. Hard-core Viet Cong, suddenly disillusioned with a philosophy that has been their life and bread for years? No. They are marginal Viet Cong at best, if Viet Cong at all, looking for a little rest from this tired war and attracted by the dollar signs of the program. People who can be bought are not going to effect change in Vietnam. We read with anguish the daily body count of "enemy" dead. We know that these "enemy" are not all combat soldiers committed to one side. Many are old men, women, and and young boys who ran when a helicopter hovered, who were hiding from the bombs in an enemy bunker, or who refused to leave their farms. We watch the development of the pacification program, from "strategic hamlet" to "revolutionary development" (an American term; in Vietnamese it is called "rural building"), and see teams of cadre operating in the villages. Who are these cadre? Young men and women, often motivated by draft exemption and the security of a government job, with three months' training in concepts that take several years to master. To the villagers, these black-pajamaed "imitation viet cong" are more interference from the government, perhaps the source of another handout. Certainly they are not a step towards "capturing

4

the hearts and minds" of the villagers. Yet, RD cadre have also
lost their lives in this war.

A road opens up, another closes. While working in Vietnam, we
must travel these roads. We have not seen any increase in security
in the past year. In Saigon and in other cities, roads are secure
but they are full of holes from the steady flow of American tanks
and trucks.

A village lives peacefully under Viet Cong control. Government
or American troops arrive to "liberate" the population. Violence
ensues, refugees are created, but the Viet Cong vanish. If the
military decides not to plow the village under (as was Ben Suc in
Operation Cedar Falls), the Viet Cong will come back and resume
their authority.

Prostitution increases, corruption increases, crime in the streets
increases, and more and more capable people join their compatriots--
either the Viet Cong or those on the American payroll. The former
have dedicated themselves to a difficult and uncomfortable struggle,
with no end in sight. The latter have sought the easier road: the
American dollar, a comfortable life, outwardly compromising their
own culture. Inwardly they have not. In their eyes the U.S. is
the exploiter to be exploited.

An election is held to legitimize a government generally detested
by the Vietnamese. Cries of fraudulence are everywhere, but the U.S.
ignores these cries in the person of Henry Cabot Lodge: "I think
these elections were as good and orderly and wholesome as our own
elections," he said after less than a week of observation. Some
results: the banning of two Saigon papers (Than Chung, Sang) on
the day after the election, the two papers which were the most out-
spoken against the government and for peace during the campaign.
"The elections are over," announced Vice President-elect Ky, after
banning all press conferences without government approval. Repression
continues.

While the U.S. has announced its dedication to the building of
democracy in South Vietnam, it continues to support a government
which jails pacifists and neutralists. The U.S. has repeatedly
announced its support for self-determination, and yet assigns advisors
to everyone from the top military command to the Department of
Waterworks in Saigon. Credibility of leaders is a problem in the
United States; in Vietnam there is no credibility. Rumors say that
the United States has a 99-year lease on Cam Ranh Bay. True? That
is not important. It is what the Vietnamese think that is important.
They have no illusions about why the U.S. is in Vietnam. Many feel
that America is in Vietnam to stop communism--at all costs. In
some ways defeating communism fits Vietnamese interests vis-a-vis
China, whom these people have fought for a thousand years. There
is no love for China, even in the North. "A unified Vietnam,"
said a Saigon youth, "under Ho Chi Minh would not succumb to China."
But they shudder when they see North Vietnam's being forced to
accept her support. Self-determination in the North, as well as
in the South, is being compromised by the American policy.

5

Conclusions: The war as it is presently being waged is self-defeating in approach.   U.S. programs are meant to gain the confidence and admiration of the Vietnamese people through the Vietnamese government. "There is more anti-Americanism here today than there was before," said an IVS volunteer returning to Vietnam again after having spent three years here from 1963 to 1966.

The U.S. continues to support a power group which has proven for five years that it is unable to bring about unity and peace in South Vietnam. "When the Americans learn to respect the true aspirations in Vietnam," said a youth leader recently, "true nationalism will come to power. Only true nationalists can bring peace to the South, talk to the North, and bring reunification," cried another youth leader, "Who is Nguyen Cao Ky? Ho Chi Minh and Vo Nguyen Giap have been fighting for Vietnam since before Ky was born. Why should they talk to him?"

What we recommend:

1. Even in our situation, normally far from the fighting, we have seen enough to say that the only monuments to this war will be the dead, the maimed, the despairing and the forlorn. The trend has been escalation of the war. We say the trend should be de-escalation.

2. Children, old people, and the sick -- not organized groups of armed men - are the most likely victims of defoliation. We say stop the spraying of herbicides.

3. Bombing stands in the way of negotiations. We have seen the results of bombing in South Vietnam, and can imagine what it has done to the North. We say stop the bombing.

4. No satisfactory conclusion of this war will come until all parties are represented in peace parleys. A movement in South Vietnam calls for the recognition of the National Liberation Front to be included in peace talks. We say recognize the National Liberation Front.

5. The United States continues to let self-interest stand in the way of self-determination in Vietnam. The U.S. must prove its commitment to compromise instead of waging an endless war of attrition. We say turn the question over to an international peace commission and be prepared to accept its recommendations.

By speaking to these questions, we have seriously jeopardized our positions in Vietnam. Some of us feel that we can no longer justify our staying, for often we are misinterpreted as representatives of American policy. Others of us wish to stay and to continue to serve the Vietnamese. It is with sadness, therefore, that we make our view known. But because above all our first concern is for the Vietnamese, there is no alternativ It is their cry and ours: End this war.

6

Respectfully yours,

Don Luce '58 *
Director, IVS Vietnam
East Calais, Vermont **

Gene Stoltzfus '63
Assoc. Dir., Community Development
Saigon
Aurora, Ohio

William Meyers '63
Team Leader
Corps IV, Can Tho
Souderton, Pennsylvania

Don Ronk '65
Team Leader
Corps I, Da Nang
Arcata, California

Roger Dee Montgomery '64
Community Development
Can Tho
Carmel, Indiana

Carl R. Adams '66
English Teacher
Da Nang
Sacramento, California

Rene Moquin '66
Community Development - Youth
Nha Trang
Orleans, Vermont

John Spragens, Jr. '66
English Teacher
Vinh Binh
Austin, Texas

David Nesmith '66
Agriculture
Hue
San Francisco, California

John Balaban '67
English Teacher
Can Tho
Hatboro, Pennsylvania

"YEAR OF ARRIVAL IN VIETNAM

Herb Ruhs '66
Community Development
Binh Duong
Louisville, Kentucky

Peter T. Klassen '67
Youth Work, Vinh Long
Oak Park, Illinois

Jerry Kliewer '66
English Teacher
Can Tho
Ulysses, Kansas

Hope Harmeling '66
English Teacher
Saigon
Beverly, Massachusetts

Bob Minnich '66
Community Development
Cao Lanh
York, Pennsylvania

James H. Rupp '66
English Teacher
Tan An, Long An
Green Bay, Wisconsin

David Anderson '67
Community Development
Binh Duong
Menlo Park, California

Daniel R. Vining, Jr. '66
English Teacher
Can Tho
Charlottesville, Virginia

Rick Pyeatt '66
Community Development
Saigon
Riverside, California

Richard Berliner
Community Development - Youth
Saigon
Silver Spring, Maryland

"HOME TOWN

7

Jay Worrall '66
Community Development
An Khe
Petersburg, Virginia

Harris Newlin '66
Agriculture
An Khe
Mooresville, Indiana

Del Epp '66
Agriculture
Pleiku
Henderson, Nebraska

Tom Amidic
English Teacher
Ninh Hoa
Upper Montclair, New Jersey

Robert Schnuckel '66
Mobile Science
Nha Trang
West Brooklin, Illinois

Thomas C. Fox '66
Refugee Worker
Tuy Hoa
Detroit, Michigan

John W. Pope '66
Education
Tuy Hoa
Jacksonville, Florida

Cathy Gammon '66
English Teacher
Can Tho
Springfield, Missouri

Jim Bigelow '66
English Teacher
Pleiku
Vienna, Virginia

Laurel Kluge '67
Mobile Science
Can Tho
Tinley Park, Illinois

Ronald Partridge '66
English Teacher
Bac Lieu
Kewanee, Illinois

Roger Hintze '66
Agriculture
Can Tho
Springfield, Minnesota

David Gitelson '66
Agriculture
An Giang
Beverly Hills, California

William Camp, Jr. '67
U.S. Army Vietnam '63-'64
Agriculture, Cao Lanh
New Preston, Connecticut

Gary Corkin '66
English Teacher
Hoi An
Portsmith, New Hampshire

Diana Gardiner '66
English Teacher
Ban Me Thuot
Hamilton, Massachusetts

Ervin Huston '66
Agriculture
Phuoc Long
Nampa, Idaho

Mark Lynch '66
Youth Work
Saigon
West Haven, Connecticut

Dennis Rothhaar '66
Refugee Worker
Cai Be
Glendale, California

Edward Rust '66
English Teacher
Nha Trang
Rockville Center, New York

8

Larry C. Peterson '67
Urban Renewal
Saigon
Napa, California

Wolfgang O. Friesen '66
Mobile Science
Hue
Newton, Kansas

Sam Delap '65
Mobile Science
Saigon
Morris City, Illinois

Len E. Ackland '67
English Teacher
Hue
Aurora, Colorado

Stephen C. Erhart '66
English Teacher
Hue
San Jose, California

Christopher Jenkins '66
Youth Work
Dalat
Gladwine, Pennsylvania

Steve Goldberg
Youth Work
Da Nang
Chicago, Illinois

Gerald Liles '66
Youth Worker
Hoi An
Richmond, Virginia

Octavius Jacob '67
Youth Worker
Hoi An
Limburg, Holland

SOURCES

Books

Ackland, Len, *A Life Shaped by Suicide and Vietnam* (Working title; expected publication date 2026).

Alex, Gary, Mike Chilton, and Frederic C. Benson, eds., *A Legacy of America's Global Volunteerism: International Voluntary Services 1953–2002*, Peace Corps Writers, 2022.

Balaban, John, trans., *Ca Dao Việt Nam: Vietnamese Folk Poetry*, Copper Canyon Press, 2003.

Balaban, John, *Remembering Heaven's Face: A Moral Witness in Vietnam*, Poseidon Press, 1991.

Branfman, Fred, *Voices From the Plain of Jars: Life Under an Air War*, 2nd ed., The University of Wisconsin Press, 2013.

Cayer, Marc, *Prisoner in Viet Nam*, translated by Stuart Rawlings, Asia Resource Center, 1990.

Cowley, Robert, and Geoffrey Parker, eds., *The Reader's Companion to Military History*, Houghton Mifflin Company, 1996.

Dudman, Richard, *40 Days with the Enemy: The Story of a Journalist Held Captive by Guerrillas in Cambodia*, Liveright, 1971.

Duncan, Donald, *The New Legions*, Random House, 1967.

Fall, Bernard B., *The Two Viet-Nams: A Political and Military Analysis*, Frederick A. Praeger, 1963.

Fall, Bernard B., and Marcus G. Raskin, eds., *The Viet-Nam Reader: Articles and Documents on American Foreign Policy and the Viet-Nam Crisis*, Vintage Books, 1965.

Hunting, Jill, *Finding Pete: Rediscovering the Brother I Lost in Vietnam*, Wesleyan University Press, 2009.

Karnow, Stanley, *Vietnam: A History*, Viking Press, 1983.

Luce, Don, and John Sommer, *Viet Nam: The Unheard Voices*, Cornell University Press, 1969.

Nguyễn, Hữu Thái, *Choices: An Insider's Account of War and Peace in Vietnam*, unpublished memoir.

Nhất, Thích Hành, *Being Peace*, Parallex Press, 2005.

Oberdorfer, Don, *Tet!: The Turning Point in the Vietnam War*, Johns Hopkins University Press, 1971.

Sagnier, Thierry J., *The Fortunate Few: IVS Volunteers from Asia to the Andes*, NCNM Press, 2015.

Schafer, John C., *Trinh Công Sơn and Bob Dylan: Essays on War, Love, Songwriting, and Religion*, Press at Cal Poly Humboldt, 2024.

Schell, Jonathan, *The Military Half: An Account of Destruction in Quang Ngai and Quang Tin*, Vintage Books, 1968.

Schlesinger, Arthur M., *The Bitter Heritage: Vietnam and American Democracy, 1941–1966*, Houghton Mifflin Company, 1967.

Sheehan, Neil, *A Bright Shining Lie: John Paul Vann and America in Vietnam*, Random House, 1988.

Related Books of Interest

Balaban, John, trans., *Ca Dao Việt Nam: Vietnamese Folk Poetry*, Copper Canyon Press, 2003.

FitzGerald, Frances, *Fire in the Lake: The Vietnamese and the Americans in Vietnam*, Little, Brown, and Company, 1972.

Halberstam, David, *The Best and the Brightest*, Random House, 1972.

Hayslip, Le Ly, and Charles Jay Wurts, *When Heaven and Earth Changed Places: A Vietnamese Woman's Journey from War to Peace*, Doubleday, 1989.

Marr, David G., *Vietnam 1945: The Quest for Power*, University of California Press, 1995.

Marr, David G., *Vietnam: State, War, and Revolution (1945–1946)*, University of California Press, 2013.

Pham, Andrew X., *Catfish and Mandala: A Two-Wheeled Voyage Through the Landscape and Memory of Vietnam*, Picador, 1999.

Articles and Congressional Hearings

Berliner, Dick, "Looking Ahead: Peace Brings to Vietnam the Things War Could Not," *Birmingham (Alabama) News,* April 30, 2000.

Berliner, Richard, "Our Biggest Item Was Soap," *Washington Daily News,* December 14, 1966.

Berliner, Richard, "President Had a Platform," *Washington Daily News,* August 3, 1965.

Berliner, Richard, "Unrest in the Philippines," *New World Outlook,* August 1970.

Berliner, Richard, "Viet Nam Lives," *HARBUS* (Harvard Business School), April 29, 1975.

Berliner, Richard A., "Congress Slow to Respond," *American Report,* April 21, 1972.

Berliner, Richard A., "Redress: Citizens Petition Congress," *American Report,* June 9, 1972.

Berliner, Richard A., "The Vietnamese 'Middle Ground,'" *Ripon Forum* V, no. 5 (May 1969): 24.

Berliner, Richard A,. "Vietnamese Refugees Settled—By Decree," *American Report,* November 26, 1969.

Berliner, Richard A,. "Will Congress Act?" *American Report,* May 5, 1972.

Berliner, Richard A., "Winning Without Daley," *American Report,* August 4, 1972.

Chomsky, Noam, *Causes, Origins, and Lessons of the Viet Nam War: Hearings Before the Committee on Foreign Relations,* United States Senate (May 9–11, 1972): 89–98.

Dole, Robert, untitled article, Dispatch News Service International, November 1969.

Erhart, Steve, "US Declares War on Rubber Trees," Dispatch News Service International, March 3, 1969.

Hersh, Seymour, "Lieutenant Accused of Murdering 109 Civilians," Dispatch News Service International, November 12, 1969.

Hersh, Seymour, "The Scene of the Crime," *The New Yorker,* March 23, 2015.

Hoskins, Janet, "What Are Vietnam's Indigenous Religions?" *Center for Southeast Asian Studies Newsletter* (Kyoto University), no. 64 (Autumn 2011): 3–6.

Howell, Leon, "Changes Come to Philippines Sugar Industry," Dispatch News Service International, November 22, 1971.

Javitz, Jacob, untitled article, Dispatch News Service International, November 1969.

Lynch, Mark, "Viet Nam: An IVS Perspective," Yale '66 at 50, June 2016.

Lý, Chánh Trung, "Why Do I Want Peace?" Crystal Erhart, trans., Dispatch [Newsletter] 1, no. 5, (February 25, 1969): 1, 6.

MacKay, William R., "Methodists Push Viet Peace," Washington Post, December 29, 1968.

Manke, Hugh, "The Expulsion of IVS—Another Casualty of War," War/Peace, December 1971.

Manke, Hugh, Subcommittee to Investigate the Problem with Refugees and Escapees, Committee of the Judiciary, United States Senate (April 22, 1971): 1–6.

Nhất, Thích Nữ Chi Mai, "Hear My Distressful Cry," Youth Bulletin: Voices of Vietnam Youth, no. 3 (June 1, 1967): 14.

Pond, Elizabeth, "Out from Cambodian Captivity: 'Don't Shoot, We Are International Journalists,'" The Christian Science Monitor, June 20-22, 1970.

Ronk, D.E., "Vietnam's Haunted Eyes," Dispatch News Service International, 1969.

Schafer, John C., "The Trình Công Sơn Phenomenon," The Journal of Asian Studies 66, no. 3 (August 2007): 597–643.

Trần, Koi Phúc, "The Betrayed Vietnamese," Dispatch News Service International, November 1969.

Unger, Jonathan, "Mao's Picture comes down—Ideas Carry On," Dispatch News Service International, November 22, 1971.

MAP AND PHOTOGRAPHS

Unless otherwise noted, all photographs were taken by the author.

INDEX

ACKNOWLEDGEMENTS

What began as an informal reminiscence for family has grown into this volume only because of the encouragement and assistance from a host of friends, colleagues, and family.

From the beginning, Carol Crawford, talented writer, editor, and mentor from Blue Ridge, Georgia, pointed me in the right direction and provided invaluable feedback as I began the journey of translating memories into memoir.

Over the course of the next five years I had the opportunity to engage with a number of colleagues from my days in Vietnam, all of whom were generous in sharing memories and offering thoughts that deepened my reflections on our work together. Many of their names appear in these pages, but I want to offer special appreciation to John Balaban, John C. Schafer, Len Ackland, Bob Minnich, Jay Worrell, Willie Meyers, Tom and Hoa Fox, Hugh Manke, and Mark Lynch.

Before I left Vietnam in 1970, Nguyễn Hữu Thái made available to me a collection of almost forty letters, poems, and essays written by Vietnamese men and women, telling of their lives as soldiers, civilians, and prisoners in South Vietnamese jails during the war. These documents, translated roughly into English, were given to me to share with Americans in whatever ways I could, in hopes that they would help people in the US understand the pain and suffering the Vietnamese were experiencing – not just from physical abuse but also from the mental anguish of being caught between the two warring parties.

The quotations that appear at the beginning of the various parts of this memoir come from the book *Being Peace*, published in 1987 and consisting of a collection of talks given by the venerable Thích Nhất Hạnh on a tour of the US in the fall of 1985. When the war came, Nhất Hạnh, with many of his fellow monks, left the monastery to engage in efforts to oppose the war and to help people affected by the war. His work led to his being exiled by the South Vietnamese government in 1966, and he went on to become a globally recognized leader in promoting mindfulness and "engaged Buddhism."

Cao Thị Như Quỳnh was gracious in correcting and confirming the Vietnamese diacritical marks on more than 120 names, and Nga Nguyễn was always available to help me with English translations of letters and documents.

In addition to those whose names are shared here, I owe an immense debt of gratitude to the many people of Vietnam who accepted me as a humanitarian and person of peace and did so much to help me learn their language, understand their culture, and appreciate the importance of their long history in shaping who they were and what they could become once they came out from under the dark cloud of foreign oppressors.

I am thankful for my literary friends, who encouraged me to write the memoir and agreed to read early drafts, providing invaluable feedback. They included Chervis Isom, Frances Moore Lappé, John Balaban, Jeannine Laverty, David Roy, and members of the Ridgeline Writing Group in Murphy, North Carolina, as well as my brother, Peter Berliner.

The journey from draft to publication was navigable only because of the invaluable assistance of Nora Gaskin Esthimer, of Lystra Books and Literary Services, whose expertise was exceeded only by her extraordinary patience, tenacity, and generous guidance.

The book would not be the same without the creative talents of Joanna Lynn Holloway, http://joannaholloway.com, who created the covers and other original artwork and provided the design. A special word of thanks goes to book designer Andrea Reider, who laid out the book and prepared it for publication.

I went to Vietnam as a volunteer but I observed Vietnam through the eyes of a reporter, an outlook instilled in me from the time I hit junior high school by both my father and my mother, who met while working on the *Springfield Republican* newspaper in Springfield,

Massachusetts. My father spent some thirty years writing pithy articles for *The Washington Daily News*, in his spare time editing my letters from summer camp and college. My mother taught me to view the world as a humanitarian; to her, no one was a stranger. This book could not have been written without access to the more than one hundred letters my parents insisted I write home while I was in Vietnam, letters my mother painstakingly typed and preserved in a thick loose-leaf binder. Excerpts from many of them appear in this memoir.

I am particularly grateful for the early encouragement given to me by my life's mate, Anne Wheeler, who persisted in telling me to write my story, despite the hundreds of books on Vietnam already in print, because every story is different. She provided excellent conceptual support, as well as a keen eye for spotting stylistic inconsistencies, grammatical miscues, and confusing sentence structures. She also helped to shepherd the complex process of interfacing with the publisher from draft to publication. Had our paths not crossed more than fifty years ago, this story would have had a very different ending.

ABOUT THE AUTHOR

The author (Birmingham, Alabama, 2025)

The son of New England parents, Richard A. Berliner grew up with two sisters and a brother in a bedroom community outside Washington, D.C. With a father who spent a career covering Capital Hill as a newspaper reporter, politics was an ever present topic of family conversations.

While a student in the 1960s at Earlham College, a Quaker school steeped in peace traditions, Berliner became interested in the Vietnam War, seeking to understand its origins and its impact. After graduation, he joined the International Voluntary Services, a non-profit organization that taught him the rudiments of the Vietnamese language and sent him to Saigon to work as a humanitarian volunteer. His work with IVS and subsequently with the Committee on Responsibility and Dispatch News Service International are covered in detail in this memoir.

After returning from Vietnam, Berliner continued to run Dispatch for two years from its Washington, D.C. office before leaving the work force to attend Harvard Business School, where he earned an MBA in 1976. Although he was determined not to go back to the D.C.

area, life took an unexpected turn when he was asked to serve as Press Secretary for Senator Edward M. Kennedy. Accepting the position on a short-term basis, Berliner returned to D.C., leaving his spouse, Anne Wheeler, in Boston, where she was set to begin law school in the fall. After reuniting with her in Boston the next year, Berliner joined the Development Office of Tufts University, where he worked until the sunny south beckoned them to her home town of Birmingham, Alabama.

In Birmingham, Berliner, now the father of two young sons, served as the founding executive director of Neighborhood Services, Inc., a catalyst for economic development in Birmingham's poorer neighborhoods. His work with communities and businesses, coupled with a stint in commercial real estate, made him the perfect fit for what became his first "permanent" position, as senior real estate officer for the University of Alabama at Birmingham.

In addition to handling real estate matters, Berliner served as liaison between the urban university and surrounding communities as the university sought to expand its footprint. He became a charter member and president of a Civitan club in the community adjacent to the university and has served as governor of the Central Alabama Civitan District. In 2012, the Birmingham Urban League honored him with its annual Friendship Recognition Award, citing his close personal and working relationships across historically deep racial and ethnic divides.

While balancing work at the university with raising a young family, Berliner continued to volunteer with a number of non-profit organizations. He founded and served as the first president of Greater Birmingham Habitat For Humanity and has served as president of the board of the Birmingham Firehouse Shelter for homeless men, his local Kiwanis and Civitan clubs, the Birmingham Commercial Real Estate Club, the Harvard Business School Alumni Club of Alabama, and YouthServe, a non-profit that creates opportunities for high school students from very different ethnic and economic backgrounds to become friends by working together on community service projects across the city.

Now officially "retired," Berliner continues to be active in community and civic affairs. He has returned to Vietnam four times since 1973 and frequently surprises members of Birmingham's broad Vietnamese community when, in the course of a casual encounter, he breaks from English into Vietnamese for a friendly conversation.

Richard and Anne reside in the Birmingham area, where they have raised two sons, shared honey from their backyard bees with friends and neighbors, and acceded to the sometimes enigmatic demands of two dogs and numerous cats for more than forty years.

COLOPHON

This book is set in Crimson, an Old Style serif typeface, designed by Sebastian Kosch and inspired by classic serifs, including Garamond, Minion, and Baskerville.

The icons used to mark the parts are traditional Vietnamese motifs. The wilted lotus (Part I) reflects struggle and loss of hope. The turtle (Part II) represents longevity and strength. The Lac bird (Part III) denotes freedom and connection. The blooming lotus (Part IV) symbolizes resilience and blossoming after adversity.